RAILROAD STATION

Guide to Revision

ab	**abbreviations**
adv	**adverb**
agr	**agreement**
ap	**apostrophe**
awk	**awkward**
cap	**capitalization**
coh	**coherence**
CS	**comma splice**
d	**diction**
dev	**development**
div	**division**
DM	**dangling modifier**
doc	**documentation**
emp	**emphasis**
frag	**sentence fragment**
FP. ∥	**faulty parallelism**
gl	**glossary**
gr	**grammar**
id	**idiom**
inf	**informal**
lc	**lower case**
MM	**misplaced modifier**
NS	**nonstandard**
P	**punctuation**
¶	**new paragraph**
no ¶	**no paragraph**
ref	**reference**
rep	**repetition**
st	**sentence structure**
sub	**subordination**
shift	**shift in perspective**
sl	**slang**
sp	**spelling**
t	**tense**
trans	**transition**
w	**wordiness**
x	**error**
∧	**omission**
-/, %, [ ]/, etc.	

English Editor: Stephen Rutter
Designer: Nancy B. Benedict

Printed in the United States of America
2 3 4 5 6 7 8 9 10—81 80 79 78 77

Library of Congress Cataloging in Publication Data

Guth, Hans Paul, 1926–
    Concise English handbook.

    Includes index.
    1. English language—Rhetoric. 2. English
    language—Grammar—1950–   I. Title.

PE1408.G934   1977   428.2   76–48897
ISBN 0–534–00480–6

Acknowledgments

I am indebted to the following for permission to reprint copyrighted materials:

American Heritage Publishing Co., Inc., for a passage from Enrique Hank Lopez, "Back to Bachimba." Copyright © 1967, American Heritage Publishing Co., Inc. Reprinted by permission from *Horizon* (Winter, 1967).
The American Scholar for passages from articles by Joseph Wood Krutch, Donald J. Lloyd, and Philip M. Wagner.

CONCISE ENGLISH HAND-BOOK

FOURTH EDITION

HANS P. GUTH

SAN JOSE STATE UNIVERSITY

WADSWORTH PUBLISHING COMPANY, INC.

BELMONT, CALIFORNIA

Check for abbreviations that should be spelled out (257–258)
Use adverb form to modify verbs and other modifiers (52–54)
Check agreement of subject and verb, pronoun and antecedent (25–31, 40–44)
Check for omission or misuse of apostrophe (274–276)
Rewrite the sentence to make it clearer or more natural (148–154)
Check for words that should be capitalized (281–282)
Strengthen sequence of ideas; show relevance of detail (165 ff., 230 ff.)
Use semicolon or period between independent clauses (296–298)
Check for awkward, inaccurate, inappropriate wording (101–105, 112–117)
Develop your point more fully—support, explain, illustrate (176 ff.)
Check dictionary for syllabication of the word (255)
Rewrite the sentence to indicate what the modifier modifies (54–56)
Check form or adequacy of documentation (323 ff.)
Check for unemphatic, anticlimactic wording or organization (143–145)
Do not punctuate as a sentence—lacks an independent clause (290–292)
Put items joined by "and," "but," "or" in same grammatical category (71–72)
Check standing of debatable usage in glossary (392 ff.)
Check for unsatisfactory forms or constructions (6 ff.)
Check for unidiomatic, un-English expression (88–90)
Wording is too informal for serious writing (23–24)
Check for faulty or unnecessary capitalization (281–282)
Shift modifier into more appropriate position or rewrite sentence (54–56)
Change nonstandard to standard form (21–22)
Check for omission or misuse of punctuation (287 ff.)
Break up into paragraphs that reflect organization (164 ff.)
Avoid confusing or unnecessary paragraph break (164 ff.)
Check reference of pronouns (40–44)
Avoid unnecessary or awkward repetition (156–157)
Check faulty predication, incomplete or mixed construction (59–67)
Check for inadequate or inappropriate subordination (134–137, 152–153)
Check for shift in time or use of pronouns, shift to passive (69–75)
Expression is too slangy for its context (103–104)
Check for spelling errors (261 ff.)
Use appropriate tense of verb (34–36, 69–71)
Strengthen transition from point to point (171–172, 235–237)
Remove deadwood (121–122, 148–149)
Correct obvious error
Correct obvious omission
Use punctuation mark indicated (see reference chart, 288)

Contents

7 Punctuation   285

6 Mechanics and Spelling   251

Contents

3   Sentence Style   129

2 Words 79

Contents

each major section correlate more directly with a major stage in the *process of composition.*

As in earlier editions, the chapter on grammar and usage presents essential terminology and describes basic features of standard written English. The chapters on words and sentence style concentrate on accurate, effective, and economical use of language. The chapters on the paragraph, the whole theme, and the research paper present essential principles of composition and rhetoric. Chapters 6 and 7 offer a concise review of mechanics; the glossaries provide brief discussions of points of usage and definitions of grammatical terms.

A book such as this must attempt to mobilize a latent consensus among people who teach, write, and write about, educated English. In preparing the present version, I have again profited greatly from the example and advice of interested colleagues. My special thanks are due to John Hanes of Duquesne University, Pittsburgh, Pennsylvania; Tyna Orren of the University of Minnesota, Minneapolis; and Mary Cermak of Federal City College, Washington, D.C.

Hans Guth

Preface

The *Concise English Handbook* provides a compact guide to written English. The basic aims of the book remain the same: to focus clearly on essentials; to provide a commonsense approach to usage; to set realistic standards for college writing; and to provide materials that students find intelligible and relevant to their needs. Improvements in the current fourth edition are designed to bring out more strongly the original intention of the book: to help promote positive competencies rather than to penalize error. Instructions focus on how things are done right; they demonstrate and reinforce positive skills needed for effective writing.

The following are features of the new fourth edition:

(1) The reference system has been *streamlined* for maximum usefulness and a clearer focus on essentials. A number of minor or debatable points have been shifted to the Glossary of Usage. In several sections, closely related points have been combined under a single heading to allow more compact presentation of essential information.

(2) Instructions to the student have been reworded throughout to make them more consistently *performance-oriented*. The boldface instructions summing up each handbook entry address themselves directly to the student's question: "What am I supposed to *do?*"

(3) The chapters on Grammar and Usage (1) and on Sentence Style (3) contain new *sentence-building* activities in addition to the more conventional sentence-correction or sentence-revision exercises.

(4) The chapters on the Paragraph (4), the Whole Theme (5), and the Research Paper (8) have been revised to make

Acknowledgments

by Germaine Greer. Copyright © 1970, 1971 by Germaine Greer.

The New Leader for a passage from "The Pentagon Papers and Historical Hindsight" by John P. Roche in *The New Leader,* July 12, 1972.

W. W. Norton & Company, Inc. for a passage from *Love and Will* by Rollo May. Copyright © 1969 by W. W. Norton & Company, Inc.

Oxford University Press, Inc., for a passage from Rachel L. Carson, *The Sea Around Us.*

Ramparts Magazine for a passage from Schofield Coryall, "New Grapes of Wrath," in *Ramparts,* March 1974.

Random House, Inc., for entries from *The Random House Dictionary of the English Language,* copyright © 1966; and for a passage from "The Future of Ecstasy" in *Cloud-Hidden, Whereabouts Unknown: A Mountain Journal,* by Alan Watts, copyright © 1970 by Alan Watts, by permission of Pantheon Books, A Division of Random House, Inc. The article originally appeared in *Playboy* Magazine, copyright © 1970 by Alan Watts.

The Reporter for passages from articles by Michael Harrington and Ken Macrorie.

Virginia Rice for passages from Paul Horgan, "Pages from a Rio Grande Notebook," *The New York Times Book Review,* copyright © 1955 by Paul Horgan.

Saturday Review for passages from articles by Frederick Lewis Allen, Henry Steele Commager, Elmer Davis, John Van Druten, James A. Michener, Edith M. Stern, and William H. Whyte, Jr.; and additional passages from articles by James K. Feibleman and Hartzell Spence.

Scientific American for a passage from "The Nature of Comets" by Fred L. Whipple. Copyright © 1974 by Scientific American, Inc. All rights reserved. Permission granted by W. H. Freeman and Company for Scientific American, Inc.

Charles Scribner's Sons for passages from "The Golden Honeymoon" by Ring Lardner in *How to Write Short Stories,* copyright 1922, 1950 by Ellis A. Lardner.

Time for passages from "Double-Dealer's Death," January 7, 1974. Reprinted by permission from *Time,* The Weekly Newsmagazine; copyright Time, Inc.

The Viking Press, Inc., for passages from John Steinback, *The Grapes of Wrath,* and from Lionel Trilling, *The Liberal Imagination.*

Acknowledgments

Appleton-Century-Crofts, Inc., for a passage from *A History of the English Language,* second edition, by Albert C. Baugh. Copyright © 1957, Appleton-Century-Crofts, Inc.

The Atlantic Monthly for passages from articles by Saul Bellow, Paul Brooks, Erle Stanley Gardner, Oscar Handlin, Alfred Kazin, Walter Lippmann, Vance Packard, and Joseph Wechsberg.

Beacon Press for a passage from "Notes of a Native Son" by James Baldwin, © 1955 by James Baldwin.

Collins + World Publishing Company for entries from *Webster's New World Dictionary of the American Language,* second college edition, copyright © 1974 by William Collins + World Publishing Co., Inc., Cleveland, Ohio.

Joan Daves for a passage from Warren Hinckle, "The Adman Who Hated Advertising" from *If You Have a Lemon, Make Lemonade.* Copyright © 1973 by Warren Hinckle.

Doubleday & Company, Inc., for passages from *The Summing Up* by W. Somerset Maugham, copyright 1938 by W. Somerset Maugham.

Clifton Fadiman for a passage reprinted by special permission from *Holiday,* copyright © 1957 by The Curtis Publishing Company.

Farrar, Straus & Giroux, Inc., for passages from Norman Podhoretz, *Doings and Undoings.* Copyright © 1953, 1954, 1955, 1956, 1957, 1958, 1959, 1962, 1963, 1964, 1965 by Norman Podhoretz.

Fortune for a passage by William H. Whyte (November 1950).

Harcourt Brace Jovanovich, Inc. for a passage from Alfred Kazin, *A Walker in the City* (Harcourt, Brace & World).

Harper & Row, Publishers, Inc., for a passage from E. B. White, *One Man's Meat,* and for passages from articles by Bruce Bliven, Heywood Broun, Robert Brustein, John Fischer, John W. Gardner, C. P. Snow, Dr. Ian Stevenson, and Philip M. Wagner.

Holt, Rinehart and Winston, Inc., for an excerpt from Lionel Trilling's introduction to *The Adventures of Huckleberry Finn* by Mark Twain, in Rinehart Editions, copyright 1948, 1950 by Lionel Trilling.

Howard Mumford Jones for permission to use a passage from an article in the *Saturday Evening Post.*

Alfred A. Knopf, Inc., for passages from Bruce Bliven, *Preview for Tomorrow,* copyright 1953, and from Alistair Cooke, *One Man's America,* copyright 1951, 1952.

Little, Brown & Company, Inc., for passages from Walter Lippmann, *The Public Philosophy.*

The Macmillan Company for a passage from Arthur M. Schlesinger, *Paths to the Present,* copyright 1949.

McGraw-Hill Book Company for passages from *The Female Eunuch*

8 The Research Paper   333

1

Grammar and Usage

For Quick Reference

Grammar is the system by which words combine into large units to convey ideas and information. In recent years, there has been much new research and controversy among grammarians. Current textbooks for school and college draw on the contributions of three major approaches:

(1) *Traditional school grammar* long dominated the teaching of grammar in the schools but today survives only in modernized versions. Traditional grammar approached grammatical study through a systematic survey of eight *parts of speech:* noun, pronoun, verb, adjective, adverb, conjunction, preposition, interjection. It relied to some extent on *meaning-based* definitions. The sentence was defined as a "complete thought." The noun was defined as the name of a person, idea, or thing; the verb was defined as expressing action or state of being.

(2) *Structural grammar* stressed the concrete, observable features that make up the *signaling system* of the language. What turns a jumbled list of words (practice—type—Mary—afternoon) into a sentence like "Mary practices her typing in the afternoon"? One obvious signal is *word order*—the arrangement of words in the sentence. Another type of signal is the use of *inflections*—the *-s* of *practices,* the *-ing* of *typing.* A third type of signal is the use of *function words*—*in, the.* Structural grammar aimed at developing the student's sentence sense by the study of the most common sentence patterns:

Subject—Verb
Dogs bark.
Subject—Verb—Object
Canadians like tea.
Subject—Verb—Indirect Object—Object
Music gives people pleasure.
Subject—Verb—Object—Object Complement
Linda called Bert a pest.
Subject—Linking Verb—Noun
Hubert is a madman.
Subject—Linking Verb—Adjective
Hubert is mad.

Subject—Verb—Object—Adjective
Noise drove Hubert mad.

(3) *Transformational grammar* attempted to go beyond the "surface" features investigated by earlier grammars. It tried to formulate the rules by which grammatical structures are generated. The basic procedure of transformational grammar is to identify first the **source sentences** from which more complex structures derive. These would be such simple statement patterns as "Jean eats," "John makes tacos," "The tacos are good." We then look at the **transformations** that change these sentences to statements about the past, or questions, or negative statements, or the like:

John made tacos.
Did Jean eat?
John does not make tacos.
The tacos were made by John.

Additional transformations help us add to one simple statement ("John made tacos") material from another ("The tacos are good") . By adding material from a second source, we produce sentences like the following:

John made *good* tacos.
John made tacos, *which Jean ate.*
Jean eats *when John makes tacos.*

The following chapter does not attempt to provide a complete grammar of the English sentence. It provides a *writer's* grammar, which aims at helping a writer identify the forms and constructions that are appropriate for written English.

5

G 1 A Bird's-Eye View of Grammar

Grammar is the study of how words work together in a sentence.

Words convey only vague meanings as long as they are loosely strung together. Tourists abroad can carry on a rudimentary conversation with foreigners after picking up a few isolated words. Foreign visitors to the United States can make some headway by taking words from a dictionary. But they will not be speaking English until they can work words into meaningful patterns like the following:

Actor	Action Verb	Target
The agent	scrutinized	my passport.

Sender	Action Verb	Address	Missive
The travel bureau	sent	me	a brochure.

Actor	Action Verb	Target	Label
Maurice	called	the trip	a disaster.

G 1a Grammatical Devices

Study the grammatical devices that help give meaning to a succession of words.

In the typical written sentence, inflections, word order, and function words combine to help the reader select among the possible meanings of words and work those words into a meaningful sequence:

A Bird's-Eye View of Grammar

- **Inflections** are *changes in the form of a word.* Inflections signal the differences in meaning between the sentences in each of the following pairs:

Stops annoy*ed* our passenger.
Stop annoy*ing* our passenger.

The physician studi*ed* burns.
The physician's study burn*ed*.

The endings spelled *s, ed,* and *ing* are the inflections most frequently used in English. Some languages, such as Latin and German, rely heavily on inflections. Originally, English was close to German in number and importance of inflected forms. Through the centuries, however, English has shed many of these. Modern English relies primarily on other grammatical devices.

- A second major grammatical device is **word order.** In English, *different arrangements of words in a sentence produce different meanings.* Compare the sentences in the following pairs:

Gentlemen prefer *blondes.*
Blondes prefer *gentlemen.*

A *tramp* called *the mayor a liar.*
A *liar* called *the mayor a tramp.*

He ate *only* the steak.
He ate the *only* steak.

- A third major grammatical device is the use of *words whose main function is to clairfy relationships among other words.* Many modern grammarians group these words together as **function words.** Function words account for the differences in meaning in the following pairs:

George set *a* poor example.
George set *the* poor *an* example.

He left the lady his estate.
He left *with* the lady *for* his estate.

G 1b   Basic Sentence Elements

Study the basic grammatical categories required to make up typical sentence patterns.

Grammarians assign words to major word classes (or **parts of speech**) according to the functions they perform. The same word may serve different functions, and belong to different word classes, in different sentences. The word *light* performs a different function in each of the following:

Turn off the *light*.
Let's *light* a candle.
She had *light* hair.
The water was *light* blue.

(1) *The basic model of the English sentence consists of only two major elements.* A complete sentence normally has at least a **subject** and a **predicate:**

Subject	Predicate
The boy	reads.
A car	stopped.
Dogs	bark.

The most important part of the subject is usually a **noun:** *car, student, bulldog, college, education.* We use nouns to name or classify things, places, people, animals, concepts. The housewife looking up entries in the Sears catalog, the chemist giving names to new plastics, the businessman naming new products—all rely on the naming function of the noun.

Here are the most important formal and structural features of nouns:

- They occur in typical noun positions: *"Dogs* bark," "I like *dogs,"* and "for my *dogs."*

- Their appearance is often signaled by noun markers such as *a, an,* and *the* (**articles**); *this, these, that,* and *those* (**demonstrative pronouns**); or *my, our,* and *your* (**possessive pronouns**). Modern grammars group these noun markers together as **determiners.**

- They typically add the inflectional *-s* to refer to more than one (plural) ; *boys, dogs, cars, ideas, preparations.* But note irregular plurals like *children* and *oxen;* unmarked plurals like *deer, sheep, offspring;* and nouns normally occurring only in the singular: *chaos, courage, rice.*

- They often show noun-forming endings (**suffixes**) like *-acy, -age, -ance, -dom, -ness, -hood: literacy, bondage, importance, wisdom, happiness, brotherhood.*

The place of nouns may be taken by noun substitutes, such as the **personal pronouns:**

He	reads.
It	stopped.
They	bark.

The predicate, the second major part of a simple sentence, makes some kind of assertion concerning the subject. (Sometimes the predicate asks a question about the subject.) The most important word, or group of words, in the predicate is the **verb:** *reads, stopped, has left, will return, is reprimanded, has been elected.* The verb signals the performance of an action, the occurrence of an event, or the presence of a condition. A noun may *name* an action: *theft, movement, investigation.* A verb refers to present, future, past, or possible performance: *steals, has moved, may investigate.*

Here are the most important formal and structural features of verbs:

- They occur in typical verb positions: "Let's *eat*," "*Eat* your cereal," and "Big fishes *eat* little fishes."

- In the present tense, most verbs add *-s* when *he, she,* or *it* could substitute for the subject (third-person singular) : "He *eats*," "She *writes*," "It *surprises* me." Many verbs have a separate inflected form for past tense: *eat—ate, sing—sang, ask—asked, investigate—investigated.*

- Typical verb-forming suffixes are *-ize* and *-en:* organ*ize,* redd*en,* sharp*en.*

- In verb forms consisting of several words, a limited number of **auxiliaries** occur. If there are several auxiliaries, they typically appear in the following order: first, a modal, if any—*will (would) , shall (should) , can (could) , may (might) ;* second, a form of *have,* if any *(has, had) ;* third, a form of *be (is, am, are, was, were, be, been) .* Here are some of the resulting combinations:

Modal	Have	Be	Main Verb
can			happen
	has		arrived
could	have		called
		is	waiting
may		be	canceled
will	have	been	sold
should	have	been	revised

(2) *In several typical sentence patterns, the predicate is completed by one or more complements.* **Complements** become essential parts of the basic structure. An action verb may carry its action across to its target (**direct object**). An action verb like *give, send,* or *write* may carry the pattern first to the destination (**indirect object**) and then proceed to the missive (direct object). A verb like *name, elect,* or *call* may carry the pattern first to a direct object and then pin a label on the direct object. (The second complement is then called an **object complement.**)

Subject	Action Verb	Complement	Complement
The student	reads	a book.	
My friend	sent	me	a letter.
Fred	called	his roommate	a liar.

In other sentences, the verb is a **linking verb,** which introduces a description of the subject. A linking verb pins a label on the subject.

Subject	Linking Verb	Complement
Schnoogle	is	a mailman.
He	may be	your brother.
The price	seemed	reasonable.
The food	tasted	good.

Grammar and Usage

The description following the linking verb is often a noun (*mailman, brother*). It may also be an **adjective.** (see G 1c.)

(3) *Several simple transformations rearrange (and sometimes omit or expand) basic sentence elements.* Thus, the **passive** makes the original *object* the subject of a new sentence. The original subject appears after *by* at the end of the pattern, or is omitted altogether. The verb is changed to its passive form, which uses the auxiliary *be* and the past principle (see G 4). The resulting pattern reverses the more common actor-action sequence by making the receiver, the target, or the result of the action the subject of the sentence.

Subject	Passive Verb	
The book	was read	(by the student).
A letter	has been sent	(by my friend).

A second transformation changes the verb to the form used in requests or commands (**imperative**) and omits the subject:

Verb	Complement
Shut	the door.
Be	a man.
Keep	quiet.

A third transformation introduces an initial *there* and postpones the subject:

	Verb	Subject
There	is	hope.
There	was	no time.
There	were	few survivors.

Note: In identifying basic sentence elements, you will have to distinguish between verbs and **verbals.** *Verbals are derived from verbs but do not by themselves function as predicates.* The most important of the verbals are the *to* forms (**infinitives**) and the *-ing* forms (**gerunds** and **present participles**). Infinitives and gerunds often serve as subjects or as complements, taking the place of nouns:

Speeding	causes	accidents.
He	refused	*to pay.*
Teachers	discourage	*cheating.*

These verbals do have some important similarities to verbs. For instance, they are often followed by objects:

Studying *grammar*	inspires	me.
Fred	refused	to pay *his dues.*
Courtesy	forbids	calling *a policeman a cop.*

The *-ing* forms are called present participles when they function as adjectives (see **G** 1c).

G 1c   Modifiers

Study the elements we use to flesh out the basic patterns.

The typical sentence contains words, or groups of words, that *develop, restrict, or otherwise modify* the meaning of the basic sentence elements. Such **modifiers** can be roughly divided into two main groups: those that modify nouns (or noun equivalents) and those that modify other parts of a sentence.

(1) All of the modifiers italicized in the following ex-

Grammar and Usage

amples modify the noun *dog* and thus belong in the first
group:

> A *shaggy* dog barred my way.
> A *big, yellow* dog was chewing the rug.
> A dog *wearing a muzzle* emerged from the door.
> A *police* dog tracked me down.
> A dog *with droopy eyes* dozed in the sun.

Of these modifiers, the first three (*shaggy, big, yellow*)
are true adjectives. An **adjective** occurs in typical adjective
positions: "a *reasonable* price," "The price is *reasonable*,"
"a very *reasonable* price." Most adjectives have distinctive
forms for use in comparisons: *small—smaller—smallest;*
good—better—best; reasonable—more reasonable—most
reasonable. Suffixes that help us derive adjectives from other
words are *-ic, -ish, -ive,* and *-ous: basic, foolish, expensive,*
courageous. In traditional grammar, however, any modifier
that modifies a noun or noun equivalent is said to *function*
as an adjective.

(2)   The second group of modifiers is illustrated in the
following sentences:

> The bell rang *twice.*
> *Suddenly* the bell rang.
> The bell rang *loudly.*
> The bell rang *at intervals.*

Twice, suddenly, and *loudly* belong to a class of words
known as **adverbs.** Many of these show the distinctive
-ly ending. *At intervals* is not formally an adverb, but in
traditional grammar it is said to serve an adverbial function.

(3)   **Combinations** introduced by *with, at, on,* and
similar words may modify either nouns or other parts of a
sentence.

The girl *from Chicago* disappeared.   (adjective function)
The girl disappeared *from Chicago*.   (adverbial function)

With, at, on, and *from* are **prepositions.** They tie a noun (or equivalent) to the rest of the sentence. Other common prepositions are *about, by, during, in, of, through, to, under, until,* and *without.* A preposition plus the noun it introduces is a prepositional phrase.

G 1d   Joining Clauses

Recognize the units that make up the larger combined sentence.

When *several subject-predicate groups combine,* they need to be distinguished from the sentence as a whole. They are traditionally referred to as **clauses.** The following sentences illustrate different ways of joining one clause to another:

My brother proposed to Elvira;	*however,*	she dislikes him.
My brother proposed to Elvira;	*but*	she dislikes him.
My brother proposed to Elvira;	*though*	she dislikes him.
My brother proposed to Elvira;	*who*	dislikes him.

Independent clauses are *self-sufficient enough to stand by themselves,* to be punctuated as complete sentences. They are still considered independent when they are joined to another independent clause by an adverbial connective or by a coordinating connective. **Adverbial connectives** are such words as *however, therefore, moreover, nevertheless, besides.* **Coordinating connectives** are such words as *and, but,* and *for.* A grammatically complete sentence ordinarily contains at least one independent clause. (See also P 2b, 2c.)

Grammar and Usage

Dependent clauses are *subordinated to the main clause* by a subordinating connective or by a relative pronoun. **Subordinating connectives** are words like *if, when, because, though,* and *whereas.* **Relative pronouns** are *who, which,* and *that.* Dependent clauses can be considered as modifiers. Those introduced by subordinating connectives usually, though not always, serve adverbial functions: "The bell rang *when I started to answer.*" Those introduced by relative pronouns usually serve adjective functions: "The bell *that had startled me* had ceased to ring." (See also P 2d.)

A special type of dependent clause, rather than being joined to the main clause, *replaces one of its nouns.* Such a clause-within-a-clause is called a **noun clause:**

Noun:	*The thief* returned my documents.
Noun Clause:	*Whoever stole my wallet* returned my documents.
Noun:	He was excited by *the news.*
Noun Clause:	He was excited by *what he had heard.*

That, frequently used as a relative pronoun, is also used to introduce a noun clause:

Osbert denied *that he had forged the check.*
That Osbert forged the check has not been proved.

Dependent clauses are often hard to recognize, because one or more elements may be missing. Especially in informal writing, *whom, which,* and *that* are often omitted. Supplying the missing element in such constructions facilitates grammatical analysis:

The speaker [*whom*] *we had invited* failed to appear.
The support [*that*] *we received* was inadequate.

Exercises

A. In the following sentences, identify the basic elements in each clause. Describe the function and grammatical category of as many other elements as you can. Point out distinctive grammatical features.

1. The water in the bowl was purple, and the goldfish were gulping for air.

2. Throughout the length of the valley, the river's course widens and narrows by turns.

3. In recent years, sport parachuting has enjoyed a small boom.

4. The only means of access was to hack one's way through hundreds of miles of jungle.

5. He painted with the suppleness of an artist who wanted a deep union with nature.

6. Many customs were common to both sides of the Rio Grande when the river became a frontier.

7. Recipes for happiness cannot be exported without being modified.

8. Uncle Alfred complained that outboard motors had driven off the fish.

9. Avoiding traffic police is easy if they ride in specially marked cars.

10. Fritz annoyed the neighbors by blowing the bugle his father had brought back from France.

11. What maintains one vice would bring up two children. (Benjamin Franklin)

12. When you are lost in the woods, remember your Indian lore.

B. The following sets of three sentences test your familiarity with basic sentence structure. The first five sets show different ways that basic sentence elements combine to make up a simple English sentence. The last five sets show sentences that *combine* information from two or more simpler statements. In each set,

Grammar and Usage

two of the sentences are very similar in their basic structure—in the way they have been put together. The remaining sentence is different. Write the letter for the different sentence after the set number.

1. (a) The school board has banned our humor magazine.
   (b) Malnutrition had become a national menace.
   (c) Bromo-Seltzer will cure that headache.

2. (a) The father gave the pair his blessing.
   (b) The Russian authorities denied his wife a passport.
   (c) His actions kept the voters happy.

3. (a) Corruption was common in high places.
   (b) The apartment was searched by the police.
   (c) His sister looked different without her wig.

4. (a) Leonard lent strangers money.
   (b) The voters elected the actor governor.
   (c) My parents named their child Miranda.

5. (a) Charitable people give generously to charities.
   (b) Please contribute freely to our special fund.
   (c) My father contributed reluctantly to the heart fund.

6. (a) A man who kicks his dog will beat his wife.
   (b) You can't tell by the looks of a cat how far it can jump.
   (c) The only thing that I like about rich people is their money.

7. (a) He can count to twenty after he takes his shoes off.
   (b) If you save one person from hunger, you work a miracle.
   (c) When the cat leaves the house, the mice have a ball.

8. (a) Children cry easily, but they also laugh a lot.
   (b) He had a perfect alibi, which made things easy for his lawyer.
   (c) Sewage pollutes the water, and exhaust fumes poison the air.

9. (a) He had forgotten where he hid the money.
   (b) She returned the car that she had borrowed.
   (c) We had found a mechanic who worked on Sundays.

10. (a) If she is there when I come home from work, I'll call you.

    (b) If you are hungry, we should find a place where we can eat.

    (c) When the session ended, they agreed on a time when they would meet again.

    C. The following *sentence-building* exercise tests your ability to recognize and use a variety of familiar building blocks for the English sentence.

1. Look at the way the italicized words add information to the two sample sentences. Fill in similar modifiers in the blank spaces left in the next two sentences. (The added elements are adjectives and adverbs.)

    Examples: The *handsome* cowboy *slowly* mounted his *magnificent* horse.

                The *tired* detective *again* questioned the *uncooperative* suspect.

    Your Turn: The _____ gentleman _____ proposed to the _____ lady.

        The _____ traveler _____ asked the _____ guide _____ questions.

2. Look at the way the italicized words add information to the two sample sentences. Fill in similar modifiers in the blank spaces left in the next two sentences. (The added elements are prepositional phrases.)

    Examples: The girl *in the Cadillac* approached the locked gate *at high speed.*

                At the other end of the swamp, Leroi was wrestling *with a huge alligator.*

    Your Turn: The stranger _____ had hidden the suitcase _____.

    _____ the news _____ had wiped out the fortune _____.

3. Look at the way the italicized words add information to the two sample sentences. Fill in similar modifiers in the blank spaces left in the next two sentences. (The added elements are "appositives.")

    Examples: Godzilla, *the fire-breathing reptile,* was fighting two giant caterpillars.

> Clark Gable, *an unforgettable screen star,* played
> in "Gone with the Wind," *a great but controversial
> movie.*

Your Turn: Marilyn Monroe, _____, experienced both success and failure in Hollywood, _____.

Tarzan, _____, travels through the
forest with Cheetah, _____.

4. Look at the way the italicized words add information to the
two sample sentences. Fill in similar modifiers in the blank
spaces left in the next two sentences. (The added elements are
"verbal phrases.")

Examples: The man *holding the gun* had stopped, *taking
careful aim at the animal.*

Fighting the storm, the little boat, *lifted by each
wave,* plowed on.

Your Turn: The girls _____ mobbed the rock
star _____.

_____, the woman _____
waved to her audience.

D. Study the way the following simple S-V-O sentences have
been built up by a variety of modifiers. Then write three S-V-O
sentences of your own—first the bare-bones version, then a version
using a variety of modifiers to help the sentence carry additional
freight.

1. A man introduces the judges.
   A young man wearing a frilly red dinner jacket introduces the
   judges.

2. A lady presents a rose.
   A very ripe young lady with lipstick on her teeth presents a
   rose to Reeves.

3. A man monitors the questions.
   A young man named Tony, who is considerably more sure of
   himself than he has reason to be, monitors the questions.

E. Write three *pairs* that each consist of two simple source
sentences. Then illustrate different ways of working the material
in each pair into a more complicated sentence. Example:

The guests had departed. Alvin tidied the room.

After the guests had departed, Alvin tidied the room.

Alvin tidied the room, for the guests had departed.

The guests had departed, so Alvin tidied the room.

The guests having departed, Alvin tidied the room.

Alvin tidied the room, the guests having departed.

G 2   Grammar and Usage

Make appropriate use of the resources of the language.

The language that educated adults use in serious conversation and in writing differs to some extent from the language they use when not on their best behavior. Students learn early that often they should say "is not" rather than "ain't," "can hardly wait" rather than "can't hardly wait," and "this kind of car" rather than "these kind of cars." Differences such as these are differences in **usage.** The study of usage investigates *choices among alternative words, word forms, and constructions.* Effective writers have learned to make the choices that will prove acceptable to their readers.

G 2a   Standard and Nonstandard   *NS*

Know how to use the kind of English that enjoys social and cultural prestige.

Standard usage is the language of education, journalism, and other white-collar occupations. You will use it in your written work except when you record or deliberately imitate **nonstandard** speech. Nonstandard speakers have usually had relatively little formal education. Their jobs often require little reading of instructions and little writing of reports. They may have few dealings with teachers, lawyers, journalists, and other presumably highly literate persons.

Here are some forms and constructions of nonstandard English:

Verb Forms:	he *don't,* you *was,* I *says; knowed, growed;* I *seen* him
Pronoun Forms:	*hisself, theirself; this here* book, *that there* car; *them* boys
Connectives:	*without* you pay the rent; *on account of* he was sick; *being as* she couldn't come
Double Negatives:	we *don't* have *no* time; a little rain *never* hurt *no* one

While nonstandard English is the natural speech in many a home and on many a blue-collar job, standard English is essential to success in school and office. Many of the features of nonstandard speech are distinctive enough to stand out, and seem clearly out of place, in writing. Nevertheless, the exact point at which nonstandard shades over into standard is a matter of dispute. Expressions like *off of* and *irregardless,* widely considered nonstandard, are frequently heard in the speech of educated people, including college teachers of English. In your *writing,* however, a simple principle applies: When in doubt, be safe. A reader who considers you half-educated because you use *irregardless* will seldom give you a chance to prove him wrong.

(See the Glossary of Usage for *as, being as, couple of,* double comparative, double negative, *hadn't ought to, learn, used to could, without.*)

G 2b   Formal and Informal   *inf*

Use different kinds of standard English for different occasions.

Relatively **informal** usages are found primarily in casual conversation, but also in writing designed to sound chatty or familiar. Relatively **formal** usages are characteristic of the language of scholarly studies, books on serious subjects, articles in serious magazines. Though more characteristic of written than of spoken English, these usages are also found in formal lectures, speeches, and discussions.

Here are some grammatical features of informal English:

Contractions:	*don't, doesn't, isn't, won't, can't; I'm, you've, they're*
Conversational Tags:	*well, . . . ; why, . . . ; now, . . .*
Pronoun Forms:	it's *me*, that's *him; who* did you invite
Pronoun Reference:	everybody took *theirs;* somebody left *their* gloves
Intensifiers:	*so* glad, *such a* surprise; *real* miserable, *awful* fast

In *informal* English, sentences often preserve some of the loose, improvised quality of speech. A speaker may start one pattern and then shift to another in midsentence. He may rethink what he is saying while he is saying it. In *formal* English, grammatical relationships in a sentence are carefully and accurately worked out: predicates logically fit their subjects; modifiers are clearly related to what they modify. The advice given in this chapter is designed to help you write the kind of formal English that is appropriate for serious writing, but that is not so extremely formal as to become stilted or affected.

(See the Glossary of Usage on *apt/liable, between/ among, blame on, can* and *may, cannot help but, couple of, different than, due to, each other/one another, get hit, it's me, less/fewer, like I said, most everybody,* possessives with verbal nouns, preposition at the end of a sentence, *providing, reason is because, shall/will,* split infinitives, *these kind, used to/didn't use to, where at, you* with indefinite reference.)

(For a discussion of formal and informal diction, see D 3.)

Exercises

A. How successful are the following attempts to reproduce in writing the forms and constructions of *nonstandard speech?* Which features of nonstandard usage do you recognize?

1. Fella says to me, gov'ment fella, an' he says, she's gullied up on ya. Gov'ment fella. He says, if ya plowed 'cross the contour, she won't gully. Never did have no chance to try her. An' the new super' ain't plowin' 'cross the contour. Runnin' a furrow four miles long that ain't stoppin' or goin' aroun' Jesus Christ Hisself.—John Steinbeck, *The Grapes of Wrath*

2. We ain't got the dog yet. It won't take but one. But he ain't there. Maybe he ain't nowhere. The only other way will be for him to run by accident over somebody that had a gun and knowed how to shoot it.—William Faulkner, "The Bear"

3. Well, anyway, they come over to help us celebrate the Golden Wedding and it was pretty crimpy weather and the furnace don't seem to heat up no more like it used to and Mother made the remark that she hoped this winter wouldn't be as cold as the last, referring to the winter previous. So Edie said

if she was us, and nothing to keep us home, she certainly wouldn't spend no more winters up here and why didn't we just shut off the water and close up the house and go down to Tampa, Florida? You know we was there four winters ago and stayed five weeks, but it cost us over three hundred and fifty dollars for hotel bill alone. So Mother said we wasn't going no place to be robbed.—Ring W. Lardner, "The Golden Honeymoon," *How to Write Short Stories*

B. Study recent columns by a columnist using a deliberately informal or humorous style. Report on his use of distinctive grammatical features of *informal English*.

G 3   Agreement

Make the subject and its verb agree in number.

Most nouns and pronouns have one form for references to a single item **(singular),** another form for references to more than one **(plural).** Often, verbs also offer us two choices: *is/are, was/were, has/have, asks/ask.* When subject and verb are both either singular or plural, they are said to agree in **number.**

Singular	Plural
The boy *goes* home.	The boys *go* home.
Love *makes* fools.	Fools *make* love.
My girl friend *was* pleased.	My girl friends *were* pleased.

(See G 5e for agreement of a *pronoun* with its antecedent.)

Grammar and Usage

G 3a Irregular Plurals

*Know which nouns borrowed from other
languages preserve irregular plurals.*

Most English nouns use the familiar *s* plural (cars,
buildings, trees, books, petitions). But some words borrowed from Greek and Latin require you to learn irregular
plural forms:

Singular	Plural	Singular	Plural
crisis	crises	criterion	criteria
thesis	theses	phenomenon	phenomena
analysis	analyses	medium	media
hypothesis	hypotheses	stimulus	stimuli

"Dat*a*" are items of information, and "bacteri*a*" are
very small organisms. The singular forms of these two
words (*datum* and *bacterium*) are rarely used, with the result that *data* now often occurs as a singular. A boy who
graduates from college becomes an "alumn*us*," a girl an
"alumn*a*." Several male graduates would call themselves
"alumn*i*," several female graduates "alumn*ae*."

Note: The following anglicized plurals are becoming
acceptable: "ind*exes*" rather than "ind*ices*," "curricul*ums*"
rather than "curricul*a*," and "formul*as*" rather than
"formul*ae*."

G 3b Confusing Singulars and Plurals

*Know how to handle expressions not clearly
either singuar or plural.*

(1) *Each, neither, either,* and *everyone* (**indefinite
pronouns**) may seem to refer to more than one person or

thing, but they are treated as singulars in formal written English:

Each of the students *is* going to receive a diploma.
Either of the plans *sounds* all right.

A number of is treated as a plural if it means "several" or "many":

A number of people *were* standing in the hallway.

(2) Expressions indicating quantity may be treated as singulars even when they seem plural in form, provided the sentence is concerned with *the whole amount* rather than with the individual units:

In those days two dollars *was* much money.

It is the most imperative social truth of our age that about one-third of the world is rich and two-thirds of the world *is* poor.—C. P. Snow, "On Magnanimity," *Harper's*

(3) Words like *audience, committee, family, group, jury, police,* and *team* are **collective nouns.** We use these as singulars when we are thinking of the group as a whole; we use them as plurals when we are thinking of the individual members of the group:

Singular: The family *is* a crucial social unit.
Plural: The family *were* seated around the dinner table.

(4) Words ending in *ics* look like plurals but are often singular. Singular are *aeronautics, mathematics, physics,* and similar words that identify a branch of knowledge or field of study:

Grammar and Usage

Mathematics *is* an indispensable tool of modern science.

Other words ending in *ics* are singular in some senses and plural in others. We say "Statistics *doesn't* appeal to me" when speaking of the *science* of statistics. We say "Statistics *don't* convince me" when speaking of statistical *data*.

G 3c   Compound Subjects   *agr*

Check for agreement in clauses that contain more than one subject.

After a **compound subject,** the verb may be plural even if each of the subjects is singular when taken by itself:

Tom and Sue *don't* smoke.
Hiking and canoeing are **fun.**

Whereas *and* actually adds one possible subject to another, *or* merely gives us a choice between two possible subjects (each of which may be singular). We say "Both his father and his mother *are* to blame" but "Either his father or his mother *is* to blame."

Note some special difficulties:

(1) *As well as, together with,* and *in addition to* do not add one subject to another. They merely show that what is said about the subject applies *also* to other things or persons:

Aunt Martha, together with her six children, *is* leaving town.

(2) Two nouns joined by *and* may be merely different parts of the *description of a single thing or person:*

Pork and beans *is* not one of my favorite dishes.
My closest friend and associate *was* a cocker spaniel.

(3) In some sentences, an *or,* an *either . . . or,* or a
neither . . . nor gives the reader a *choice between a singular subject and a plural one.* Make the verb of such a sentence agree with the subject closer to it:

Either laziness or excessive social obligations *have kept* him
from his work.

G 3d Blind Agreement

agr

*Do not make the verb agree with a word that
stands in front of it but is not its subject.*

Avoid **blind agreement.** Check especially for *a plural
noun* that comes between a singular subject and its verb.
Beware of faulty agreement whenever the subject of a sentence is one thing singled out among several, one quality
shared by several members of a group, or one action affect-
ing different things or persons:

Only one of my friends *was* ready [not *"were* ready"] in time.

The usefulness of his remedies *has been* questioned [not
"have been questioned"].

Understanding the opponent's motives *is* important [not *"are*
important"].

When for some reason *the subject follows the verb,* do
not make the verb agree with a stray noun that stands in
front of it:

Sleeping in the cradle *were* two rosy-cheeked infants.
(Who was sleeping? The infants *were* sleeping.)

In the very first chapter *occur* several incredible incidents.
(What occurs? Incidents *occur.*)

G 3e Agreement After *There* and *It*

Check for agreement in sentences starting with "there is," "there are," "it is," and the like.

After *there,* the verb agrees with the **postponed subject**—that is, with whatever is "there":

Singular: There *was* much *work* to be done.
Plural: There *were* scattered *rumblings* of dissent.

In formal usage, the plural verb is required even when followed by a compound subject of which each part is singular:

On the crown of the hill, there *are* a miniature plaza, miniature cathedral, and miniature governor's palace.—Arnold J. Toynbee, "The Mayan Mystery," *Atlantic*

Note: It is a pronoun and can function as the subject. After *it,* the verb is *always* singular:

It's your last chance.
It *was* the Joneses.

G 3f Agreement After *Who, Which,* and *That*

Check for agreement problems caused by relationships between several clauses.

Who, which, and *that* often serve as subjects in **adjective clauses**—that is, dependent clauses that modify a noun or pronoun. The verb following the *who, which,* or *that* agrees with the *word being modified:*

Singular: I hate a man who *stares* at me.

Plural: I hate men who *stare* at me.

Note: Formal English requires agreement in combinations like "one of those who know" and "one of those who believe." "Jean is *the only one* of those girls *who goes* to college for an education" means that one girl *goes* to college for an education but that the others don't. "Jean is one of *those girls who go* to college for an education" means that a number of girls go to college for an education and that Jean is one of them.

G 3g   Logical Agreement   *agr*

Where meaning requires it, observe agreement in other sentence elements in addition to verbs.

Often, you have to carry through agreement in number from the subject not only to the verb but also to the remainder of the sentence. (See G 5e for agreement of pronoun and antecedent.)

Illogical: Average newspaper *readers* go through their whole *life* knowing a little about everything but nothing well.

Revised: Average newspaper *readers* go through their whole *lives* knowing a little about everything but nothing well.

Illogical: My more studious *friends* are wise like *an owl* and always look up to higher things.

Revised: My more studious *friends* are wise like *owls* and always look up to higher things.

(See the Glossary of Usage on *these kind.*)

Exercises

A. In a college dictionary, look up the plural forms of the following nouns: *antenna, appendix, beau, cactus, cello, cherub, nucleus, oasis, stigma, vertebra.* Check whether the following forms are singular or plural or both: *addenda, agenda, apparatus, candelabra, deer, dice, Saturnalia, series, species, strata.*

B. In each of the following sentences, you can solve an agreement problem by changing a single word—usually the verb or first auxiliary. Write the changed form of the word after the number of the sentence.

1. The description of his appearance and manners hint at his hidden emotions.

2. For these men, the years spent in the armed forces has been a waste of time.

3. My sister and older brother belongs to my mother's church.

4. As one walks farther up the street, the style of the buildings change.

5. The humor that is mixed in with the characters and their lives add a certain luster to the book.

6. In the display window, there is two old sewing machines and a tailor's dummy dressed in a faded white dress.

7. The deep thinkers among the students attempt to solve all the world's problems by the use of their powerful mind.

8. These responsibilities entrusted to me has helped me develop my character.

9. A sharp increase in thefts are occurring on the beaches and in the campgrounds of this area.

10. The general attitude of the people I asked were very evasive.

11. The political science courses one takes in college often shows that the nation's great thinkers were people with human failings.

12. The significance of many of the words used by Shakespeare are hard to understand.

13. I am not one of those who believes in indiscriminate force to restore law and order."

14. A list of all the chores a housewife does in an average week show that she needs more energy than most men.

15. One of the first situations that challenge the reader's stereotypes arise as Elisa is working at a drive-in restaurant.

C. Select *appropriate forms,* paying special attention to common sources of faulty agreement.

1. In many of my classes the attitude of the students *(1) was/ (2) were* very poor.

2. The benefits that the city has derived from its new industries *(3) is/ (4) are* negligible.

3. Cooking, as well as sewing or cleaning, *(5) has/ (6) have* always bored me.

4. I was raised in a home where smoking and excessive drinking *(7) was/ (8) were* not permitted.

5. Getting along with one's neighbors *(9) is/ (10) are* not always easy.

6. The qualities that a girl looks for in a future husband *(11) is/ (12) are* determined in part by her family background.

7. The World's Fair dazzled everyone who *(13) was/ (14) were* there.

8. The ability to talk about something other than money and children *(15) is/ (16) are* important if a marriage is to last.

9. Colleges have to make provision for students who are below average academically but who nevertheless *(17) wants/ (18) want* a college education.

10. Using words like *dichotomy* and *schizophrenia (19) is/ (20) are* no sign of superior intelligence.

11. She was one of those hostesses who *(21) makes/ (22) make* no attempt to entertain the guests.

Grammar and Usage

12. His father felt that five dollars *(23) was/ (24) were* more than sufficient as a monthly allowance.

13. According to the judge, neither of the witnesses *(25) was/ (26) were* guilty of perjury.

14. We soon realized that our supply of food and fuel *(27) was/ (28) were* dangerously low.

15. Weapons like the bow and arrow, the spear, or the knife *(29) was/ (30) were* among the first major human inventions.

G 4 Verb Forms

Use verb forms appropriate to serious written English.

The most important verb forms are those traditionally grouped together to form the system of tenses. The **tenses** of a verb are the various *forms that indicate primarily different relationships of events in time:*

Active

		Progressive
Present	I ask	(I am asking)
Past	I asked	(I was asking)
Future	I shall (will) ask	(I shall be asking)
Perfect	I have asked	(I have been asking)
Past Perfect	I had asked	(I had been asking)
Future Perfect	I shall (will) have asked	(I shall have been asking)

	Passive	
Present	I am asked	(I am being asked)
Past	I was asked	(I was being asked)
Future	I shall (will) be asked	——
Perfect	I have been asked	——
Past Perfect	I had been asked	——
Future Perfect	I shall (will) have been asked	——

Most English verbs, the *regular verbs,* have two basic forms (**principal parts**). The first form is the plain form of the verb (*consent, smoke, depart, investigate, organize*). Standing by itself, it can form the **present tense.** This "simple present" may point to something actually happening now, something done regularly or habitually, or something about to happen in the immediate future:

We *consent.*
I *smoke* a pack a day.
They *depart* tonight.

The plain form can combine with *will* or *shall* in the **future tense:**

He *will* talk to you later.

The plain form plus *-ing* makes up the present participle, used in the various tenses of the **progressive** construction. The progressive construction normally indicates that at a given time an action or event is in progress:

We *are considering* your request.
Her husband *was painting* the house.

Grammar and Usage

The second basic form of a verb can stand by itself as the **past tense,** which indicates that an action took place in the past and came to an end in the past. To form this "simple past," regular verbs add *-ed* or *-d* to the plain form:

> He *consented*.
> We *asked* him.
> They *investigated* him thoroughly.

Regular verbs make the *-ed* form do double duty as a verbal (past participle) combining with the various forms of *have* to make up the **perfect tenses.** The present perfect ("I *have considered* your request") describes something that may have happened in the fairly recent past and that has a bearing on the present. The past perfect ("I *had considered* his request very carefully") describes something that had already happened when *other* events in the past took place. (See G 10a for sequence of tenses and shifts in tense.)

G 4a   Irregular Verbs gr

Know the standard forms of irregular verbs.

Irregular verbs often have not two but three basic forms. The simple past is often different from the past participle: *run—ran—run; know—knew—known; go—went—gone.* Pay special attention to verbs whose basic forms are *confusing in spelling or in sound.* Here is a brief list:

Present	Past	Perfect
begin	began	have begun
bend	bent	have bent
blow	blew	have blown

break	broke	have broken
bring	brought	have brought
burst	burst	have burst
choose	chose	have chosen
come	came	have come
deal	dealt	have dealt
dig	dug	have dug
do	did	have done
draw	drew	have drawn
drink	drank	have drunk
drive	drove	have driven
eat	ate	have eaten
fall	fell	have fallen
flee	fled	have fled
fly	flew	have flown
freeze	froze	have frozen
go	went	have gone
grow	grew	have grown
know	knew	have known
lead	led	have led
run	ran	have run
see	saw	have seen
send	sent	have sent
sing	sang	have sung
speak	spoke	have spoken
swim	swam	have swum
take	took	have taken
throw	threw	have thrown
wear	wore	have worn
write	wrote	have written

Sometimes you have a *choice of two acceptable forms:*

They gracefully *dived* (or *dove*) into the pool.
She *dreamed* (or *dreamt*) of a sloe-eyed Arab prince.
He *lighted* (or *lit*) his cigarette.
Your prediction *has proved* (or *has proven*) wrong.
The ship *sank* (or *sunk*) within minutes.

Grammar and Usage

Business *thrived* (or *throve*) as never before.
The sleepers *waked* (or *woke*) refreshed.

Note: In a few cases different forms for the same tense correspond to *differences in context or in meaning.* For instance, it is "The picture was *hung*" but "The prisoners were *hanged*"; "The sun *shone*" but "The boy *shined* my shoes."

G 4b   *Lie, Sit,* and *Rise*   𝒢𝓇

Know the standard forms of lie, sit, and rise.

Some verbs have doubles just different enough to be confusing:

(1) *Lie—lay—lain* indicates that somebody or something is situated somewhere. The same basic forms are used in the combination *lie down.*

On hot days the animals *lie* in the shade.
A letter *lay* on the floor.
He *should have lain down.*

Lay—laid—laid indicates that somebody is placing something somewhere. Use it when you can substitute *place* or *put.*

I wish I *could lay* my hands on him.
The weary travelers *laid down* their burdens.
You *should have laid aside* some money for emergencies.

(2) *Sit—sat—sat* indicates that someone is seated. *Sit down* follows the same scheme.

Though he told me that he seldom *sat* while at work, he *has sat* for an hour exactly where he *sat down* when he looked for a place to *sit.*

Set—set—set, one of the few verbs with only one basic form, belongs with *lay* as a possible substitute for *place* or *put*. You, yourself, *sit,* or *sit down;* you *set,* or *set down,* something else:

> When you *have set* the alarm, *set* it down by the cot I *set* up.

(3) *Rise—rose—risen* means "get up" or "go up." *Raise—raised—raised* refers to lifting something or *making* it go up:

> Since you *rose* this morning, the tax rate *has risen* ten cents.
>
> Though he *is* always *raising* his prices, he *has* not *raised* the salaries of his employees.

Exercise

Select verb forms appropriate to formal written English.

1. If a teacher *(1) lays/ (2) lies* a hand on an unruly student, he is likely to be sued by the student's parents.

2. In discussions touching on religious issues, many perplexing questions can be *(3) raised/ (4) risen.*

3. After the class *(5) sat/ (6) set* down, Mrs. Warner wanted to know who had *(7) wrote/ (8) written* "The Student's Lament."

4. The picture showed two elderly gentlemen *(9) setting/ (10) sitting* at a table and playing chess.

5. While the boys *(11) swam/ (12) swum* in the clear, cold water, I *(13) sat/ (14) set* in the canoe watching them.

6. While *(15) setting/ (16) sitting* up a new filing system, we must have *(17) mislaid/ (18) mislain* your letter.

7. The report has been *(19) laying/ (20) lying* on his desk all summer; at least I saw it *(21) lay/ (22) lie* there last week.

8. When I *(23) saw/ (24) seen* the deserted entrance, I *(25) knew/ (26) knowed* that the performance had already *(27) began/ (28) begun.*

9. The Park Department finally *(29) sat up/ (30) set up* benches for visitors who might want to *(31) set down/ (32) sit down.*

10. Satisfied with the conditions *(33) sat/ (34) set by* the negotiators, the rebels *(35) laid down/ (36) lay down* their arms.

G 5   Reference of Pronouns

To make a pronoun stand for the right noun,
place the right pronoun in the right position.

When you use a pronoun like *he, it,* or *this,* it should be clear to your reader who or what *he, it,* or *this* is. A pronoun has to refer clearly to its **antecedent,** the thing or person for which the pronoun is a substitute.

G 5a   Ambiguous Reference   *ref*

Do not let a pronoun point to more than one
possible antecedent.

Look at the use of *she* and *her* in the following example: "Mary was friendly to my sister because *she* wanted *her* to be *her* bridesmaid." Which of the two girls was getting married, and which was going to be a bridesmaid? The sentence is **ambiguous;** it confuses the reader because of an unintended double meaning.

Reference of Pronouns

Ambiguous:	After *Father* brought *Junior* back from the game, we took pictures of *him*.
Clear:	We took pictures of *Father* after *he* brought *Junior* back from the game.
Clear:	We took pictures of *Junior* after *Father* brought *him* back from the game.

If a *they* is preceded by two plural nouns, you can sometimes avoid ambiguity by *making one of them singular:*

Ambiguous:	*Students* like *science teachers* because *they* are realistic and practical.
Clear:	A *student* usually likes his *science teachers* because *they* are realistic and practical. (*They* can no longer be mistakenly referred to *students*.)

Similarly, one of two singular nouns might be changed into a plural:

A *writer* must necessarily talk to his *readers* [better than "to his *reader*"] in simple language if *his* vocabulary is limited.

Note: The *farther removed* a pronoun is from its antecedent, the greater the danger of ambiguous reference. Do not make a reader go back through several sentences in a paragraph to check what *he, this,* or *they* stands for.

G 5b   Reference to Modifiers   *ref*

**Make pronouns refer to one of the basic
elements of a sentence rather than to a modifier.**

The following sentence would sound absurd: "During the summer, Grandfather worked on a river boat, but in the winter *it* usually froze over." The *it* seems to refer to the boat, but boats do not freeze over. Similarly absurd sentences may result when a pronoun is expected to refer to a **possessive**:

Ambiguous: I reached for the *horse's* bridle, but *it* ran away.
(The bridle seems to be running away.)

Clear: The *horse* ran away after I reached for *its* bridle.
(The possessive has been changed to a pronoun, and the noun put where it is needed to prevent confusion.)

Note: Reference to a possessive accounts for the awkwardness of sentences like the following: "In *John Steinbeck's* novel *The Grapes of Wrath*, he describes the plight of the marginal farmer." Better: "In *his* novel . . . *John Steinbeck* describes . . ."

G 5c Vague *This* and *Which* *ref*

Avoid ambiguity caused by idea reference.

Vague **idea reference** results when a *this* or *which* refers to the overall idea expressed in the preceding statement:

Ambiguous: I knew that Bob was cheating, but the other students were not aware of *this*.
(Were they unaware of the *cheating*, or of my *knowing* about it?)

A vague *this* can be easily supplemented: "this assumption," "this outrage." A vague *which* is more difficult to improve. You may find it easier to do without it:

Ambiguous:	I have received only one letter, *which* frightens me.
Clear:	Receiving only one letter frightened me.
Clear:	The letter (the only one I received) frightened me.

G 5d   Implied Antecedents   *ref*

Eliminate indirect reference.

In informal conversation, we often make a pronoun refer to an antecedent that we have not actually mentioned. We expect its identity *to be understood.* We say, "In London, *they* have a great deal of fog." *They* means "Londoners" or "the people living in London."

Avoid the orphaned *it* or *they,* which refers to an *implied idea* in a sentence like the following: "My mother was a teacher; therefore, I have also chosen *it* as my profession." The *it* stands not for "teacher" but for "teaching":

Revised:	My mother was a teacher; therefore, I have also chosen *teaching* as my profession.
Ambiguous:	The prisoner's hands were manacled to a chain around his waist, but *they* were removed at the courtroom door. (What was removed? The prisoner's hands?)
Revised:	The prisoner's hands were manacled to a chain around his waist, but *the manacles* were removed at the courtroom door.

G 5e   Indefinite Antecedents   *ref*

In formal usage, treat indefinite expressions that are singular in form as singular antecedents.

Treat the **indefinite pronouns**—*everybody (everyone)*, *somebody (someone)*, *nobody (no one)*, *anybody (any-*

Grammar and Usage

one), *one*—consistently as singular. Informal English typically uses a singular verb after these words but then often
switches to a plural pronoun.

Formal: Someone left *his* (or *her*) gloves [not *"their* gloves"].

Formal: After hours everybody does as *he* (or *she*) pleases [not
        "as *they* please"].

Formal: Nobody should meddle in affairs that are none of *his*
        (or *her*) business [not "none of *their* business"].

Formal: One must honor *his* (or *one's*) obligations [not *"their*
        obligations"].

Consistently treat as singulars expressions like *a person, an individual, the typical student,* or *an average American.* These may seem to refer to more than one person but
are singular in form.

Faulty: A *person* can never be too careful about *their* use of
        language.

Revised: A *person* can never be too careful about *his* (or *her*)
        use of language.

Faulty: A *student* is here in college to study, but *they* are usu-
        ally poorly prepared for this task.

Revised: A *student* is here in college to study, but *he* (or *she*)
        is usually poorly prepared for this task.

Note: None started as the equivalent of "no one," but
today either singular or plural forms after it are acceptable:

None of the students *has his* (or *her*) books ready [or *"have
their* books ready"].

Exercise

In some of the following sentences, you can solve problems of pronoun reference by changing one or two of the pronouns. Write the changed pronouns after the number of the sentence. In other cases, you will have to rewrite part or all of the sentence.

1. In today's world, the sight of a parent spending enough time with their child is rare indeed.

2. When a person leaves home and goes to school, they are on their own.

3. Although most Americans were in support of the Allies, they tried to remain neutral.

4. Universities provide many services to the community surrounding it.

5. A student who follows my advice should find themselves doing well in school.

6. The average individual respects the wishes of the group because they hate to be considered odd.

7. My father is extremely intelligent, though he does not always express it in a verbal form.

8. Each woman has their own reason for getting an education.

9. All his clothes look tailor-made, and it gives him an air of distinction.

10. A teacher has office hours so they can help their students.

11. A fireman came up behind the policeman, but his first effort to reach my perch at 'the center of the roof was almost disastrous.

12. The English taught in elementary school included a weekly spelling test, but they did little to improve my oral use of language.

13. Newspapers give prominence to youths who get into trouble, which pins a bad label on all young people.

14. The person does not want anyone to know what they have

done, so they go to church and confess their sins to a priest in a confessional.

15. Society feels that a college degree is necessary to success and therefore pushes everyone into it.

G 6   Pronoun Forms

Use pronoun forms in accordance with the conventions of written English.

Pronouns have alternative forms, used depending on the function of the pronoun in the sentence. *I* and *he* are **subject forms,** identifying the person that the predicate says something about. *Me* and *him* are **object forms,** identifying the object of a verb or preposition. Only half a dozen pronouns have a distinct object form: *I—me; we—us; he—him; she—her; they—them; who—whom.*

Subject	Object	Object of Preposition
I congratulated	*him.*	
He recommended	*me*	to *them.*
They prejudiced	*her*	against *me.*

A third possible form typically indicates that the object of an action is identical with the performer. *Himself, themselves, myself, ourselves,* and similar forms are **reflexive forms:**

He cut *himself.*
They asked *themselves* what had gone wrong.

They are also used as **intensives,** for emphasis:

> The dean told me so *himself.*
>
> We should also weigh the testimony of the accused men *themselves.*

G 6a   Subject and Object Forms   *gr*

> *Use the pronoun forms for subject and object as appropriate in written English.*

Formal use of these forms differs to some extent from what we commonly hear in informal and nonstandard speech.

(1) Choose the standard form when a pronoun is *one of several subjects or objects in a clause:*

> My brother and *I* [not "*me* and my brother"] were reading comic books.
> (Who was reading? *I* was reading.)
>
> She asked my brother and *me* [not "my brother and *I*"] to dry the dishes.
> (Whom did she ask? She asked *me.*)

(2) Be careful with *pronoun-noun combinations* like *we Americans—us Americans* or *we girls—us girls:*

> *We boy scouts* are always eager to help. (*We* are eager.)
>
> He told *us boy scouts* to keep up the good work. (He told *us.*)

(3) Object forms are required *after prepositions* (with *her;* because of *him;* for *me*). Use the object form for a pronoun that is the second or third object in a prepositional phrase:

47

This kind of thing can happen to you and *me* [not "to you and *I*"].

I knew there was something between you and *her* [not "between you and *she*"].

(4) *As* and *than* are treated as connectives even when most of the clause they presumably introduce is missing. To decide whether they should be followed by the subject form or the object form, *reconstruct the missing clause:*

He is as tall as *I* (am).
I owe you as much as (I owe) *them*.
Her sister was smarter than *she* (was).
I like her better than (I like) *him*.

(5) In formal usage, subject forms are required *after linking verbs,* which introduce not an object of an action but a description of the subject:

The only ones not invited were *she* and a girl with measles.

The need for this use of the subject form seldom arises except after "it is," "it was," "it must be," and so on. (See the Glossary of Usage for *it's me/it is I.*)

Note: Formal English avoids the use of the reflexive pronoun as a substitute for the plain subject form or object form:

My friend and *I* [not "and *myself*"] were the last ones to leave.

I asked both his wife and *him* [not "and *himself*"] to come over after dinner.

G 6b   *Who* and *Whom*

Know how to use who *and* whom.

Who and *whom* are easily confused because their function in a sentence is not always obvious. Furthermore, *who* is increasingly replacing *whom* in speech.

Spoken: Tell me *who you are thinking of.*

Written: It is good for the sanity of all of us to have *someone whom we continue to think of* as Mister even though we address him by his given name.—Philip M. Wagner, "Mencken Remembered," *The American Scholar*

Observe the following guidelines in your writing:

(1) When *who* or *whom* occurs *at the beginning of a question, who* asks a question about the subject. *Whom* asks a question about an object:

Subject: *Who* did it? *He* did.

Object: *Whom* did you meet? I met *him.*

Object: To *whom* should I write? To *him.*

In more complicated questions, it may not be obvious whether a *who* inquires about a subject or about an object. However, the *he*-or-*him* test will always work:

Who do you think will win? (I think *he* will win.)
Whom did you expect to come? (I expected *him* to come.)

(2) *Who* and *whom* may *introduce dependent clauses.* To apply the *he*-or-*him* test to a dependent clause, separate it from the rest of the sentence:

Grammar and Usage

Subject:	Ask her / *who* wrote the letter. (*He* wrote the letter.)
Subject:	We approached the man / *who* was waiting. (*He* was waiting.)
Subject:	Here is a nickel for / *whoever* gets there first. (*He* gets there first.)
Object:	*Whom* we should invite / is a difficult question. (We should invite *him*.)
Object:	She knew my brother, / *whom* I rarely see. (I rarely see *him*.)
Object:	He knew few people / on *whom* he could rely. (He could rely on *them*.)

(See the Glossary of Usage for *"who, which,* and *that"* and for "possessives with verbal nouns.")

Exercises

A. Which of the italicized pronoun forms are appropriate to formal English? Which are inappropriate?

1. A teacher should not be condescending just because *he* knows more than *us* students.

2. Jack constantly enriched the conversation of my friends and *I* with brilliant comments.

3. People *who* are asked to "play *themselves*" in a movie often find that a good actor can portray their type more effectively than *them*.

4. My brother and *I* had no respect for the people with *whom* we worked, and soon we had no respect for *ourselves*.

5. I am tired of *his* spreading rumors about a rift between the board and *I*.

6. People *whom* I had not seen for months or *whom* I knew very slightly telephoned to advise *me* to get off the newly formed committee.

7. People *who* cannot suffer can never grow up, can never discover *who* they are. (James Baldwin)

8. Grandmother disapproved of John, *who she* felt lacked some of the qualities of a gentleman.

9. Every reader occasionally encounters a fictional character with *whom* he can immediately identify.

10. Giles would argue for hours with *whoever* was willing to listen to *him*.

B. In each of the following sentences, change one pronoun to a form more appropriate to formal written English. Write the changed form after the number of the sentence.

1. After dinner, us children would go to the first floor to play, explore, and talk.

2. When my mother punished my sister and I, she always suffered more than we did.

3. My cousin, who I had not seen for several years, worked there and knew how to get things done.

4. My sister is better than me at learning foreign languages.

5. I stopped at Jane's house because I had some letters for she and her mother.

6. I recognize the man's face; it was him who started the riot.

7. Every year, my father takes my brother and I on a camping trip.

8. This information should remain strictly between you and I.

9. The new ruler surrounded himself with subordinates on who he could rely.

10. Visitors from outer space might smile at the technology that us earthlings possess.

G 7 Modifiers

Check the form and position of modifiers.

Modifiers help us build up bare-bones sentences (see G 1c). Modifiers range all the way from single words to elaborate verbal phrases:

Adjectives:	The *dutiful* son married the *wealthy* girl.
Adverbs:	Jean will *probably* leave *early*.
Verbal Phrase:	The man *waiting in the dark doorway* was her ex-husband.

G 7a Adjectives and Adverbs   *gr*

In formal English, use the distinctive adverb form.

Most adverbs are distinguished from the corresponding adjectives by the *-ly* ending: *bright—brightly, cheerful—cheerfully, considerable—considerably, frequent—frequently, happy—happily, rapid—rapidly, rare—rarely, single—singly.* However, some adverbs, such as *fast, much, thus,* and *well,* have no distinctive ending. Some words ending in *-ly* are not adverbs but adjectives: a *friendly* talk, a *lonely* life, a *leisurely* drive, a *manly* reply.

Use distinctive adverb forms in sentences like the following:

Adverb:	In my absence, the town had changed *considerably*.
Adverb:	A teacher must be firm if he wants to be taken *seriously*.

Note the following special problems:

(1) *Good* and *bad* used as adverbs are commonly heard in informal speech but are widely considered non-standard. In formal English, "I don't hear so good" would be "I don't hear *well*." "I write pretty bad" would be "I write *badly*."

Objectionable:	This morning, the motor was running *good*.
Formal:	This morning, the motor was running *well*.

The adverb *well,* however, may do double duty as an adjective, in the sense of "healthy," "not ill": "He looks *well*"; "I don't feel *well*."

(2) Formal usage prefers "talks *loudly*" to "talks loud," "go *slowly*" to "go slow," or "come *quickly*" to "come quick," though both the long form and the short form of these adverbs have long been standard English.

Note: Not every word appearing next to a verb is necessarily an adverb. Linking verbs are followed by adjectives that point back to the subject:

His habits are *expensive.*
Most of the bottles were *empty.*
The speaker seemed *nervous.*

Here are some other verbs that may function as linking verbs and may thus be followed by adjectives:

Genevieve *turned* pale.	Honeysuckle *smells* sweet.
The heat *grew* oppressive.	The soup *tasted* flat.
He *became* rich overnight.	His hands *felt* moist.
Your fears *will prove* silly.	Sirens *sound* frightening.
The accused *remained* silent.	Your friend *looks* ill.

Grammar and Usage

G 7b   Adverbs to Modify Modifiers gr

In formal usage, use the distinctive adverb form to modify either an adjective or another adverb.

In "a *poorly* informed American," *poorly* is an adverb modifying the adjective *informed*. The man's supply of information is poor, though he himself may be wealthy.

Adverb + Adjective: a surprising*ly* beautiful bird
a hopeless*ly* retarded student
an impressive*ly* versatile actor

Adverb + Adverb: You sang admirab*ly* well.
He answered surprising*ly* fast.
She worked incredib*ly* hard.

Many everyday expressions use adjective forms instead of adverb forms as informal **intensifiers:** "He speaks *awful* fast." "Dean Howard is *real* popular." "I am *dreadful* sorry." In formal English, *omit* such intensifiers altogether or use a formal intensifier like *very*. Use *fairly* to replace the informal *pretty* in "pretty old."

G 7c   Misplaced Modifiers MM

Place modifiers so that they point clearly to what they modify.

Notice the changes in meaning that result from changes in the position of modifiers:

Adverb: The car *almost* broke down on every trip we took.
(It never quite did.)

The car broke down on *almost* every trip we took.
(It did frequently.)

Prepositional Phrase:	The man *with the ax* opened the door.
	The man opened the door *with the ax*.
Verbal:	Jerry married a wealthy wife *yearning for high social status*.
	Yearning for high social status, Jerry married a wealthy wife.

Watch out for the following:

(1) **Misplaced modifiers** seem to point to the wrong part of the sentence. Usually you can simply shift the modifier to a more appropriate position, though you may sometimes have to recast the sentence as a whole:

Misplaced:	He looked at the tree he had felled *with his hands in his pockets*.
	(It is hard to fell trees with one's hands in his pockets.)
Revised:	*With his hands in his pockets,* he looked at the tree he had felled.
Misplaced:	*Being made of stone,* the builder expected the house to stand for a century.
	(They called him Old Stoneface, no doubt.)
Revised:	Since *the house* was made of stone, the builder expected it to stand for a century.

(2) A **squinting modifier** seems to point two ways at once:

Squinting:	I feel *subconsciously* Hamlet wanted to die.
	(Are you talking about *your* subconscious feelings—or Hamlet's?)
Revised:	I feel that Hamlet *subconsciously* wanted to die.

(3) A **dangling modifier** is left dangling—what it supposedly points to is not part of the sentence. A dangling modifier is usually a verbal—a *to* form (infinitive) or *-ing*

form (participle). Revise by bringing back into the sentence what the verbal is supposed to modify.

Dangling: *To do well in college,* good grades are essential.

Revised: To do well in college, *a student* needs good grades.

Dangling: Often, *after convincing a girl to finish school,* she finds few openings in the field of her choice.

Revised: Often, after *her friends* have convinced her to finish school, a girl finds few openings in the field of her choice.

Note: Some verbal phrases are not intended to modify any one part of the main sentence. These are called **absolute constructions.** The most common ones are the many generally acceptable expressions that *clarify the attitude or intention of the speaker:*

> *Generally speaking,* traffic is getting worse rather than better.
> He had numerous children—seven, *to be exact.*
> *Considering the location,* the house is not a bad bargain.

Formal English, more frequently than informal English, uses verbals that *carry their own subjects along with them:*

> *The air being warm,* we left our coats in the car.
> *Escape being impossible,* he prepared for the worst.

Exercises

A. In most of the following sentences, one word should be changed to the distinctive adverb form. Write the changed word after the number of the sentence. If no word needs to be changed, write "No."

1. When the woman began to talk, she spoke nervously and very defensive.
2. Although his batting average was very low, his occasional hits always seemed to come at pressure points in our games.
3. He was tired and unable to think logical.
4. I read the questions as careful as the time allowed.
5. Toward the end of the story, the events unfold very sudden as they sometimes do in real life.
6. The children were becoming less cautious and more brave on their bicycles.
7. My father regarded life more serious than most people do.
8. Macbeth interpreted the prophecies of the weird sisters very literal.
9. During the time Judy spent in France, her French improved considerable.
10. No matter what dish George prepared, it tasted flat.
11. His survey was as complete as the time allowed.
12. All the girls performed admirably, but Judy did exceptionally well.
13. I had to talk fast and furious before the householder could slam the door in my face.
14. An experienced cryptographer can decipher a simple code very easy.
15. My father didn't do very good in school because he had to work on my grandfather's farm.

B. Point out the misplaced or dangling modifiers that make most of the following sentences unsatisfactory. Your instructor may ask you to rewrite some or all of the unsatisfactory sentences.

1. Leaving town, the weather got worse.
2. This morning I wrote to my family for the first time since I have come here on the back of a postcard.
3. The winds brought storms that bent small trees to the ground on the hillsides.

4. The car was towed away by John, having exploded on Interstate 59.

5. Unsure of my future, the army was waiting for me.

6. After ringing for fifteen minutes, the President's secretary answered the phone.

7. Brushing the aides aside, the reporter insisted on the promised interview with the senator.

8. Enjoying the party, the curfew hour was ignored.

9. Lacking a college education, the manager constantly made comments about the importance of the working people and the knowledge to be gained from living.

10. After being around Nick for only a short time, it was easy to see he was no ordinary person.

11. These magazines clearly appeal to women readers with stories about torrid love affairs.

12. Sometimes a student studies only so that he can prove in class the professor is wrong just to be showing off.

13. When traveling during the night without sufficient lighting, other motorists will have difficulty seeing the vehicle.

14. Such magazines as *Argosy, Adventure,* and *True* have on their covers brightly colored pictures of men fighting wars or hunting in wild country.

15. Several reporters sat with coffee cups discussing the day's events.

G 8   Confused Sentences

Avoid garbled sentences resulting from hasty writing, inaccurate copying, or careless typing.

Even when the reader can make out the intended meaning, he or she will be annoyed at being temporarily tripped up by a defect that the writer should have caught in revision.

G 8a   Omission and Duplication   *st*

Check your sentences for omitted or duplicated elements.

Make sure you have transcribed each sentence in full, without omitting minor sentence elements like *a, the, has, be,* or *am.* Make sure you have not awkwardly repeated minor elements, especially connectives like *that* or *when:*

> I think *that* because he is ill *(that)* he will not come.
>
> When school starts in the fall *(that is when)* most parents sigh with relief.

Many hastily written sentences lack some essential part:

Hasty: After my sister moved to Ohio, her little girl contracted polio, but did not cause paralysis.
(It was not *the girl* that didn't cause paralysis, but the disease.)

Revised: After my sister moved to Ohio, her little girl contracted polio, but fortunately *the disease* did not cause paralysis.

G 8b   Mixed Construction   *st*

Do not confuse different ways of expressing the same idea.

The experienced writer will try out various possible constructions and select the one that seems to fit best. The inexperienced writer may plunge ahead, confusing the various possibilities. The result is known as **mixed construction:**

Grammar and Usage

Mixed:	In case of emergency should be reported to the head office.
Consistent:	*In case of emergency, report* to the head office.
Consistent:	*Emergencies should be reported* to the head office.
Mixed:	The department manager *rejected him to be* one of his assistants.
Consistent:	The department manager *rejected his application.*
Consistent:	The department manager *did not want him to be* one of his assistants.
Mixed:	The course was canceled *because of* not enough students registered.
Consistent:	The course was canceled *because not enough students registered.*
Consistent:	The course was canceled *because of insufficient enrollment.*

Note: In informal English, an adverbial clause starting with *because* sometimes appears as the subject of a verb. Formal English requires a noun clause starting with *that:*

Mixed:	*Because people enjoy watching a light comedy* does not mean that our society is in a state of decay.
Consistent:	*That people enjoy watching a light comedy* does not mean that our society is in a state of decay.

G 8c   Faulty Predication   *st*

Make sure that what the predicate says can logically apply to the subject.

Suppose you say, *"The choice* of our new home *was selected* by my mother." What was actually selected? Not a choice, but a home.

Confused Sentences

Logical:	The choice *was made* by my mother.
Logical:	*The home* was selected by my mother.
Faulty:	At the beginning of the year, *the participation* in club activities is always *overcrowded.* (The meetings—not the participation—are overcrowded, though the fact that many people participate is the reason for the overcrowding.)
Logical:	At the beginning of the year, *our club meetings* are always overcrowded.

G 8d   Faulty Equation   *st*

> **Use a linking verb to equate two things that are logically equal.**

In informal English, such equations are often loose and illogical. "His job *is* a mail carrier" is illogical because a mail carrier is a person, not a job. Formal English would require *"He* is a mail carrier" or "His job is *that of* a mail carrier."

Faulty:	*A woman* going to college to increase her knowledge is as valid a reason as a man going to college to become a dentist or a lawyer. (A woman is a reason?)
Revised:	*A woman's* going to college . . . (Going to college to increase her knowledge is a reason.)

A common type of faulty equation makes a linking verb introduce an **adverbial clause.** Children, for instance, will say, "A zoo is *when you go to look at animals."* "When you go to look at animals" is not logically a description of a zoo; normally it would indicate *when* an action takes place or a condition occurs.

Faulty: Punishment is *when you are told to stand in the corner.*

Satisfactory: When you are told to stand in the corner, you are being punished.

Satisfactory: Punishment is a means of keeping children out of mischief.

Linking verbs often cause faulty equation when they introduce **prepositional phrases** that would normally indicate the circumstances of an action. Use an infinitive (or similar noun equivalent) instead:

Our only hope *is to convince* your parents [not *"is by convincing* your parents"].

Their method of selection *was to question* the candidates carefully [not *"was by questioning* the candidates"].

G 8e   Faulty Appositives   *st*

Make sure that your appositives can be equated with the nouns they modify.

An **appositive** is a noun placed next to another noun: "John, *a sophomore,* came to see me." Here, John and the sophomore are identical. However, it does not make sense to say, "There was only *one telephone call, a friend* of yours." A friend can *make* a telephone call, but we would not say that he *is* one.

Faulty: We have only one *vacancy, a mathematics teacher.*
            (A teacher is not a vacancy, and a vacancy is not a teacher.)

Revised: We have only one *vacancy,* a *position* for a mathematics teacher.
            (What is actually vacant is a *position* for a teacher.)

Exercise

In the following sentences, point out all instances of hasty writing, mixed construction, faulty predication, and faulty apposition. Label each sentence *S* (satisfactory) or *U* (unsatisfactory). If your instructor desires, revise unsatisfactory sentences.

1. Parents view sex as sacred and should be reserved for marriage alone.

2. By cutting the number of jurors in half greatly reduces the time used in selecting a jury.

3. He was watched by the owner, a little man who peeped over the counter with a wrinkled face.

4. Committing suicide in the story pointed out that the weak cannot survive in this world.

5. Scientists know how to distill drinking water from salt water, but the cost of such a project is too unprofitable.

6. One good example of romantic love triumphing against odds is when there is an interracial marriage.

7. I saw him eat three hot dogs and drank three cokes.

8. I suddenly realized that we were no longer on level ground and that the road was tilting upward on great concrete stilts.

9. In my experience, the older a man is, the more chivalrous and the more gallantry he possesses.

10. Nowadays, the idea of love is begun at a very tender age.

11. Radical opinions are too biased and will not accept realistic compromise.

12. Because little of the pledged money actually came in, the repertory company had to give up its noble experiment.

13. My father first met his business partner in the army, for whom he drove a jeep and was his immediate supervisor.

14. The players up for the team were about even in ability and was a hard decision to make.

15. A person who fails in various things might give him an inferior feeling.

G 9 Incomplete Constructions

In formal English, spell out relationships merely implied in various informal constructions.

In written English, we avoid shortcuts common in informal speech. Check constructions like the following for logical completeness.

G 9a Incomplete Comparison *st*

Complete incomplete comparisons.

Normally, *more, better,* and *whiter,* the **comparative forms,** establish a comparison between at least two elements:

Carpenters make more money than *teachers.*
Half a loaf is better than *a slice.*

Most, best, and *whitest,* the **superlative forms,** establish a comparison within a group of at least three elements:

The annual classic at Le Mans is the most dangerous *automobile race in Europe.*

(1) In formal English, don't make the reader find out for himself *what is being compared with what.* Watch for incomplete comparisons resulting from the use of *more* and *the most* as intensifiers: "That girl has *more* luck" (than who or than what?). "I had *the most* wonderful experience" (of the day? of the year? of a lifetime?). "I saw *the*

most exciting play" (the most exciting play of the season? the most exciting play ever produced?) .

(2) Some sentences compare things *that are not really comparable:* "The skin of her cheeks was as soft as a child." Actually, her skin was as soft as a *child's* (skin) , or as soft as *that* of a child. Check for logical balance in sentences like the following:

Illogical: *Her personality* was unlike *most other girls* I have known in the past.

Logical: *Her personality* was unlike *that* of most other girls I have known.

Illogical: *The teachings* of Horatio Alger reached a wider audience than *Whitman.*

Logical: The *teachings* of Horatio Alger reached a wider audience *than those of* Whitman.—Saul Bellow, "The Writer as Moralist," *Atlantic*

(3) Some camparisons mention *three comparable items* without making it clear which two are being compared. "Tom liked Dick better than Harry" may mean two different things:

Clear: Tom liked Dick better than Harry *did.*

Clear: Tom liked Dick better than *he liked* Harry.

(See the Glossary of Usage for informal *so* and *such.*)

G 9b   Contraction of Coordinate Elements   *st*

In telescoping coordinate elements, omit only identical items.

When several items of the same kind are coordinated by a connective like *and* or *but,* we often omit forms that would cause unnecessary duplication. But such omission may cause truncated sentences.

(1) If one of *several verbs* in a sentence appears in a shortened form, fill in the complete forms first and omit only identical items. In "It *can be done* and *will be done,*" the *be done* after *can* is identical with that after *will.* You can therefore omit it and say: "It *can* and *will be done.*" But avoid "It *can* and *has been* done." The complete forms are *can be done* and *has been done.*

| Incomplete: | The patient *was given* an injection and the instruments *made* ready. |
| Complete: | The patient *was given* an injection, and the instruments *were made* ready. |

(2) A special kind of unsatisfactory telescoping occurs in *double-barreled comparisons* of the *as-good-if-not-better* type: "My theme is as good if not better than yours." The complete forms would be *as good as* and *better than.* Formal English would require "My theme is as good *as,* if not better *than,* yours." Less awkward and equally acceptable is shifting the second part of the comparison to the end of the sentence:

My theme is as good as yours, *if not better.*

(3) When you coordinate *several prepositional phrases,* keep prepositions that are not identical but merely express a similar relationship:

| Satisfactory: | I have great *admiration and respect* for him. |
| | (Taken up separately, the two prepositions would prove identical: "admiration *for* him" and "respect *for* him.") |

Incomplete Constructions

Unsatisfactory: I have great *respect and faith* in him.
(Taken up separately, the two phrases would require different prepositions: "respect *for* him" and "faith *in* him.")

Notice the use of different prepositions in the following examples:

She was jealous *of* but fascinated *by* her rival.

His behavior during the trial adds *to* rather than detracts *from* my admiration for him.

Exercise

Check the following sentences for incomplete constructions. Point out unsatisfactory comparisons and unsatisfactory contraction. Label each sentence S (satisfactory) or U (unsatisfactory). If your instructor desires, revise unsatisfactory sentences.

1. In much of Europe, American films are more popular than any other country.
2. Women on the whole understand children better than men.
3. The light at the intersection of Sixth and Grove will turn green exactly six seconds after the intersection of Wright and Grove.
4. Few of my friends were preoccupied or even interested in making a living.
5. Children seem to like the so-called adult Westerns as much as adults do.
6. Unlike America, traveling abroad is a rare luxury in many foreign countries.

7. Mike never has and never will succeed in making his restaurant something more than a place to eat food.

8. The United States has more television sets to the square mile than any other country in the world.

9. Year after year, American colleges produce more physical education teachers than mathematics.

10. The Secretary of State usually attracts more criticism than any member of the President's cabinet.

11. Critics of our schools must realize that they can and are doing great harm by indiscriminate attacks.

12. Unlike a track coach, a history teacher seldom has a newspaper article written about him when his students do exceptional work.

13. Most young children learn a second language more readily than an older person does.

14. The impact of American books, magazines, and comics in Great Britain is much greater than British publications in the United States.

15. A good background in the liberal arts is excellent preparation for such practical professions as engineers and lawyers.

G 10   Consistency

Do not confuse your readers by unmotivated shifts in tense, reference, or grammatical perspective.

The need for consistency makes a writer guard against confusing shifts in perspective. Like a road full of unexpected twists and turns, sentences that lack consistency slow down and confuse the reader.

G 10a   Shifts in Tense   *shift*

***Be consistent in your use of verb forms that
indicate the relationship of events in time.***

(1) Avoid *shifting from past to present* when something becomes so real that it seems to be happening in front
of you:

> We *disembarked* at noon and fought our way through the
> jungle in the sultry afternoon heat. Suddenly, there *is* a tiger! I
> *aim* my rifle and *pull* the trigger! Nothing *happens*—the gun
> *wasn't* loaded. Luckily, one of my bearers *saved* me from the con-
> sequences of my carelessness.

Tell the whole story as though it were happening now:
"We *disembark* . . . *fight* our way . . . one of them *saves*
me." (Or, describe *everything* in the past.)

(2) Avoid shifts in perspective when two events happen *at different times or during different periods:* "When
I *saw* the *F* on my report card, I *was* terribly disappointed,
because I *studied* very hard." If studying hard was a matter
of past history by the time the student received his grade,
the **sequence of tenses** would be more accurate like this:

> I was terribly disappointed, because I *had studied* very hard.

Formed with *have* or *has,* the **present perfect** indicates
that something has happened prior to events taking place
now: "He *has finished* his supper and *is getting* up."
Formed with *had,* the **past perfect** indicates that something
happened in the relatively distant past, prior to *other*
events in the past: "He *had finished* his supper and *was
getting* up." A confusing shift results when a writer disre-
gards these relations:

Grammar and Usage

Shift: Last March, the Secretary of the Air Force told the committee what *has happened* to air transport in this country.

Consistent: Last March, the Secretary of the Air Force told the committee what *had happened* to air transport in this country.

          (The secretary could not have told the committee what *has happened* since he testified and up to the present time.)

(3) *Avoid shifts resulting from failure to observe the distinction between direct and indirect quotation.* What the speaker felt or observed at the time he spoke would occur in the present tense in direct quotation: He said, "I *feel* fine." It would occur in the past tense in indirect quotation: He said that he *felt* fine. What the speaker felt *before* he spoke would occur in the past (or perhaps in the present perfect) when quoted directly: He said, "I *felt* fine." It would occur in the past perfect when quoted indirectly: He said that he *had felt* fine.

Failure to adjust the tenses in indirect quotations can lead to sentences like the following:

> Her husband admitted that he *was* [should be *"had been"*] a confirmed bachelor.
>
> Mr. Chamberlain said that there *will be* [should be *"would be"*] peace in our time.

When *a statement made in the past formulates a general truth,* the present tense is plausible:

Galileo said that the earth *moves* and that the sun *is* fixed; the Inquisition said that the earth *is* fixed and the sun *moves;* and Newtonian astronomers, adopting an absolute theory of space, said that both the sun and the earth *move.*—A. N. Whitehead, *Science and the Modern World*

(4) *Avoid inconsistent combinations between forms that indicate differences in attitude toward possible events* (called differences in **mood**). In the following sentences, note the differences between factual reference to a possibility and the **conditional,** which makes the same possibility seem less probable, or contrary to fact.

Inconsistent:	If he *comes* to this country, the army *would* draft him.
Factual:	If he *comes* to this country, the army *will* draft him.
Conditional:	If he *came* to this country, the army *would* draft him.

G 10b   Shifts in Reference   *shift*

Be consistent in the way you refer to yourself and others.

The least ambiguous pronoun you can use to refer to yourself is of course *I, me,* or *my* (**first person singular**). Writers who want to speak directly to their readers can call them *you* (**second person singular** and **plural**) and use *we* to refer to both the readers and themselves:

You will agree that *we* must do everything in our power.

As *you* no doubt remember, *we* have witnessed several similar incidents during the past year.

But *you* also appears as an informal equivalent of *one* or *a person,* referring not so much to the reader as to people in general:

Formal:	*One* cannot be too careful.
Informal:	*You* can't be too careful.

71

Confusion results when a writer shifts to the indefinite, generalized *you* after he has already identified the person he has in mind in some other way: "I don't want to be a famous actress. *I* would rather lead my own life without people always knowing what *you* are doing." The easiest way to avoid this kind of shift is to use *you* only to mean "you, the reader."

Similar in effect to shifts to *you* are shifts to the **imperative,** the request form of verbs: *"Come* in." *"Put* it down." *"Leave* him alone." Imperatives are most appropriate in directions and exhortations. They startle the reader when they suddenly break into ordinary expository prose:

Shift: High schools *should stop* educating all students at the same rate. *Give* aptitude tests for placement and then *separate* the students accordingly.

Consistent: High schools *should stop* educating all students at the same rate. They *should give* aptitude tests for placement and then *separate* the students accordingly.

G 10c   Shifts to the Passive   *shift*

Avoid shifting to the passive when the person in question is still the active element in the sentence.

Some sentences confuse the reader by shifting from an **active** construction (*"He built* the house") to a **passive** one (*"The house was built* by him") :

Inconsistent: He *returned* to the office as soon as *his lunch had been eaten.*

             (This sounds as though his lunch might have been eaten by somebody else.)

Consistent: He *returned* to the office as soon as he *had eaten* his lunch.

Unsatisfactory shifts to the passive are especially frequent after an impersonal *one* or *you:*

Inconsistent: As *you scan* the area of your backyard, a small patch of uninhabited earth *is located.*

Consistent: As *you scan* your backyard, *you locate* a small patch of earth.

G 10d   Faulty Parallelism   *FP*

Use parallel grammatical structure for elements serving the same function in a sentence.

Sentence elements joined by *and, or,* and *but* have to be **parallel;** they have to fit into the same grammatical category. If you put an *and* after *body,* the reader expects another noun: "body and *chassis,*" "body and *soul.*" If you put an *and* after *swore,* he expects another verb: "swore and *affirmed,*" "swore and *raved.*" The same principle applies to other elements:

Infinitives: Two things that a successful advertisement must accomplish are *to be noticed* and *to be remembered.*

Participles: I can still see my aunt *striding* into the corral, *cornering* a cow against a fencepost, *balancing* herself on a one-legged milking stool, and *butting* her head into the cow's belly.

Clauses: The young people *who brood* in their rooms, *who forget* to come down to the dining hall, and *who burst out* in fits of irrationality are not worrying about who will win the great game.—Oscar Handlin, "Are the Colleges Killing Education?" *Atlantic*

Faulty parallelism results when the second element does not fit the expected pattern. For instance, *"ignorant and a miser"* is off balance because it joins an adjective and a noun. You could change *ignorant* to a noun ("He was an *ignoramus* and a miser") or *miser* to an adjective ("He was ignorant and *miserly*").

Faulty: My grandfather liked *the country* and *to walk* in the fields.

Parallel: My grandfather liked *to live* in the country and *to walk* in the fields.

Faulty: He told me *of his plans* and *that he was leaving*.

Parallel: He *informed* me of his plans and *told* me that he was leaving.

Look especially for the following:

(1) Sentences sound awkward when a noun appears in coordination with an adjective as the modifier of *another noun:*

Faulty: The schools must serve *personal and society* needs as they evolve.

Parallel: The schools must serve *personal and social* needs as they evolve.

(2) Lack of parallelism is especially obvious after **correlatives:** *either . . . or, neither . . . nor, not only . . . but also, whether . . . or.*

Faulty: I used to find him either *on the porch* or *dozing* in the living room.

Parallel: I used to find him either *sitting* on the porch or *dozing* in the living room.

Faulty: We wondered whether *to believe* him or *should we try* to verify his story.

Parallel: We wondered whether we should *believe* him or *try* to verify his story.

(3) **Avoid faulty parallelism** *in a series of three or more elements.* Often a writer will lead his reader into what looks like a conventional series only to trip him up by making the last element snap out of the expected pattern:

Faulty: He liked to *swim, relax,* and *everything peaceful.*

Parallel: He liked *swimming, relaxation,* and peaceful *surroundings.*

If the elements in a faulty series are not really parallel in *meaning,* the revision might break up the series altogether:

Faulty: Her new friend was *polite, studious,* and *an only child.*

Parallel: Her new friend was *a gentleman, a scholar,* and *an only child.*

Broken Up: Her new friend, *an only child,* was a gentleman and a scholar.

Exercises

A. Check the following passages for unnecessary or confusing shifts in perspective. Label each sentence *S* (satisfactory) or *U* (unsatisfactory). If your instructor desires, revise unsatisfactory sentences.

Grammar and Usage

1. Things like this make a person face reality and wonder what your destiny could possibly be.

2. We gathered some old rags, and a bucket and soap were placed near the car.

3. The harder I push, the tighter I grip the wrench, the more the blood dripped from my scraped knuckles, and the angrier I became.

4. The more I think about capital punishment, the more one question kept entering my mind.

5. It was soon discovered by the students that if you didn't work fast you were put in the slow learning group.

6. Suddenly the sky darkens, a breeze springs up, and a premonitory rumble rolls across the lake.

7. Men are not qualified to speak of good if evil has never been examined.

8. A true gentleman behaves the way he does because courtesy has to him become second nature.

9. As the world grew dark, he dreams of a place he will never see.

10. To the early Christians, endurance meant seeing one's loved ones thrown to wild beasts without losing faith in your God.

11. Parents must take an active interest in what their children are doing. Coach a ball team or be a den mother to a girl scout group.

12. As I walk by the shop, the owner, not having anything to do, was looking out of the window.

13. The police were warning us that if the crowd did not calm down arrests will be made.

14. My favorite television program was already in progress. Right in the middle of a dramatic scene, the station goes off the air.

15. Millions of people every day rush off to jobs they detest.

B. Check the following sentences for parallel structure. Label each sentence *S* for satisfactory, or *FP* for faulty parallelism. Your instructor may ask you to revise some or all of the unsatisfactory sentences.

1. Her parents kept telling her Joe was poor, lazy, and his hair was too long.

2. He blamed me for not giving him a chance to succeed and I ruined his big chance for him.

3. The affluent American has a large income, a nice house, and lives in the nice part of town.

4. The book made me remember the bombings in Germany, the dismembered bodies, and the fire and fury of war.

5. She got her opinions by listening to her teachers and then evaluate their ideas.

6. The boy described how he was beaten by his masters, taken advantage of by the older servants, and the meager meals of bread and porridge he received.

7. In many gangster movies, the hero deceives the police, moves in the best society, and comes to a bad end only because his mother-in-law shoots him for having slapped her daughter.

8. To most readers, the word *home* suggests security and comfort as well as a place to live.

9. The success of a television program depends on how well the program has been advertised, the actors taking part, and is it comedy or serious drama.

10. Students come to college to have fun, find a husband or wife, get away from home, and many other ridiculous reasons.

11. Objective tests can never be a true test of a student's ability and failing the majority of those who would otherwise do well.

12. My father thought that young girls should not go to dances, see young men only in the company of a chaperone, and many other old-fashioned prejudices.

13. At the beginning, the story focuses on whether the old man will capture the large beautiful fish or will the fish elude him.

Grammar and Usage

14. O'Neill's last plays are alive with archetypal American experience and anguished family biography.

15. Teen-agers assert their independence through the way they dress, comb their hair, and their tastes in music.

2
Words

For Quick Reference

Good writers know the power of words. They marvel at the resources of language and exploit them in their work. The layman typically notices words only when something goes wrong:

> Leprosy invaded Europe in the Middle Ages and was very *popular* among the poor.
>
> Contralto is a *low* form of music that only ladies sing.
>
> In Platonic love, sexual relations are *illuminated.*

Though amused by such verbal accidents, experienced writers study words with a more positive interest. They know that in order to study and write in any major field they have to learn its language. A student of physics has to know terms like *velocity, inertia, hydraulic, ratio,* and *proton.* A student of literature has to become familiar with terms like *myth, protagonist, didactic,* and *allegory.*

In order to use words with confidence, good writers do more than look for a single basic meaning. They become aware of the *different uses* to which a word is put, and the *different effects* it may have on a reader. Effective writers know that words can work for them, but also *against* them. They know when words do their job, but not well—like a knife used in eating peas. They are always looking for words that will help them say what they want to say more clearly, more directly. They look for words that are fresh and vigorous rather than stale and tired. The following chapter is designed to help a writer improve his or her command of vocabulary and diction; that is, of word resources and word choice.

D 1   College Dictionaries

To make the best use of your dictionary, familiarize yourself fully with how it provides information.

College dictionaries provide information not only on the full range of meaning of a word but also on its history, implications, and possible limitations. The following dictionaries are widely recommended:

- *Webster's New World Dictionary* (NWD) makes a special effort to explain the meanings of words simply and clearly, using "the simplest language consistent with accuracy and fullness." Historical information *precedes* current meanings, so that the reader is given a sense of how a word developed. Lists of idioms provide an excellent guide to how a word is used in characteristic phrases. Throughout, informal and slang uses of words are so labeled.

- The *Standard College Dictionary* (SCD) was first published in 1963. Usually, the most *frequent* (rather than

vocabulary entry	**beau·ty** (byōō′tē), *n., pl.* **-ties** for 2–6. **1.** a quality that is present in a thing or person giving intense aesthetic pleasure or deep satisfaction to the senses or the mind. **2.** an attractive, well-formed girl or woman. **3.** a beautiful thing, as a work of art, building, etc. **4.** Often, **beauties.** that which is beautiful in nature or in some natural or artificial environment. **5.** a particular advantage: *One of the beauties of this medicine is the absence of aftereffects.* **6.** a person or thing that excels or is remarkable of its kind: *His black eye was a beauty.* [ME *be(a)ute* < OF *beaute*; r. ME *bealte* < OF, var. of *bellet* < VL **bellitāt-* (s. of **bellitās*) = L *bell(us)* fine + *-itāt- -ITY*] —**Syn. 1.** loveliness, pulchritude, comeliness, fairness, attractiveness. **2.** belle. —**Ant. 1.** ugliness.

pronunciation
syllabication dot

synonym lists

part of speech and inflected forms	**be·gin** (bi gin′), *v.*, **be·gan, be·gun, be·gin·ning.** —*v.i.* **1.** to proceed to perform the first or earliest part of some action; commence or start. **2.** to come into existence; originate: *The custom began during the Civil War.* —*v.t.* **3.** to proceed to perform the first or earliest part of (some action): *Begin the job tomorrow.* **4.** to originate; be the originator of: *Civic leaders began the reform movement.* [ME *beginn(en)*, OE *beginnan* = *be- BE- + -ginnan* to begin, perh. orig. to open, akin to YAWN] —**be·gin′ner,** *n.*

etymology

synonym study	—**Syn. 3.** BEGIN, COMMENCE, INITIATE, START (when followed by noun or gerund) refer to setting into motion or progress something that continues for some time. BEGIN is the common term: *to begin knitting a sweater.* COMMENCE is a more formal word, often suggesting a more prolonged or elaborate beginning: *to commence proceedings in court.* INITIATE implies an active and often ingenious first act in a new field: *to initiate a new procedure.* START means to make a first move or to set out on a course of action: *to start paving a street.* **4.** inaugurate, initiate. —**Ant. 1.** end.

antonym

variant spelling	**be·la·bor** (bi lā′bər), *v.t.* **1.** to discuss, work at, or worry about for an unreasonable amount of time: *He kept belaboring the point long after we had agreed.* **2.** to scorn or ridicule persistently. **3.** *Archaic.* to beat vigorously. Also, *Brit.,* **be·la′bour.**

hyphenated entry	**belles-let·tres** (*Fr.* bel le′tᴿ³), *n.pl.* literature regarded as a fine art, esp. as having a purely aesthetic function. [< F: lit., fine letters] —**bel·let·rist** (bel le′trist), *n.* —**bel·let·ris·tic** (bel′li tris′tik), *adj.* —**Syn.** See **literature.**

word element	**bene-,** an element occurring in loan words from Latin where it meant "well": *benediction.* [comb. form of *bene* (adv.) well]
consecutive definition numbers	**be·neath** (bi nēth′, -nēᴛ́ħ′), *adv.* **1.** below; in or to a lower place, position, state, or the like. **2.** underneath: *heaven above and the earth beneath.* —*prep.* **3.** below; under: *beneath the same roof.* **4.** further down than; underneath; lower in place than: *the first drawer beneath the top one.* **5.** inferior in position, rank, power, etc.: *A captain is beneath a major.* **6.** unworthy of; below the level or dignity of: *beneath contempt.*

usage note	**bent**[1] (bent), *adj.* **1.** curved or crooked: *a bent bow; a bent stick.* **2.** determined, set, or resolved (usually fol. by *on*): *to be bent on buying a new car.*

example contexts	**bet·ter**[1] (bet′ər), *adj., compar. of* **good** *with* **best** *as superl.* **1.** of superior quality or excellence: *a better coat.* **2.** morally superior; more virtuous: *He's no better than a thief.* **3.** of superior value, use, fitness, desirability, acceptableness, etc.: *a better time for action.* **4.** larger; greater: *the better part of a lifetime.* **5.** improved in health; healthier: *Is your mother better?* —*adv., compar. of* **well** *with* **best** *as superl.* **6.** in a more excellent way or manner: *to behave better.* **7.** to a greater degree; more completely or thoroughly: *I probably know him better than anyone else.* **8.** more: *I walked better than a mile to town.* **9. better off, a.** in better circumstances. **b.** more fortunate; happier. **10. go (someone) one better,** to exceed another's effort; be superior to. **11. had better,** would be wiser or more reasonable to; ought to: *We had better stay indoors today.* **12. think better of, a.** to reconsider and decide more favorably or wisely: *She was tempted to make a sarcastic retort, but thought better of it.* —*v.t.* **13.** to make better; improve; increase the good qualities of. **14.** to improve upon; surpass; exceed: *We have bettered last year's production record.* **15. better oneself,** to improve one's social standing, financial position, or education. —*n.* **16.** that which has greater excellence: *the better of two choices.* **17.** Usually, **betters.** those superior to one in wisdom, social position, etc. **18. for the better,** in a way that is an improvement: *His health changed for the better.* **19. get the better of, a.** to get an advantage over. **b.** to prevail against. [ME *bettre*, OE *betera*; c. OHG *bezziro* (G *besser*), Goth *batiza* = *bat-* (akin to BOOT[2]) + *-iza* comp. suffix] —**Syn. 13.** amend; advance, promote. See **improve.**

idiomatic phrases

Explanation of dictionary entries
(From *Random House Dictionary*)

the oldest) meaning of a word appears first. Coverage of informal English and slang is excellent and up to date, with authoritative notes on debatable points of usage. Like the NWD, the *Standard College Dictionary* has introductory materials on the history of English and on modern approaches to the study of language.

- *Webster's New Collegiate Dictionary* is published by the G. & C. Merriam Company, whose collection of several million citation slips has been called "the national archives of the language." The *Collegiate* is based on *Webster's Third New International Dictionary,* the most authoritative and comprehensive unabridged dictionary of current American English. Historical information precedes meanings, which are presented in the order of their development. The Merriam-Webster dictionaries have abandoned the practice of labeling words informal as too arbitrary or subjective. They make only sparing use of the label "slang." Unlike the NWD and the SCD, the *Collegiate* lists names of people and places in separate indexes at the end of the book.

- The college edition of the *Random House Dictionary,* like the SCD, aims especially at students who use the dictionary as a guide to the preferences of conservative teachers. Thus, both informal English and slang are marked; usage notes "recognize the existence of long-established strictures." As in the SCD, the most frequently encountered meanings of a word come first.

- The *American Heritage Dictionary* is an impressive recent addition to the list of established college dictionaries. It aims at providing a "sensible" (moderately conservative) guide to edited English. It presents word meanings in a "natural flow" from a central meaning and gives exceptionally full treatment to word history.

The ideal dictionary would tell the users in plain English what they want to know. In practice, dictionaries try to give information that is technically accurate and yet intelligible to the layman. Look at the following sample entries. How much help would you get from each?

bi·o·de·grad·a·ble (-di grā′də b'l) *adj.* [BIO- + DEGRAD(E) + -ABLE] capable of being readily decomposed by biological means, esp. by bacterial action: said of some detergents with reference to disposal in sewage

From *Webster's New World Dictionary*

bio·de·grad·able \-di-′grād-ə-bəl\ *adj* [²*bi-* + *degrade* + *-able*] : capable of being broken down esp. into innocuous products by the action of living beings (as microorganisms)

From *Webster's New Collegiate Dictionary*

D 1a   Synonyms and Antonyms   *d*

Use the dictionary to help you distinguish between closely related terms.

Often, a dictionary indicates meaning by a **synonym,** a word that has nearly the same meaning as the word you are looking up. Thus, your dictionary may give "sad" or "mournful" as a synonym for *elegiac,* or "instructive" as a synonym for *didactic.* Often, your dictionary will explain a word by giving an **antonym,** a word of approximately opposite meaning. *Desultory* is the opposite of "methodical." *Hackneyed* is the opposite of "fresh" or "original."

Synonyms are seldom simply interchangeable. Their areas of meaning overlap, but at the same time there are subtle differences. *Burn, char, scorch, sear,* and *singe* all refer to the results of exposure to extreme heat, but whether a piece of meat is charred or merely seared makes a difference to the person who has it for dinner.

Look at the way the following entry tries to distinguish among words like *feeling, passion,* and *emotion.* How would you state the differences in your own words?

> *SYN.*—**feeling,** when unqualified in the context, refers to any of the subjective reactions, pleasurable or unpleasurable, that one may have to a situation and usually connotes an absence of reasoning [I can't trust my own *feelings*]; **emotion** implies an intense feeling with physical as well as mental manifestations [her breast heaved with *emotion*]; **passion** refers to a strong or overpowering emotion, connoting especially sexual love or intense anger; **sentiment** applies to a feeling, often a tender one, accompanied by some thought or reasoning [what are your *sentiments* in this matter?]

From *Webster's New World Dictionary*

D 1b   Denotation and Connotation   *d*

Use the dictionary as a guide to the associations of words.

Many words **denote**—that is, point out or refer to—very nearly the same objects or qualities. At the same time, they **connote**—that is, suggest or imply—different attitudes on the part of the speaker. *Cheap* and *inexpensive* both mean low in price. However, we may call an article "cheap" to suggest that we consider it shoddy or inferior; we may call it "inexpensive" to suggest that we consider it a good bargain. *Unwise* and *foolish* both indicate a lack of wisdom. However, calling a proposal "unwise" suggests a certain amount of respect for the person who made it; "foolish" suggests ridicule and contempt.

Here is how a dictionary handles the connotations of synonyms of *plan:*

> *SYN.*—**plan** refers to any detailed method, formulated before-hand, for doing or making something (vacation *plans*); **design** stresses the final outcome of a plan and implies the use of skill or craft, sometimes in an unfavorable sense, in executing or arranging this (it was his *design* to separate us); **project** im-plies the use of enterprise or imagination in formulating an am-bitious or extensive plan (they've begun work on the housing *project*); **scheme,** a less definite term than the preceding, often connotes either an impractical, visionary plan or an underhand intrigue (a *scheme* to embezzle the funds).

From *Webster's New World Dictionary*

D 1c   Context   *d*

Use the dictionary as a guide to the context where a given meaning is appropriate.

The **context** of a word may be another word ("square meal"), a whole sentence or paragraph ("Square your pre-cepts with your practice"), a whole article or book (a treat-ment of squares in a book on plane geometry), or a situa-tion (a police officer directing a pedestrian to a square).

Here is an entry showing a word used in different con-texts:

> **apt** (apt), *adj.* **1.** inclined; disposed; given; prone: *too apt to slander others.* **2.** likely: *Am I apt to find him at home?* **3.** unusually intelligent; quick to learn: *an apt pupil.* **4.** suited to the purpose or occasion: *an apt metaphor.*

From *The Random House Dictionary*

In an unfamiliar context, familiar words may have a new or different meaning. For instance, an author praising modesty and thrift may describe them as "homely virtues." Looking up the word, you will find that its original meaning, as you might expect, is "associated with the home." Favorable associations of domestic life account for such meanings as "simple," "unpretentious," "intimate"; unfavorable associations account for such meanings as "crude," "unpolished," "ugly."

D 1d   Grammatical Labels d

Use the dictionary as a guide to the functions a word can serve in a sentence.

For instance, *human* is usually labeled both as an **adjective** (adj.) and as a **noun** (n.), with some indication that the latter use ("a human" rather than "a human being") is not generally accepted as appropriate to written English. *Annoy* is labeled a **transitive verb** (v.t.); it is incomplete without an object. In other words, we usually annoy somebody or something; we don't just annoy. *Set* also is usually transitive (*"set* the bowl on the table"), but it is labeled **intransitive** (v.i.) when applied to one of the celestial bodies. In other words, the sun doesn't set anybody or anything; it just sets.

D 1e   Idiom id

Use the dictionary as a guide to idiomatic phrases.

A word often combines with other words in an expression that becomes the habitual way of conveying a certain idea. Such expressions are called **idioms.** To write idiomatic

English, you have to develop an ear for individual phrases and ways of saying things. For instance, we *do* a certain type of work, *hold* a job or position, *follow* a trade, *pursue* an occupation, and *engage in* a line of business.

Study the following list of idiomatic phrases all using the word *mind*. Can you think of half a dozen similar phrases all using the word *eye,* or the word *hand?*

—**bear** (or **keep) in mind** to remember —**be in one's right mind** to be mentally well; be sane —**be of one mind** to have the same opinion or desire —**be of two minds** to be undecided or irresolute —☆**blow one's mind** [Slang] to undergo the hallucinations, etc. caused by, or as by, psychedelic drugs —**call to mind 1.** to remember **2.** to be a reminder of —**change one's mind 1.** to change one's opinion **2.** to change one's intention, purpose, or wish —**give (someone) a piece of one's mind** to criticize or rebuke (someone) sharply —**have a (good** or **great) mind to** to feel (strongly) inclined to —**have half a mind to** to be somewhat inclined to —**have in mind 1.** to remember **2.** to think of **3.** to intend; purpose —**know one's own mind** to know one's own real thoughts, desires, etc. —**make up one's mind** to form a definite opinion or decision —**meeting of (the) minds** an agreement —**never mind** don't be concerned; it doesn't matter —**on one's mind 1.** occupying one's thoughts **2.** worrying one —**out of one's mind 1.** mentally ill; insane **2.** frantic (*with* worry, grief, etc.) —**put in mind** to remind —**set one's mind on** to be determined on or determinedly desirous of —**take one's mind off** to stop one from thinking about; turn one's attention from —**to one's mind** in one's opinion

From *Webster's New World Dictionary*

A special problem for inexperienced writers is the idiomatic use of **prepositions.** The following list reviews idiomatic uses of some common prepositions:

abide *by* (a decision)
abstain *from* (voting)
accuse *of* (a crime)

acquiesce *in* (an injustice)
adhere *to* (a promise)
admit *of* (conflicting interpretations)

Words

agree *with* (a person), *to* (a proposal), *on* (a course of action)

alarmed *at* (the news)

apologize *for* (a mistake)

aspire *to* (distinction)

assent *to* (a proposal)

attend *to* (one's business)

avail oneself *of* (an opportunity)

capable *of* (an action)

charge *with* (an offense)

collide *with* (a car)

compatible *with* (recognized standards)

comply *with* (a request)

concur *with* (someone), *in* (an opinion)

confide *in* or *to* (someone)

conform *to* (specifications)

deficient *in* (strength)

delight *in* (mischief)

deprive *of* (a privilege)

derived *from* (a source)

die *of* or *from* (a disease)

disappointed *in* (someone's performance)

dissent *from* (a majority opinion)

dissuade *from* (doing something foolish)

divest *of* (responsibility)

find fault *with* (a course)

identical *with* (something looked for)

ignorant *of* (a fact)

inconsistent *with* (sound procedure)

independent *of* (outside help)

indifferent *to* (praise or blame)

infer *from* (evidence)

inferior *to* (a rival product)

insist *on* (accuracy)

interfere *with* (a performance), *in* (someone else's affairs)

jealous *of* (others)

long *for* (recognition)

object *to* (a proposal)

oblivious *of* (warnings)

part *with* (possessions)

partial *to* (flattery)

participate *in* (activities)

persevere *in* (a task)

pertain *to* (a subject)

preferable *to* (an alternative)

prevail *on* (someone to do something)

prevent someone *from* (an action)

refrain *from* (wrongdoing)

rejoice *at* (good news)

required *of* (all members)

resolve *on* (a course of action)

rich *in* (resources)

secede *from* (the Union)

short *of* (cash)

succeed *in* (an attempt)

superior *to* (an alternative)

threaten *with* (legal action)

wait *for* (developments), *on* (a guest)

Exercises

A. Compare *three* of the major college dictionaries by investigating the following:

1. Read the definitions of *dada, kitsch,* and *gobbledygook.* Are they clear and informative?

2. Study the order of meanings for *coy, nice, operate.* How does the order differ, and why?

3. Compare the treatment of synonyms (if any) for *dogmatic, prompt,* and *train* (v.) .

4. What and where are you told about Dreyfus, Prometheus, Niels Bohr?

5. How does the dictionary deal with *Aryan, dago, nigger?*

B. What's new in dictionaries? How up to date, or how far behind, is your dictionary in its coverage of the following words? For those that are missing, write a short definition that would help a dictionary editor bring the dictionary up to date.

aerospace	cosmonaut	residuals
airbag	holding pattern	schlock
anchorman	honky	skydiving
black muslim	hydrofoil	tax shelter
bluegrass	kibbutz	tokenism
body stocking	minibike	unisex
chicano	payload	

C. Study the synonyms in the following sets. What meaning do all three words have in common? How do they differ? Which are differences in connotation?

gaze—stare—ogle
settlement—compromise—deal
loyalty—allegiance—commitment
obedient—docile—obsequious
revolt—revolution—mutiny
intelligent—clever—shrewd
juvenile—youngster—adolescent

feminine—womanly—effeminate
imaginary—fantastic—visionary
fatherly—paternal—paternalistic

D. How does your dictionary distinguish among the changing meanings of each of the following words? Show how context determines your choice of the meaning appropriate in each phrase.

bay leaves, at *bay*, *bayed* at the moon, *bay* window, bomb *bay*, a breeze from the *bay*

head of lettuce, *head* the procession, a *head* of steam, *heads* or tails, over the listeners' *heads*, went to his *head*, *heads* of government, *head* off complaints, not have a *head* for figures

car of recent *make*, *make* the beds, *make* money, *make* excuses, *makes* my blood boil, *make* a speech, *makes* easy reading, *made* him a sergeant

repair a car, *repaired* to the meeting, in good *repair*, *repair* the damage

straight to the point, *straight* alcohol, *straight* party line, the comedian's *straight* man, *straight* hair, thinking *straight*

a *tender* smile, *tender* an apology, legal *tender*

E. Check your answers to the following questions by consulting your dictionary:

1. Is *incompetent* used as a noun?

2. Which of the following words are used as verbs: *admonition, loan, lord, magistrate, minister, sacrilege, spirit, war?*

3. Are the following words used as adjectives: *animate, predominate, very?*

4. What idiomatic prepositions go with the following words when they are used as verbs: *glory, care, marvel?*

5. Are the following used as intransitive verbs: *entertain, censure, promote?*

F. Point out and correct any unidiomatic use of prepositions:

1. To seek a good grade at someone else's expense would be a violation to our standards of conduct.

2. During the past fifty years, deaths caused by highway accidents have been more numerous than those incurred from two world wars and the war in Korea.

3. Plans for cost reduction have been put to action by different agencies of the federal government.

4. Several families volunteered to take care for the children of flood victims.

5. Only the prompt help of the neighbors prevented the fire of becoming a major disaster.

6. During the first years of marriage we had to deprive ourselves from many things that other people take for granted.

7. The arrival of the ship to its destination caused general rejoicing.

8. Though I support Mr. Finchley's candidacy, I take exception with some of his statements.

9. We Americans do not hesitate in waving our flag if the occasion arises.

10. The people of this country naturally shun at the thought of having any kind of censorship imposed upon their newspapers.

11. As an instrument of the popular will, the senate suffers from defects inherent to its constitution.

12. A businesswoman cannot succeed unless she takes heed to the preferences of her customers.

D 2   Word History

Let the history of a word help you understand its uses, meanings, and associations.

College dictionaries often summarize the **etymology** of a word. They briefly trace its origin and history. Your dictionary is likely to relate the word *lock* to corresponding words in earlier English (ME. = Middle English; AS. = Anglo-Saxon or Old English), in other Germanic languages (G. = German; ON. = Old Norse or Early Scandinavian), and in the hypothetical common parent langauge of most European languages (IE. = Indo-European). Here is the etymology of a word that came into English from Latin by way of Old French:

fe·male (fē'māl) *adj.* [ME., altered after MALE < *femelle* < OFr. < L. *femella*, dim. of *femina*, a woman < IE. base **dhē-*, to suck, suckle, whence L. *felare*, to suck, *filius*, son, *fetus*, progeny, Gr. *thēlazein*, to suckle]

From *Webster's New World Dictionary*

In addition to tracing words to other languages, the etymologist is concerned with **semantic change**—gradual changes in meaning. The most complete record of such changes is the unabridged *New English Dictionary on Historical Principles,* reissued in 1933 as the *Oxford English Dictionary* (OED). This monumental reference work gives the earliest date a word occurs and then provides quotations tracing its development down through the centuries.

The most extensive changes in vocabulary come about through contacts between different cultures. Armed conquest, colonial expansion, and international trade make words move from one language to the other. Roughly three-fourths of the words in your dictionary were absorbed into English from foreign sources. When the Anglo-Saxon tribes came to England from continental Europe during the period between A.D. 450 and 600, they spoke Germanic dialects, close to the dialects from which modern Dutch and German are derived. The American tourist coming to Germany can still easily recognize the German equivalents of *arm, drink, father, fish, hand,* or *house.* However, the basic Germanic vocabulary of **Anglo-Saxon** or **Old English** was enriched and modified by words from other languages throughout early English history.

D 2a   Latin and Greek

Know some of the most common Latin and Greek roots.

English has borrowed heavily from Latin and Greek. Latin had been the language of the Roman empire. It became the official language of the Roman Catholic Church, which established itself in England in the seventh century and remained the supreme spiritual authority until the sixteenth century. English early absorbed Latin words related to the Scriptures and to the doctrines and ritual of the church, such as *altar, candle, chalice, mass, palm, pope, shrine, relic,* and *rule.* Other early borrowings were related to church administration, the everyday life of monks and the clergy, and the church-controlled medieval system of education.

Greek was the language of the literature, philosophy, and science of ancient Hellenic culture, flourishing both in Greece proper and in other parts of the Mediterranean world. Either in the original Greek or in Latin translation, this body of knowledge exercised a continuous influence on Western civilization during the Middle Ages and Renaissance. Modern philosophical, scientific, and technological terminology draws heavily on Latin and Greek roots. Examples of words absorbed either directly from Greek or from Greek through Latin are: *anonymous, atmosphere,*

catastrophe, chaos, climax, crisis, enthusiasm, and *skeleton.*
Examples of words absorbed from Latin are: *contempt,
gesture, history, incredible, index, individual, intellect,
legal, mechanical,* and *rational.*

(1) *Latin and Greek Roots.* Knowledge of a common
Latin or Greek root often provides the key to a puzzling
word. For instance, the Greek root *phys-* usually refers to
the body or to material things. The Greek root *psych-*
usually refers to the mind or the soul. This distinction explains *physician* (heals the body) and *psychiatrist* (heals
the mind), *physiology* (study of bodily functions) and *psychology* (study of mental functions), *physical* (characteristic of material reality) and *psychic* (going beyond material reality).

Here is a brief list of common Latin and Greek roots.
Explain how each root is used in the sample words given
for it:

auto-	*self*	autocratic, automatic, automobile, autonomy
capit-	*head*	capital, decapitate, per capita
carn-	*flesh*	carnal, carnivorous, incarnation, carnival
chron-	*time*	anachronistic, chronometer, synchronize
culp-	*fault*	culpable, culprit, exculpate
doc-	*teach*	docile, doctor, doctrine, indoctrinate
graph-	*write*	autograph, graphic, geography, orthography
hydr-	*water*	dehydrate, hydrant, hydraulic, hydrogen
jur-	*swear*	conjure, juror, perjury
man-	*hand*	manacle, manicure, manual, manufacture

phon-	*sound*	euphony, phonetics, phonograph, symphony
terr-	*land*	inter, terrestrial, subterranean
urb-	*city*	suburb, urban, urbane
verb-	*word*	proverb, verbal, verbiage, verbose
vit-	*life*	vitality, vitamin
vol-	*wish*	volition, voluntary, volunteer

(2) *Common Prefixes and Suffixes.* Especially useful is a knowledge of the most common Latin and Greek **prefixes** and **suffixes**—syllables attached at the beginning or at the end of a word to modify its meaning. A common prefix like *sub-,* meaning "below" or "beneath," helps to explain not only *substandard* and *subconscious* but also *submarine* (below the sea) and *subterranean* (beneath the surface, underground). The suffix *-cide* means "killer" or "killing" in *homicide* (of a human being), *suicide* (of oneself), *fratricide* (of a brother), *parricide* (of a parent), and *insecticide* (of insects).

Here is a brief list of Latin and Greek prefixes:

bene-	*good*	benediction, benefactor, benefit, benevolent
bi-	*two*	bicycle, bilateral, bisect
contra-	*against*	contraband, contradict, contravene
ex-	*out, out of*	exclude, exhale, expel
extra-	*outside*	extraordinary, extravagant, extrovert
omni-	*all*	omnipotent, omnipresent, omniscient
per-	*through*	percolate, perforate, permeate
poly-	*many*	polygamy, polysyllabic, polytheistic

Words

pre-	*before*	preamble, precedent, prefix
re-	*back*	recall, recede, revoke, retract
tele-	*distant*	telegraph, telepathy, telephone, television
trans-	*across, beyond*	transatlantic, transmit, transaction, transcend

D 2b   Borrowings from Other Sources

Recognize some of the sources of the English vocabulary.

Here are some kinds of historical information that you will find in a good dictionary:

(1) Over the centuries, *thousands of words were absorbed into English from French.* England was conquered by the French-speaking Normans in the years following 1066. At the beginning of the so-called **Middle English** period, about 1150, the Norman conquerors owned most of the land and controlled the most important offices in state and church. The language of law, administration, and literature was French. When the native English of the conquered people gradually reestablished itself, thousands of French words were retained. Many of these words were associated with the political and military role of the aristocratic Norman overlords: *castle, court, glory, mansion, noble, prince, prison, privilege, servant, treason, treasure, war.* But hundreds of other words absorbed into Middle English were everyday words like *avoid, branch, chair, demand, desire, disease, envy, praise, table, uncle.*

Note: Many French words passed into English through the hands of English poets who found them in medieval French poetry and romance. Some of these words preserve a poetic and often old-fashioned flavor: *chevalier* for "knight," *damsel* for "girl," *fealty* for "loyalty," *paramour* for "sweetheart," *travail* for "toil."

(2) A number of foreign languages have influenced the vocabularies of *special fields of interest.* Since the consolidation of **Modern English** (about 1500), numerous words have come into English from French, Italian, Spanish, and various other sources. French elegance, artistry, and military organization gave us words like *apartment, ballet, battalion, cadet, caress, corps, façade, infantry, negligee, patrol.* Italian opera and symphonic music provided terms like *cantata, concert, falsetto, sonata, solo, soprano, violin.* From Spain, which pioneered in the discovery and exploitation of new continents, came words like *alligator, banana, cannibal, cocoa, mosquito, Negro, potato, tobacco, tomato,* some of them absorbed into Spanish from New World sources.

(3) Modern English has a number of foreign words in *different stages of assimilation.* If they are still felt to be foreign rather than English, your dictionary may put a special symbol in front of them, or label them "French," "Italian," or whatever is appropriate. How does your dictionary handle the following Russian words: *troika, tovarich, apparatchik?*

Exercises

A. Find the original meaning of each of the following words: *attenuate, circumlocution, cornucopia, egregious, metaphysics, philosophy, premise, protract, recalcitrant, translucent.*

How does the original meaning help explain the current use of each word?

B. Report on the history of *five* of the following. What language does each term come from? How did it acquire its current meaning?

brunette	gossip	non sequitur
carnival	habeas corpus	propaganda
crescendo	Halloween	pundit
cynic	husband	troglodyte
dollar	laissez faire	vaudeville

C. Explain the meaning of the common element in each of the following sets. How does the common element help explain each word in the set?

anesthetic—anarchy—anemic
antibiotic—biography—biology
audio-visual—audition—inaudible
biennial—centennial—perennial
century—centipede—percentage
cosmic—cosmopolitan—microcosm
disunity—discord—dissent
eugenics—eulogy—euphonious
heterogeneous—heterosexual—heterodox
magnify—magnificent—magnitude
prelude—interlude—ludicrous
synchronize—symphony—sympathy

D. Indicate the basic meaning of each Latin and Greek prefix used in the following words: *ambivalent, antedate, antipathy, circumvent, concord, hypersensitive, international, introvert, malpractice, multimillionaire, neofascist, postgraduate, pseudoscientific, retroactive, semitropical, ultramodern, unilateral.*

E. What are the meanings of the following expressions? How many of them does your dictionary consider foreign rather than English? *Ad hoc, aficionado, auto-da-fé, blitz, corpus delicti, coup de grace, cum laude, de jure, enfant terrible, ersatz, eureka, fait accompli, hara-kiri, hoi polloi, pax Romana, quod erat demonstrandum, tour de force, Zeitgeist.*

D 3   Varieties of Usage

Recognize words that are appropriate only to certain situations or limited to specific uses.

Dictionaries use **restrictive labels** to show that a word is used only under certain circumstances and that it can be out of place when used without attention to its limitations. In the following dictionary entry, six of the nine principal meanings of *brass* are preceded by restrictive labels:

brass (bras, bräs), *n.* **1.** any of various metal alloys consisting mainly of copper and zinc. **2.** an article made of such an alloy. **3.** *Mach.* a partial lining of soft metal for a bearing. **4.** *Music.* **a.** an instrument of the trumpet or horn family. **b.** such instruments collectively. **5.** *Brit.* **a.** a memorial tablet or plaque incised with an effigy, coat of arms, or the like. **b.** *Slang.* money. **6.** *Furniture.* any piece of ornamental or functional hardware. **7.** *U.S. Slang.* **a.** high-ranking military officers. **b.** any very important officials. **8.** *Informal.* excessive assurance; impudence; effrontery. —*adj.* **9.** of or pertaining to brass. [ME *bras*, OE *bræs*; c. OFris *bres* copper, MLG *bras* metal] —**brass′ish,** *adj.*

— subject label
— geographic label
— usage label

From *Random House Dictionary*

D 3a   Nonstandard Words   *NS*

Recognize words that suggest nonstandard speech rather than educated usage.

Usage labels provide a guide when roughly synonymous choices have different associations. One choice may suggest the folk speech of factory and barracks ("nohow"); the other may suggest the standard English of school and office ("not at all"). Words like *anywheres* and *nohow* are either not listed in your dictionary at all or labeled illiterate, **nonstandard,** or vulgate. Like nonstandard grammatical patterns, they are often associated with low social standing or a lack of formal education. (See **G** 2a.)

D 3b   Informal Words   *unf*

Recognize words that sound too informal for systematic exposition or argument.

Some dictionaries label informal words **colloquial.** The word does *not* mean "local" but "characteristic of informal speech." People use colloquial language when at ease and with their friends; as a result, it tends to sound relaxed and folksy. But the man who is most comfortable in a robe and slippers puts on a tie and a business suit when going to the office on Monday morning. Similarly, a writer has to be able to use formal language in formal situations.

Informal	Formal	Informal	Formal
boss	superior	kid	child
brainy	intelligent	mean	ill-natured
bug	germ	skimpy	meager
faze	disconcert	sloppy	untidy
flunk	fail	snoop	pry
folks	relatives	snooze	nap
hunch	premonition	splurge	spend lavishly
job	position	stump	baffle

Other familiar words are generally acceptable in one sense but colloquial in another. Colloquial are: *alibi* in the sense of "excuse," *aggravate* in the sense of "annoy," *funny* in the sense of "strange," and *mad* in the sense of "angry."

Informal language uses qualifiers like *kind of* (hard), *sort of* (easy), *a lot, lots;* abbreviated forms like *ad, bike, exam, gym, phone.* It uses many **phrasal verbs,** verbs that combine a short basic verb with one or more prepositions: *check up on, chip in, come up with, cut out* (noise), *get across* (a point), *take in* (a show), *take up with* (a person). Informal English usually contains a liberal sprinkling of catchall words like *nice, cute, awful, wonderful,* or *terrible.* It is fond of **figurative expressions** like *have a ball, polish the apple, shoot the breeze, hit the road.*

Colloquial expressions can set a casual, leisurely tone:

There was a broad streak of mischief in Mencken. He was forever *cooking up* imaginary organizations, having *fake* handbills printed, inventing exercises in pure nonsense.—Philip M. Wagner, "Mencken Remembered," *The American Scholar*

To reject the book because of the immaturity of the author and the *bugs* in the logic is to throw away a bottle of good wine because it contains bits of the cork.—E. B. White, "A Slight Sound at Evening," *Yale Review*

But often, colloquialisms suggest a put-on folksiness, the public-relations heartiness of some advertisers and some political candidates (Uncle Sam from a billboard: "My folks mostly drive Ford V-8s"). Many college teachers expect the student to keep expository writing free of a colloquial tinge.

D 3c   Slang   *sl*

Use slang only in the most informal kinds of writing or for special effects.

No one can fix the exact point at which informal language shades over into slang, but generally the latter is more drastic in its disregard for what makes language formal and dignified. Slang often has a vigor missing in more pedestrian diction. The figurative expressions it substitutes for less imaginative formal terms are often apt: *blowhard, gumshoe, drunk tank, downer, spaced out, whirlybird.* Often a slang expression has no very satisfactory formal equivalent: *come-on, eyewash, runaround, stuffed shirt.* Many slang terms appeal to the user's love of the grotesque: *beat one's brains out, blow one's top, chew the fat, fly off the handle, hit the ceiling, kick the bucket, lay an egg.*

Slang is the major resource of many a humorous writer:

Despite that great wellspring of love and pity I have for the afflicted and the misbegotten, and those who have been *just plain took,* I find it hard to get worked up over the plight of those *gaffers* who play golf on the city's links. Little boys lurk in the brush, and when one of the superbly conditioned athletes knocks a *nifty* their way, they keep the ball. Then, if things haven't changed since my day, they sell the balls to other superbly conditioned athletes, who then *scream like banshees* when the golfball connoisseurs *steal 'em* again. Since grabbing the little thieves by the scruff of their necks and *beating the bejabbers out of them* would obviously be in violation of their civil rights, we must look elsewhere for a solution.

Remember that the humor in slang is often crude. Calling a person "fatso" or "skinny" or "bonehead" may be funny, but it also suggest a lack of tact or respect.

D 3d   Fancy Words   *d*

> **Avoid words that are pompous, affected, or stilted.**

Students whose writing has been criticized as slangy or colloquial sometimes have difficulty finding middle ground.

Trying to avoid excessive informality, they may go to the opposite extreme.

Stilted: I sincerely believe that the government should *divulge* more on the subject of socialism and its *cohorts,* because its *impetus* has reached a frightening *momentum.*

Do not imitate writers who habitually prefer the fancy word to the plain word, the elegant flourish to the blunt phrase. Here is a brief list of words that can make your writing seem affected:

Fancy	Plain	Fancy	Plain
adumbrate	hint	nuptials	wedding
ameliorate	improve	obsequies	funeral
astound	amaze	presage	predict
betrothal	engagement	pulchritude	beauty
commence	begin	quaff	drink
concomitant	result	residence	home
demise	death	tome	volume
emolument	pay, reward	vernal	springlike
eschew	avoid	vista	view

Exercises

A. Which of the following expressions would you expect to carry *restrictive labels?* Check your answers with the help of your dictionary. *Barf, go Dutch, hang-up, goof off, high-falutin, jalopy, mooch, narc, persnickety, shyster, skin flick, windbag.*

B. Arrange the expressions in each group in order *from the most formal to the most informal.* Be prepared to defend your decisions. (Your instructor may ask you to check your own judgments against those of your dictionary.)

1. live it up, live on little, live up to a promise
2. dress up for a party, dress down an offender, dress a wound
3. dream up a scheme, a cherished dream, dreamboat
4. tear up the bill, tear into someone, that tears it
5. hook up the microphone, got him off the hook, did it on his own hook
6. crack a book, her voice cracked, crack down on crime
7. have a go at it, go through with it, go for blondes
8. skip town, skip a grade, children skipping down the path
9. deal cards, make a deal, big deal!
10. sweat shirt, sweat out a decision, no sweat

C. Much slang comes and goes. Which of the following are still current? Select five and write a sentence or two about each to help a dictionary editor complete a coverage of recent student slang.

rap	jive	bread
jock	bag	the man
gig	busted	yak
gyp	dude	lid
rip-off	tripping	
bummer	zonked	

D. Point out *colloquialisms and slang expressions* and comment on their appropriateness. If your instructor desires, rewrite the sentences, avoiding all expressions that are not appropriate to formal written English.

1. Travelers who wish to see the true Paris should not go at a time when it is swamped by tourists.
2. Modern medicine has found ways of licking many dread diseases.

3. Psychologists have discovered that many young people get a kick out of cutting up in front of a group.

4. Our unlimited material resources will avail us nothing unless we keep alive the gumption that comes down to us from colonial farmers.

5. When the refugees were told that the train was going to leave in ten minutes, there was a mad rush to the station.

6. Parents only confuse a child by bawling him out every time he commits a minor mistake.

7. When Lovelace fails to suggest a definite date for the wedding, Clarissa begins to suspect that he is only pulling her leg.

8. Sent to size up our new allies, he found most of them in good shape.

9. The concert was scheduled to start at eight o'clock, but unfortunately the soloist did not show up.

10. In view of the late hour, we decided we better shove off and get some shuteye.

E. Observe the language used by your friends or fellow students to find *six current slang expressions* not listed in your dictionary. Define them, explain their use, and indicate what, if anything, they reveal about the speaker's attitude.

D 4   Words in Limited Use

Recognize words that have only regional currency or are no longer in general use.

Dictionaries use restrictive labels to show that a word is not current throughout the English-speaking world, or not current at this time, or familiar mainly to specialists.

Words

D 4a   Regional Labels   *d*

Notice geographic labels for words in use mainly in one region.

During the centuries before travel, books, and finally radio and television exercised their standardizing influence, languages gradually developed regional varieties. Sometimes, as in the case of German and Dutch, they grew far enough apart to become separate languages.

Here are the types of regional variation that you are likely to encounter:

(1) *Vocabulary differs somewhat from one English-speaking country to another.* American travelers in England notice the British uses of *tram, lorry, lift, torch, wireless, fortnight.* Here is a passage with many British terms:

> A scale or two adhered to the *fishmonger's* marble slab; the *pastrycook's* glass shelves showed a range of interesting crumbs; the *fruiterer* filled a long-standing void with fans of cardboard bananas and a "Dig for Victory" placard; the *greengrocer's* crates had been emptied of all but earth by those who had somehow failed to dig hard enough. . . . In the *confectioner's* windows the ribbons bleached on dummy boxes of chocolate among fly-blown cutouts of pre-war blondes. *Newsagents* without newspapers gave out in angry red chalk that they had no matches either.—Elizabeth Bowen, *The Heat of the Day*

(2) *Like most European languages, British English varies greatly from area to area.* Such regional varieties within a country are called **dialects.** Students of English literature usually encounter some dialect writing. For instance, a poet to whom a pretty girl is a "bonny lass," a church a "kirk," and a landowner a "laird" is using one of the dialects of Scotland and Northern England rather than standard British English.

(3) *American speech shows some regional differences.* By and large, the constant intermingling of settlers from

many areas, and the rapid growth of mass media of communication, have kept these American dialects from drifting very far apart. Here are some of the words that your dictionary is likely to mark as dialectal: *dogie, poke* (bag), *reckon* (suppose), *tote* (carry), *you all.*

D 4b   Obsolete and Archaic   *d*

Know how dictionaries label words no longer in common use.

Some words, or meanings of words, have gone out of use altogether. They are called **obsolete**. Examples of obsolete meanings are *coy* (quiet), *curious* (careful), *nice* (foolish). Some words or meanings are no longer in common use but still occur in special contexts. Such words and meanings are called **archaic**. The King James version of the Bible preserves many archaisms that were in common use in seventeenth-century England: *thou* and *thee, brethren, kine* (cattle).

In the following dictionary entry, five of the numbered meanings of *brave* are labeled obsolete:

brave (brāv) *adj.* **brav·er, brav·est 1.** Having or showing courage; intrepid; courageous. **2.** Making a fine display; elegant; showy. **3.** *Obs.* Excellent. — *v.* **braved, brav·ing** *v.t.* **1.** To meet or face with courage and fortitude: to *brave* danger. **2.** To defy; challenge: to *brave* the heavens. **3.** *Obs.* To make splendid. — *v.i.* **4.** *Obs.* To boast. — *n.* **1.** A man of courage. **2.** A North American Indian warrior. **3.** *Obs.* A bully; bravo. **4.** *Obs.* A boast or defiance.

From *Standard College Dictionary*

Here are some archaisms familiar to readers of poetry and historical fiction:

Words

anon	(at once)	*fere*	(companion)
brand	(sword)	*forsooth*	(truly)
childe	(aristocratic youth)	*methinks*	(it seems)
erst	(formerly)	*rood*	(cross)
fain	(glad or gladly)	*sprite*	(ghost)

D 4c   Neologisms   *d*

Be cautious in using words that have recently come into the language.

Lexicographers, who at one time resisted the introduction of new words, now compete in their coverage of **neologisms,** or newly coined expressions. Many new words serve a need and rapidly become generally accepted: *bookmobile; cybernetics, astronaut, supersonic, transistor.* But many other coined words make conservative readers squirm. Avoid copywriters' words like the following:

jumboize	paperamics	outdoorsman
moisturize	usership	

Many new words are part of an impersonal *bureaucratic jargon* that lacks the life and color of real human language. Memos and reports often use words made up, by people with tin ears, on the model of *escapee, personalize, finalize, socioeconomic.* (See D 6c.)

D 4d   Subject Labels   *d*

Watch for technical terms that are not likely to be familiar to outsiders.

Labels like *Law, Naut.* (nautical), or *Mach.* (machinery) are called subject labels. The **technical terminology** or, on a less formal level, the **shoptalk** of a trade or profession requires explanation in writing for the general reader. The math student will have no difficulty with *set, natural number, integer, rational number,* and *number sentence.* But the layman would want them explained.

Exercises

A. Which of the following words have regional or dialect uses? (And where are they used?) Which of these words (or which of their uses) are archaic? Which are obsolete? *Bloke, bonnet, boot, bower, complected, costermonger, coulee, cove, dogie, favor, gentle, goober, goodman, hackney, petrol, quid, thorpe, trolley, tube.*

B. E. B. White, in an article on Maine speech, discussed the following expressions among others: *tunk* a wedge, *soft* weather, *dozy* wood, people *from away,* a *snug* pasture, *gunkhole, nooning.* Write a paper in which you discuss a number of expressions that you associate with a specific region. For instance, investigate dialect features that set your own native speech apart from that of a region where you now live.

C. Linguists have recently begun to study (and to argue about) black English and English as spoken by Spanish-speaking Americans. Investigate and prepare a report on five or six expressions familiar to blacks or Spanish-Americans but little known among your Anglo friends.

D. Discuss the use of newly coined words in current advertising. Show which of these you think may eventually become standard English and explain why.

E. What special fields of interest do the following technical terms represent? Which of the terms would you expect the average high school graduate to know? *A priori, brochure, calorie, camshaft, crochet, de facto, denouement, graupel, lien, plinth, solstice, sonata, spirit, symbiosis, tachistoscope, thyroid, transubstantiation, valence, venireman, ventricle.*

F. A student investigating Post Office shoptalk discussed the following terms: *swing room, star route, merry-go-round, Tour Three, fat stock, confetti, shedders, scheme man, nixie clerk.* Investigate and report on Post Office shoptalk in your area. Are any of the same terms in use? Are any of the terms recorded in general or specialized dictionaries? *Or* conduct a similar investigation of shoptalk in one of the following areas: railroading, trucking, flying.

D 5   Expressive Language

> *Use the exact words needed to convey your intended meaning.*

Effective writing is clear, fresh, graphic, and concrete. Learn to revise your writing for more effective, more expressive word choice.

D 5a   Accurate Words   *d*

> *Aim at accurate words and exact shades of meaning.*

Hastily written words often express the intended meaning almost but not quite:

Hasty: *The news* about widespread corruption was first *exposed* by the local press.

Revised: The news about widespread corruption first *appeared* in the local press. (Evildoers or shortcomings are "exposed," but news about evildoers is "printed," "presented," or "reported.")

Check your papers for the following:

(1) Watch out for words easily *confused* because closely related in sound or meaning.

> The work was sheer *trudgery* (should be *drudgery*).
> Similar choices *affront* every student (should be *confront*).
> He grew up in a *staple* environment (should be *stable*).

(2) Watch out for *garbled idioms:*

Garbled: Unemployment *played* an important *factor.*

Should Be: Unemployment *played* an important *role.*

Garbled: Many young people have *lost their appeal for* fraternities.

Should Be: Fraternities have *lost their appeal* for many people.

(3) Watch out for words with the wrong *connotation:*

Inexact: Life in the suburbs *subjects* a family to the beauties of nature.

Revised: Life in the suburbs *brings* a family *closer* to the beauties of nature. (The connotations of *subject* are unfavorable; it implies that we are exposed to something unwillingly.)

D 5b   Specific Words   *d*

Use specific, informative words.

Instead of a colorless general word like *building,* use a more expressive word like *barn, mansion, warehouse, bun-*

galow, *tenement, shack, workshop,* or *cabin. Tenement* carries more information than *building.* It also comes closer to concrete experience, making it possible for the reader to visualize an actual structure. When words remain unnecessarily general, readers are too far removed from what they can see, hear, and feel.

General: All the animals of the farm joined in singing "Beasts of England."

Specific: The whole farm *burst* out into "Beasts of England" in tremendous unison. The cows *lowed* it, the dogs *whined* it, the sheep *bleated* it, the horses *whinnied* it, the ducks *quacked* it. (George Orwell)

Good writers have at their fingertips the right word for specific objects, shapes, sounds, textures, motions:

sand crabs, *wriggling* and *scuttling* . . . heavy little creatures, shaped like *scarabs,* with *grey-mottled* shells and orange underparts . . . (John Steinbeck)

a big, squarish *frame house* that had once been white, decorated with *cupolas* and *spires* and *scrolled* balconies in the heavily lightsome style of the seventies . . . (William Faulkner)

D 5c Figurative Words *d*

Use figurative expressions to make writing graphic and colorful by exploiting similarities between different things.

A compressed but explicit comparison, introduced by *as* or *like,* is called a **simile.** An implied comparison that uses one thing as the equivalent of another is called a **metaphor.** Literally, *monkey* refers to a small, long-tailed animal. Metaphorically, it may mean a person who, like a monkey, is agile, mischievous, imitative, or playful.

(1) *Figurative expressions should be apt.* The implied analogy must fit:

Apt: Putting the hubcap back on the rim is *like putting an undersized lid on an oversized jar.* (As one side of the hubcap is pounded into place, the opposite side pops out.)

Inept: Lacking the ignition of advertising, our economic engine would run at a slower pace. (An engine without ignition would not run at a slower pace; it would just be dead.)

(2) *Figurative expressions should be consistent.* When several figurative expressions appear closely together, they should blend into a harmonious whole rather than clash because of contradictory associations. Avoid the **mixed metaphor:**

Consistent: Fame cannot spread wide or endure long that is not *rooted* in nature, and *manured* by art. (Samuel Johnson)

Mixed: America's colleges are the *key* to national survival, and the future of the country lies in their *hands.*
(Keys do not have hands.)

Mixed: Enriched programs give the good student a chance to *dig* deeper into the large *sea* of knowledge.
(Most people do their digging on solid ground rather than at sea.)

(3) *Figurative expressions should not call excessive attention to themselves.* Avoid metaphors that are strained enough to become distracting:

Extravagant: When the average overmothered college student is removed from parental control, the severance of the umbilical cord causes him to bleed to death, psychologically speaking.

115

D 5d   Fresh Words   *d*

Phrase ideas freshly in your own words.

Many phrases that may once have been striking have become trite through overuse. Such tired phrases are called **clichés.** They make the yawning reader feel that nothing new is being said and that there is little point in paying attention.

Trite: He was always *wrapped up* in his own thoughts and feelings.

Fresh: Only the *cocoon* of his own thoughts and feelings existed for him.

Trite: The dean let us have it, *straight from the shoulder.*

Fresh: The dean spoke to us directly and urgently, *like a scout just returned from the enemy camp.*

To the cliché expert, ignorance is always "abysmal," fortitude "intestinal," and necessity "dire." Daylight is always "broad," silence "ominous," and old age "ripe." People make a "clean break" and engage in "honest toil" till the "bitter end." They make things "crystal clear"; they wait "with bated breath"; they work "by the sweat of their brow."

Here are some of the clichés that at times spill over into student writing:

believe it or not	dire straits
better late than never	easier said than done
beyond the shadow of a doubt	the facts of life
bolt out of the blue	few and far between
burn the midnight oil	fine and dandy
couldn't care less	the finer things
crying shame	first and foremost
	free and easy

get in there and fight
good time was had by all
green with envy
in one fell swoop
in the last analysis
it goes without saying
it stands to reason
last but not least
the last straw
let's face it
malice aforethought
nature's glory
off the beaten track
pride and joy
proud owner

rear its ugly head
rude awakening
a shot in the arm
sink or swim
a snare and a delusion
sneaking suspicion
something tells me
straight and narrow
strike while the iron is hot
tender mercies
to all intents and purposes
truer words were never
     spoken
truth is stranger than fiction
up in arms

Exercises

A. Make sure you can distinguish between the confusing words in the following pairs: *antic—antique; biography—bibliography; clique—cliché; connive—conspire; difference—deference; ethical—ethnic; feudalism—fatalism; gentle—genteel; literal—literary—literate; manners—mannerisms; sensible—sensitive; specie—species.*

B. Write down a *more accurate* word for the word italicized in each sentence.

1. Diane had only a small knowledge of the problem *coherent* [inherent] in being a woman.

2. If not used, the muscle becomes *anthropoid.* [atrophied]

3. Justice prevails when a criminal is *righteously* punished for wrongdoing.

4. The March of Dimes was originally organized to help those *inflicted* with infantile paralysis. [afflicted]

Words

declining

5. By *defying* to participate in saluting the flag, people are showing disrespect to our country.

6. Abortion is quickly becoming more acceptable but still considered by many *immortal*.   *immoral*   *yelps*

7. The dog went bounding down the steps, emitting *whelps* at every leap.   *I puppy*

8. Our next *fiascle* took place in Hollywood.   *fiasco*

9. My dilemma is whether to describe the three incidents separately or *incarcerate* them all in one short story.   *incorporate*

10. He tried for years to win the *disparaging* strife against alcohol.   *discourage* *I laughed at*

11. She could not find the key. "Damn," she *scoffed*, and started to pound on the door.   *cursed* *I to laugh*

12. The chairman *contributed* the low attendance to poor publicity.   *att*

13. A good listener can listen to teachers and retain the knowledge they have *expelled*. *expounded*

14. Sick people can no longer pay for their hospital costs without a tremendous *drain* being put on their families.   *strain*

15. In later chapters, the hero's wife fades *in* the background.   *to*

C. How many different figurative expressions can you find in the following passage?

The sixties was the decade when the frightened cry of "Timber!" was everywhere in the unclean air of publishing. The flow of competive daily newspapers dried up, and magazines great and small fell like the trees chopped down for the paper to print them. Now that the flagship *Life* has joined its lessers in the Sargasso Sea of bestilled publications, some conventional wisdom prevails as to how American publishing became trapped in such an economic rathole: spiraling production costs, quadrupling postage rates, blood-sucking competition for advertising dollars from television, the general malaise of the economy, mass circulations sustained at uneconomical cut rates, the decline of print, et cetera. None of these reasons, to my way of thinking, explains the big picture.—Warren Hinckle, "The Adman Who Hated Advertising," *Atlantic*

D. Look at the use of figurative expressions in the following sentences. Which work well to help the author make his point? Which are mixed or overdone? (Your instructor may ask you to find more apt figurative expressions to replace the unsatisfactory ones.)

1. When I moved to the new school, many new faces dotted this horizon of experience.

2. Slapping on a price freeze to stop inflation could become a one-way street to a Pandora's box of problems. *allusion*

3. To be the son of a great man can be a disadvantage; it is like living next to a huge monument.

4. The sexual liberation of women unleashed a Pandora's box of wails from husbands who were exposed as inadequate lovers.

5. Education is certainly not a precise instrument. When you increase the supply, you don't get the same immediate effect as when you press on the accelerator of your automobile.

6. In successful education, the cornerstone is motivation, the vehicle is reading, and the outcome is a self-generating learner.

7. Sexual satisfaction was now the female's oyster, and any man who from sheer exhaustion or rebellion chickened out was a louse.

8. When the number of people on the gravy train exceeds the number pushing it, the great big train of economic well-being on which all of us ride will come to a stop.

9. An industrial world thinks it wants only a pinch of intelligence to season a great plateful of mechanical aptitudes. (Jacques Barzun)

10. I was dismayed to find that the place associated with my favorite childhood memories had succumbed to the clutch of change.

11. America's unsolved social problems stand there like milk

bottles on the steps of the White House, waiting for the next President to take them in.

12. English teachers, fascinated with avant-garde literature, have sown a whirlwind of literary filth which has since grown into wholesale obscenity on the part of too many young people.

E. Rewrite the following sentences to *eliminate clichés*. Try to make your phrasing fresh enough to revive the reader's attention.

1. They will have to get his signature by hook or by crook.

2. Catching the street corner pusher has become small potatoes. The major effort is now international, and it is a pathway strewn with political pitfalls.

3. Cleopatra squeezes Antony under her thumb, while Octavia pulls the rug from under him in front of Caesar and his troops.

4. After one more defeat, she will have to throw in the sponge.

5. The reporter swallowed their story hook, line, and sinker.

6. The typical organization man knows which side his bread is buttered on.

7. Party platforms never get down to brass tacks.

8. In trying to revitalize our neighborhoods, we too often throw out the baby with the bath water.

9. When we are asked to change administrations in the midst of a serious international crisis, we should remember that it is unwise to change horses in midstream.

10. The opposing candidate is a Johnny-come-lately who entered the campaign only at the urging of influential backers.

D 6 Directness

A writer must know how to be blunt and direct.

At times, a writer will be deliberately indirect for tactical reasons. More common is the kind of careless indirectness that for no good reason slows down the reader.

D 6a Redundancy   *w*

Avoid wordiness.

Try to substitute one word that gives your meaning exactly for two words that give it blurrily. The most easily spotted kind of wordiness is **redundancy,** or unnecessary duplication. The phrase *basic fundamentals* is redundant because *basic* and *fundamental* mean nearly the same thing. In the following sentences one or the other way of expressing the same idea should be omitted:

> We left *in the morning* at about six o'clock A.M.
> *As a rule,* the weather was *usually* warm.
> There is more to it than *seems apparent.*
> *Physically,* he has not grown much in *height.*
> *In my opinion, I think* you are right.

Here are some sources of wordiness other than direct duplication:

(1) *All-purpose nouns* like *situation, angle, factor, aspect, line,* or *element* are often mere padding:

Padded: When I first came to Smith College, *there was a situation where* some students lived in better housing than others.

121

Words

Concise: When I first came to Smith College, some students lived in better housing than others.

Padded: Another *aspect* that needs to be considered is the consumer relations *angle*.

Concise: We should also consider consumer relations.

(2) *Roundabout transitions* sometimes take the place of simple phrases like *for example, however,* and *therefore:*

Wordy: *In considering this situation we must also take into account the fact that* other students do not feel this way.

Economical: Others, *however,* do not feel this way.

Wordy: *Taking these factors into consideration, we must conclude that* your request is unjustified.

Economical: *Therefore,* your request seems to us unjustified.

(3) Introductory phrases like *the fact that* or *the question whether* can often be trimmed without loss:

Wordy: *The question of whether* churches should unite agitates people of many denominations.

Economical: *Whether* churches should unite agitates people of many denominations.

D 6b   Euphemisms   *d*

Prefer plain English to euphemisms and weasel words.

Much roundabout diction results from the desire to be elegant. Refined or impressive names for unpleasant or prosaic things are known as **euphemisms.** The most familiar euphemisms are those for elementary facts of human existence.

(birth)	*blessed event, new arrival*
(pregnancy)	*to be expecting*
(age)	*senior citizens, the elderly*
(death)	*pass on, expire, the deceased, mortal remains*

Euphemisms are "beautiful words"—words more beautiful than what they stand for. Often they are required by politeness or tact. When referring to people you respect, you will prefer *stout* to *fat, intoxicated* to *drunk,* and *remains* to *corpse.* Often, however, euphemisms mislead, or even deliberately deceive. Plumbers become "sanitary engineers," file clerks "research consultants," undertakers "funeral directors," translators "language facilitators," and fortune tellers "clairvoyant readers." In much public-relations prose and political propaganda, euphemisms cover up facts that the reader is entitled to know: *straitened financial circumstances* for "bankruptcy"; *planned withdrawal* for "disorganized retreat"; *resettlement* for "forcible removal."

Many readers are annoyed by such evasive tactics: they will be grateful when you call a spade a spade.

Euphemism	Blunt
immoderate use of intoxicants	heavy drinking
lack of proper health habits	dirt
deteriorating residential section	slum

D 6c   Jargon   *d*

Do not try to impress your reader with pretentious pseudo-scientific language.

Much inflated diction results from a writer's using two highbrow words where one lowbrow word would do. Jar-

Words

gon reflects the desire to make the trivial seem important. It cultivates an impressive pseudo-scientific air by using indirect, impersonal constructions and technical-sounding Latin and Greek terms.

Jargon: Procedures were instituted with a view toward the implementation of the conclusions reached.

Plain English: We started to put our ideas into practice.

Jargon: Careful consideration of relevant data is imperative before the procedure most conducive toward a realization of the desired outcomes can be determined.

Plain English: Look before you leap.

Jargon addicts say "Reference was made" rather than "I mentioned"; "the hypothesis suggests itself" rather than "I think." They prefer *magnitude* to "size," *methodology* to "methods," *interrelationship* to "relation." They discuss simple everyday happenings in terms of "factors," "phases," "aspects," "situations," "criteria," "data," "problems," "facets," "phenomena," "structures," "levels," and "strata."

Obviously, many scientific and scholarly subjects call for language that is technical, precise, impersonal. Jargon is the *unnecessary* use of technical language in order to borrow the prestige of science and scholarship.

Pompous: A drastic reappraisal and reassessment of our present position on a number of issues, including the location of our offices, is being given meaningful consideration in order to maximize our opportunities and those of our clients in a National Capital filled with flux.

Plain Fact: The company is moving its offices.

D 6d   Flowery Diction *d*

Avoid language that is flowery or overdone.

Flowery and extravagant diction interferes with a writer's doing justice to a subject. Flowery diction results from an attempt to give a poetic varnish to prose. Some writers cannot resist the temptation to call a policeman a "minion of the law," an Irishman a "native of the Emerald Isle," a colonist who served in the War of Independence a "gallant warrior defending our infant republic."

Flowery:	The respite from study was devoted to a sojourn at the ancestral mansion.
Plain English:	I spent my vacation at the house of my grandparents.
Flowery:	The visitor proved a harbinger of glad tidings.
Plain English:	The visitor brought good news.

Exercises

A. What makes each of the following sentences wordy? Your instructor may ask you to rewrite these sentences.

1. The war against alcohol lasts enduringly forever.
2. Mormons fleeing persecution founded the beginning of our community.
3. In due time, a new fad will eventually replace this current craze.
4. The mail-order house claimed the product would increase sexual virility among men.

5. The fact that the college forces one to pay for membership in a student organization seems to me a coercion of the student's funds.

6. Some of today's popular music seems to revert back to music popular thirty years ago.

7. The weather bureau announced that at times there would be occasional rain.

8. The reason that married students have high grades academically is that they have a definite goal in the future to come.

9. In the modern world of this day and age, economical operation has become an indispensable condition for business success.

10. The act of effective teaching is an art that not many teachers are capable of doing.

B. Investigate the *current use of euphemisms* in one major area, such as education, medicine, or the funeral industry. Examine such euphemisms for intention, appropriateness, effect.

C. Do you ever say to yourself: "There must be a simpler way of saying this"? Translate the following examples of jargon into plain English.

1. The author uses the main character as the narrator of the story in that this character is telling about an incident that has happened to him previously in his life that made him feel like a fool for doing this act.

2. One way in which private schools are better than public schools is that in attending a private school, one achieves good study habits to follow.

3. To be frank about it, today an inadequacy can bring about the ruination of a person in later life when it happens in education.

4. In many instances, and circumstances in common day speech and word usage, one will hear words and ideas expressed that do not denote the proper meaning, or thought that they were intended to generate.

5. The results she had on people through her outward actions, was merely a small incident as compared to the effect the example she set had on them.

6. In these two books, there are basic differences in character representation that are accountable only in terms of the individual authors involved.

7. Further insight into the article discovered that the writing insinuated a connection between the conviction of the accused and his working class background.

8. Advertisements similar to those of Certs and Ultra-Brite are creating a fallacy in the real cause of a person's sex appeal.

9. The fact that we are products of our environmental frame of reference ensures that each of us has deeply ingrained within the fiber of our being preconceived ideas which influence our thoughts, actions, and reactions.

10. We say we believe in democracy while denying the partaking of its first fruits, justice and equality, to diverse members of our society. This is true in many aspects of our lives, but especially so in the context of racial prejudice.

D. Study the language used by your favorite *sports writer, fashion analyst, or society editor.* Write a brief report, providing samples of characteristic diction.

3

Sentence Style

For Quick Reference

A writer's most basic tool is the sentence. The most basic fact about the English sentence is that it gives the writer a tremendous range of *choice*. Each of the following sentences states the same idea in a different way:

The old man recited the verses with many a splendid gesture.

With many a splendid gesture, the old man recited the verses.

The verses were recited by an old man gesturing splendidly.

A man—old, gesturing splendidly—was reciting verses.

There was an old man reciting verses, gesturing splendidly.

The man who recited the verses with many a splendid gesture was old.

When you work on sentence style, you focus on what helps your sentences carry their message. You work on what makes sentences *effective*. You practice writing sentences that come right to the point. You practice choosing among the available sentence resources those that are right for the job. You develop an ear for the kind of well-built sentence that reads right—that makes the reader want to write in the margin: "Well said!"

S 1   Sentence Building

Write sentences that clearly signal important relationships.

Many simple sentences are built on the "Who does what?" model. When such a sentence moves with few or no modifiers from subject to verb and from there to one or more complements, we are likely to encounter few problems of clarity or proper perspective.

My friend waited outside the restaurant.
The relatives of the deceased *crowded the room.*
The heavens declare the glory of God.

Sentence Style

Our problem is to maintain the same clarity and direct-ness in sentences that carry more, and more complicated, information.

S 1a   Effective Predication   *st*

Rewrite weak sentences on the "Who does what?" model.

Try to make the subject name the key agent. Then make the predicate state the key point.

Weak: *One crucial factor* in the current revolution in our social structure *is the relationship* between the white policeman and the black community.
(Subject and predicate carry little of the meaning; they are semantic blanks.)

Stronger: *The white policeman* standing on a Harlem street corner *finds himself at the very center* of the revolu-tion now occurring in the world.—James Baldwin, *Nobody Knows My Name*
(Sentence structure now makes the "crucial factor" also *grammatically* crucial—by making *policeman* the subject of the sentence.)

Watch out especially for sentences in which nouns end-ing in *-ment, -ion, -ism,* and the like, serve as the subject of the sentence. Often these refer to actions, events, and activi-ties that could be more vigorously expressed by a verb, with the agent clearly identified and serving as the subject.

Weak: Violent *arguments* frequently *took place.*

Revised: *We* often *argued* violently.

Weak: *A certain element* of confusion *was present.*

Revised: *The speaker confused us.*

Weak: *A criticism* which is prevalent against modern poetry *is* that *its appeal is* only to the super-sophisticated.

Revised: *Many critics charge* that *modern poetry appeals* only to the super-sophisticated.

To make the subject and predicate of a main clause carry your main point, eliminate tag statements like "The simple fact is that . . ." and "the question now confronting us is whether . . ."

Weak: *The question* now confronting us *is* whether we should yield to intimidation, and thus encourage other groups to resort to the same tactics.

Revised: *Should we yield* to intimidation, and thus encourage other groups to resort to the same tactics?

S 1b   Effective Coordination   *st*

Use coordination when two ideas are about equally important.

In sentences like the following, both clauses are about equally relevant to the general trend of the report or argument:

We tried to locate the files, *but* we were unsuccessful.

Our press is essentially provincial in this country, *and* except for a few syndicated columnists the reputation of our newspaper reporters is mainly local.

If you doubt the appropriateness of a coordinating connective like *and* or *but,* test the sentence by inserting a parenthetical "equally important":

Effective: Under one of the plans, a reservist spends only six months on active duty, *but* [equally important] he remains in the Ready Reserve for seven and one-half years.

Sentence Style

Excessive coordination often results from the overuse of *and*. Note that it merely says "more of same," without indicating any specific relationship. It is appropriate when the clause that follows really gives us "more of same" by reinforcing the same point:

A tart temper never mellows with age, *and* a sharp tongue is the only edged tool that grows keener with constant use.—Washington Irving, "Rip Van Winkle"

And is also appropriate when events follow each other "as they happen," without emphasis on cause and effect or other logical relations:

There was a shock, *and* he felt himself go up in the air. He pushed on the sword as he went up and over, *and* it flew out of his hand. He hit the ground *and* the bull was on him.—Ernest Hemingway, "The Undefeated"

But avoid *and* when it merely makes a sentence ramble on, without preparing the reader for what is coming:

Rambling: A member of the Reserve has to participate in weekly drills, *and* he may be called up in emergencies, which came as an unpleasant surprise to me, *and* you would do better to stay away from it.

S 1c   Effective Subordination   *sub*

Use subordination when details, reasons, or qualifications accompany a main point.

Subordinating connectives (*when, while, since, because, if, though*) and relative pronouns (*who, which,* and *that*) can make the material they subordinate seem of secondary importance. They fit well when the main clause states a major point, with the dependent clauses establishing relations in place, time, or logic:

The edge of the cape was wet with blood *where* it had swept along the bull's back as he went by.—Ernest Hemingway, "The Undefeated"

Remember the following points:

(1) Effective subordination *clarifies relationships in a* sentence. Merely placed next to each other, the following two statements may seem disjointed: "Kroger organized a counterfeiting ring. He had studied printing in Germany." When one is subordinated to the other, the connection between them becomes more obvious:

Effective: Kroger, *who had studied printing in Germany,* organized a counterfeiting ring.

(2) Unskillful subordination *blurs emphasis. "I was ten* when we moved to Alaska" focuses the reader's attention on you and your age. "When I was ten, *we moved to Alaska"* focuses the reader's attention on Alaska. **Upside-down subordination** results when the wrong item seems to stand out. When tucked away in a subordinate part of a sentence, important information may catch the reader unaware and, as a result, have an ironic effect. *Avoid upside-down subordination when no irony is intended:*

Upside-Down: The salary was considered good by local standards, *though* it was not enough to feed and clothe my family.

Sentence Style

Improved:	*Though* considered good by local standards, my salary was not enough to feed and clothe my family.
Upside-Down:	He had a completely accident-free record up to the last day of his employment, *when* he stepped on a power line and almost lost his life.
Improved:	On the last day of his employment, *after* ten years without a single accident, he stepped on a power line and almost lost his life.

S 1d   Effective Modifiers   *sub*

Use modifiers to help a sentence carry added freight.

A skillful writer often uses modifying words and phrases where an inexperienced writer might use separate clauses. Observe the tightening of relationships in the following pair:

Routine:	We caught two bass. We hauled them in briskly, as though they were mackerel. After we pulled them over the side of the boat, we stunned them with a blow on the back of the head.
Effective:	We caught two bass, *hauling them in briskly* as though they were mackerel, *pulling them over the side of the boat* in a businesslike manner without any landing net, and *stunning them with a blow on the back of the head.*—E. B. White, *One Man's Meat*

The following sentences, from a bull-fighting story by Ernest Hemingway, illustrate the effective use of one or more modifiers *at different positions* in the sentence:

* breaking up subject and verb:

The horse, *lifted and gored,* crashed over with the bull driving into him.

Manuel, *lying on the ground,* kicked at the bull's muzzle with his slippered feet.

Manuel, *facing the bull, having turned with him each charge,* offered the cape with his two hands.

● at the end of the sentence:

Manuel walked towards him, *watching his feet.*

The bull was hooking wildly, *jumping like a trout, all four feet off the ground.*

● at the beginning of the sentence:

Now, *facing the bull,* he was conscious of many things at the same time.

Heads up, swinging with the music, their right arms swinging free, they stepped out.

Arrogant, swinging, they looked straight ahead as they marched.

● more than one position:

The bull, *in full gallop,* pivoted and charged the cape, *his head down, his tail rising.*

Exercises

A. Study the following model sentences. They make exceptionally full use of the *sentence resources* that we can draw on to help load a sentence with information. For each of the model sentences, write a sentence of your own on a subject of your own choice. As much as you can, follow the sentence structure of the original. Try to come close—you need not follow the model sentence in every detail.

Model 1: Your photographs will be more artistic if you use the film that has chromatic balance.

Sample Imitation: Your checks will be more welcome if you draw them on an account that has money in it.

Model 2: Everyone is a moon and has a dark side which he never shows to anybody. (Mark Twain)

Model 3: John, being bored and having a crowd, picked this time to play the fool again.

Model 4: Sitting in the study hall, she opened the lid of the desk and changed the number pasted up inside from seventy-seven to seventy-six.

Model 5: The fullback held the ball lightly in front of him, his knees pumping high, his hips twisting as he ran toward the end zone.

B. Rewrite the following sentences for *more effective predication*.

1. A conscientious teacher's satisfaction is incomplete unless he reaches a full realization of his goals.

2. As the result of unruly demonstrations, repeated interruptions of the committee's deliberations took place.

3. The conclusion is inevitable that considerable impairment of our country's military strength has come about.

4. A plan for safe driving is of no use if the cooperation of the individual driver is not present.

5. The accumulation of pressures to conform is so great that the student is in constant awareness of their presence.

6. The contribution of the alumni to the growth of the college will be in proportion to their information about its educational needs.

C. Write three simple, short sentences built on the "Who-does-what" model. Then *add* to each sentence, building up relevant details. Examples:

A girl plays "Silent Night."

A *small skinny black* girl plays "Silent Night" *with two fingers on an untuned piano in a sunken garage.*

A dog zig-zags.

A dog, *tail held high,* zig-zags *among the tailless creatures in search of its master.*

D. Rewrite the following passages, making effective use of *subordination or modifiers.*

1. Campus elections are ridiculous. Nobody qualified runs. I refuse to have anything to do with them.

2. Piloting a boat is easy. It is like driving a car. The controls are about the same.

3. The monkey family is large. It includes monkeys, baboons, lemurs, and apes. The animals in the monkey family are closely related to man. They are imitative. They can be trained to perform simple tasks. However, their intelligence is low.

4. My father came from a wealthy family, and my mother came from a very poor home, and it was strange that she held the purse strings in the family.

5. Many high school teachers follow a textbook word for word, and they go over each page until everyone understands it. In college, many teachers just tell the student to read the textbook, and then they start giving lectures on the material covered in the text, but they don't follow it word for word.

E. Study the following sentences as examples of different basic jobs a sentence can do. For each model sentence, write a sentence of your own that follows as closely as possible the basic structure of the original.

1. (a sentence that fills in examples)

Women are beginning to read a good deal about their own place in history, about the determined struggles of the suffragettes, the isolation of Virginia Woolf, and the heroism of Rosa Luxemburg. (Lucy Komisar)

Pattern: (People) are beginning to hear (read) a good deal
about _____, about _____.

2.   (a sentence that specifies)

Prayer that craves a particular commodity, anything less than
all good, is vicious. (Emerson)
Pattern: (Something) that _____ is _____.

3.   (a sentence that traces a process)

We begin as children; we mature; we leave the parental nest;
we give birth to children who, in turn, grow up, leave and
begin the process all over again. (Alvin Toffler)
Pattern: We _____; we _____; we _____.

4.   (a sentence that sums up the high point of a story)

When a Sunday dinner came, I went to the table and tried
to act as if there wasn't a thing different, but when I saw my
little red hen in the dish, I wished I was somewhere else.
(Student theme)
Pattern: When _____ came, _____.

5.   (a sentence that points out a contrast or a paradox)

Most people would prefer just about any kind of work to
that of a domestic servant; yet the mindless, endless, repeti-
tious drudgery of housekeeping is the central occupation of
more than fifty million women. (Lucy Komisar)
Pattern: Most people (agree) (believe) (prefer) _____;
yet _____.

S 2   Sentence Variety

Keep your sentences from becoming plodding and monotonous.

An effective writer uses sentences of different length and structure for variety and emphasis.

S 2a   Sentence Length   *st*

Use short sentences to sum up a point; use long sentences for detailed explanation and support.

A short, incisive sentence is often appropriate for summing up a key idea or for giving pointed advice. The following sentences are quotable, emphatic, to the point:

Economy is the art of making the most of life. (G. B. Shaw)
As long as possible live free and uncommitted. (Thoreau)
Perversity is the muse of modern literature. (Susan Sontag)

A complex, elaborate sentence is often appropriate for detailed explanation or argument. The following sentences from Thoreau's "Civil Disobedience" are carefully worked out, with all ifs and buts fully stated:

There will never be a really free and enlightened State until the State comes to recognize the individual as a higher and independent power, from which all its own power and authority are derived, and treats him accordingly.

It is not a man's duty, as a matter of course, to devote himself to the eradication of any, even the most enormous wrong; he may still properly have other concerns to engage him; but it is his

141

duty, at least, to wash his hands of it, and, if he gives it no thought longer, not to give it practically his support.

Remember the following points:

(1) Excessive use of *short, isolated sentences* can make your writing sound immature:

Choppy: Many teachers can give students information. Very few can inspire students to learn. Information is of little use to students. Soon they will leave college. Then they will forget what they have memorized. They must be inspired to learn on their own.

Improved: Many teachers can give students information, but few can inspire them to learn. When students leave college, the information they have memorized will be of little use and will soon be forgotten. What they need most is the ability to learn on their own.

(2) Your writing will gain in clarity and emphasis if you occasionally make your reader stop short at a *concise, memorable statement of an important point*. Notice the emphatic short sentences in the following passages:

With the great growth in leisure-time activities, millions of Americans are turning to water sports: fishing, swimming, water skiing, and skin diving. *Clean water exhilarates and relaxes.*—Vance Packard, "America the Beautiful—and Its Desecraters," *Atlantic*

Bennett was always facing the wonder of the actualities of living. It was wonderful to him that we live as we do, that time will pass and change us, that we will die and perhaps die painfully, that life is what it is. *He never decorates or embroiders. He is wholly materialistic. Common sense is the salt of his plate.* We are never swept away, but we are curiously won over, and we, too, are filled with wonder at the slow unspinning of life.—John Van Druten, "My Debt to Arnold Bennett," *Saturday Review*

(3) A short sentence can be especially effective if it sets off an important conclusion or a *key observation at the end of a passage composed of longer sentences:*

They have a constitutional right, of course, to tell us what we must do to be saved; as they have always done. Twenty years ago they were telling us the direct opposite of what they tell us now; but they were just as sure then as now that they had the sole and sufficient key to salvation, and that those who did not accept it were forever damned. *One becomes bored.*—Elmer Davis, "History in Doublethink," *Saturday Review*

S 2b Varied Word Order   *rep*

Use variations from normal word order to keep your sentences from being too much alike.

Though most of your sentences will follow the subject-verb sequence, there will usually be enough variety in the remaining sentence elements to prevent tiresome repetition. Monotony is most likely to result when a number of sentences start with the same subject, especially a pronoun like *I* or *he:*

Monotonous: A good example of a topic drawn from personal experience is a bus accident I once had. I wrote a paper about this experience of mine. I remembered the events which took place during the accident. I could describe them well. After all, I had experienced them. It was a shocking experience. I will never forget it. The facts stand out in my memory because it was so shocking.

(1) *Make a modifier that usually occurs later in the sentence precede the subject.* The **introductory modifier** can bring variety into a group of plodding sentences:

Varied: He reversed the direction of the canoe. *After a few seconds* he stopped paddling. *Slowly* he made the canoe drift to the bank. *When within a yard of the shore,* he grabbed one of the overhanging branches.

Varied: The Trans World Terminal stems from the work of contemporary architects like Corbusier of France and Nervi of Italy, masters of the curve in concrete. *Like a true eagle,* this building is all curves and muscle, no right angles. *Built of reinforced concrete,* the whole structure swoops and turns and rises.—Ken Macrorie, "Arriving and Departing," *The Reporter*

(2) To gain emphasis, *shift a complement to a more emphatic initial position.* The **introductory complement** is normal in exclamations beginning with *what* or *how:* "*What stories* that man told!" "*What a liar* you are!" "*How true* that is!" In other sentences, the introductory complement is especially effective when it takes up something mentioned earlier:

Effective: The committee has asked me to resign. *That* I will never do.

Effective: Mr. Schlumpf fried two small pieces of fish. *One of these* he fed to his cat. *The other* he ate himself.

Effective: We really should not resent being called paupers. *Paupers* we are, and *paupers* we shall remain.

Note: Like other attention-getting devices, the introductory complement sometimes attracts attention to the speaker rather than to what he or she is saying. Sometimes the construction smacks of old-fashion oratory:

More patient wife a husband never had.
Gone are the days of my youth.
Such deeds of glory we shall see no more.

(3) *Shift the predicate of the main clause toward the end* and work some of the modifiers into the sentence earlier. Such treatment may strengthen a sentence especially if a **final modifier** is a belated qualification or concession, unexpectedly weakening the main point:

Weak: Richard Wagner became one of the most successful composers of all time in spite of the jeers of his contemporaries. (This version may make your readers remember the jeers rather than the man's success.)

Improved: Richard Wagner, *though jeered at by his contemporaries,* became one of the most successful composers of all time.

Note: A **loose** sentence finishes one major statement *early* but then leads on to further points or further detail. It is an expandable or cumulative sentence that looks as if it might have been built in stages:

Loose: *Comedy usually moves toward a happy ending,* and the normal response of the audience to a happy ending is "this should be," which sounds like a moral judgment. —Northrop Frye, *Anatomy of Criticism*

In a **periodic** sentence, an essential part of the main statement is *held in suspense* until the end. The sentence ends when the main statement ends. Everything else is worked into the sentence along the way, contributing its share to the main effect. A periodic sentence has an air of finality; it makes the main idea stay with us:

Periodic: *Even Tom Jones,* though far more fully realized, *is still deliberately associated,* as his commonplace name indicates, *with the conventional and the typical*—Northrop Frye, *Anatomy of Criticism*

Exercises

A. Study the following models as examples of *short, memorable* sentences. Then write two sentences of your own that follow as closely as possible the structure of the original. Write the first one about a personal trait or quality, the second one about a type of person. Make your sentences fit the following patterns:

Model 1: Curiosity, like all other desires, produces pain as well as pleasure. (Samuel Johnson)

(Pattern: _____, like _____, _____.)

Model 2: The man with a new idea is a Crank until the new idea succeeds. (Mark Twain)

(Pattern: The person with _____ is _____ until _____.)

B. Study the following models as examples of *long, elaborate* sentences carrying along a great many details. For each example, write a similar sentence of your own, carrying nearly as much freight as the original. (You need not follow the structure of the original in detail.)

Write your first sentence about a setting, the second about a writer (or artist, or movie star, or other celebrity), the third about an activity (or kind of performance).

1. The backstage of New York's Hunter College Auditorium is now crowding up with photographers, glistening men in briefs, technicians, an official looking for a lost trophy, and an amazingly built woman just barely wearing a leopard-skin bathing suit who, as it happens, is Miss Nude America and will compete in the Miss Body Beautiful contest.—Robert M. Strozier, "Cadillac Calves and Lovely Square Pecs," *Atlantic*

2. The boys in his books got ahead by outwitting thieves and sharpers—yet he himself, a mild and generous little man who gave freely of his earning to newsboys and bootblacks on the New York streets (the sort of boys who were his favorite

heroes) , was an easy mark for impostors.—Frederick Lewis Allen, "Horatio Alger, Jr.," *Saturday Review*

3. An interview need not be an ambush to be good, but it should set up a situation in which the subject can be surprised by what he says—that is, a situation in which he has to do some audible thinking.—Richard Todd, "Speaking in a Public Capacity," *Atlantic*

C. Study the following examples of how a *short summary* sentence and a *long elaborating* sentence can work together. Then write three pairs of your own that similarly give your reader "the long and the short of it."

> *Training is everything.* The peach was once a bitter almond; cauliflower is nothing but cabbage with a college education. (Mark Twain)

> *Newspapers give a distorted view of life.* They overemphasize the unusual, such as a mother giving birth to quintuplets, the development of a Christmas tree that grows its own decorative cones, the minting of two pennies which were only half engraved, gang fights, teen-age drinking, or riots.

D. Study the variations in sentence style in the following passages. Describe the functions performed or the effects produced by sentences of different *length*. Which passages make use of variations in *word order?*

1. Why conform to a group? Why throw away your birthright for a Greek pin or a peace button, for security and nonentity? This goes especially for the typical college student, who merely wants to do what "everyone else is doing." What everyone else is doing isn't best. It's merely common. One of the synonyms of "common" is "vulgar."

2. The dictionary can neither snicker nor fulminate. It records. It will offend many, no doubt, to find the expression *wise up,* meaning to inform or to become informed, listed in the Third International with no restricting label. To my aging ears it still sounds like slang. But the evidence—quotations from the *Kiplinger Washington Letter* and the *Wall Street Journal*—

convinces me that it is I who am out of step, lagging behind. (Bergen Evans)

3. The production of a work of art is not the result of a miracle. It requires preparation. The soil, be it ever so rich, must be fed. By taking thought, by deliberate effort, the artist must enlarge, deepen and diversify his personality. Then the soil must lie fallow. Like the bride of Christ, the artist waits for the illumination that shall bring forth a new spiritual life. He goes about his ordinary avocations with patience; the subconscious does its mysterious business; and then, suddenly springing, you might think from nowhere, the idea is produced. (W. Somerset Maugham)

S 3   Awkward Construction

Avoid constructions that make for an indirect, awkward, wooden style.

Effective sentences may be long and complicated, as long as the words and structural relationships convey meaning clearly and directly. On the other hand, the grammatical equipment even in short sentences may become so heavy that it interferes with communication.

S 3a   Deadwood   *awk*

Prune your sentences of deadwood.

Often a sentence runs more smoothly after it has been trimmed down. Avoid unnecessary *there are*s and *who were*s:

Awkward:	*There are* many farmers in the area *who* are planning to attend the meeting *which is* scheduled for next Friday.
Improved:	Many farmers in the area plan to attend the meeting scheduled for next Friday.

Other sentences can be cleared of deadwood by effective use of pronouns:

Awkward:	A child of pre-school age often shows a desire to read, but *the child's* parents often ignore this *desire*.
Improved:	Often a child of pre-school age shows a desire to read —*which his* parents ignore.

Some connectives, prepositions, and pronouns are unnecessary or unnecessarily heavy:

Awkward:	I wrote little, *because of the fact that* my childhood had been *an* uneventful *one*.
Improved:	I wrote little, because my childhood had been uneventful.

S 3b   Awkward Passive   *awk*

Avoid the passive when it makes sentences heavy or roundabout.

An active sentence is modeled on the "agent-action-target" relationship: "The woodcutter *felled* the tree." A passive sentence reverses this perspective and looks at the action from the point of view of the original object: "The tree *was felled* by the woodcutter." As a result, the passive is appropriate when the recipient or target of an action seems *more important than the performer:*

Sentence Style

The unpretentious monarchs of Scandinavia and the Low Countries are respectfully accepted by their sober subjects.—Kingsley Martin, "Strange Interlude," *Atlantic*

The passive is equally appropriate when the originator or the performer of an action is *unimportant, irrelevant,* or *hard to identify:*

Some of John's brain cells *were damaged* when he was a small child.

In World War II, millions of people *were driven* from their homes.

Students often *overuse* the passive under the mistaken impression that it will make their sentences more formal, more scholarly. Practice translating such pseudo-formal passives back to the active:

Pseudo-Formal: Although Bradley Hall *is* regularly *populated* by students, close study of the building as a structure *is* seldom *undertaken.*

Direct: The students *passing* through Bradley Hall seldom *pause to study* its structure.

Pseudo-Formal: My experiences at writing *were* greatly *increased* due to two large essays due each week.

Direct: I *wrote* more than ever, *having to turn in* two long essays each week.

Unnecessary use of the passive can make it hard for the reader to visualize actions or events. Since the agent or performer is often *omitted* from a passive sentence, the reader may find it hard to determine the person responsible for an action or idea:

Evasive: A plan for popular election of Supreme Court justices *is* now *being advanced.* (By whom? The passive spreads a protective cloak of anonymity around the authors of the proposal.)

Evasive: The racial problem is clearly one that *could and should have been solved* decades ago. (By whom?)

(On *shifts* to the passive, see G 10c.)

S 3c   Impersonal Constructions   *awk*

Avoid impersonal constructions that obscure the identity of the forces at work.

The impersonal *one,* the *it* without antecedent, and *there-is* or *there-are* sentences are most appropriate when the identity of persons or forces initiating an action is of secondary importance. We naturally say "it rains" or "it snows" when we are interested in the process and its results rather than in its causes. But guard against the *unnecessary* use of such constructions.

(1) The **impersonal *one*** is often a tiresome substitute for fuller identification of the persons concerned, especially if their identity is indirectly revealed by modifiers:

Roundabout: *When teaching, one* should be patient.

Improved: *Teachers* should be patient.

Roundabout: *As a father, one* should not spoil his children.

Improved: *Fathers* should not spoil their children.

Roundabout: *If one is a citizen of a democracy, she* should exercise her voting rights.

Improved: *A citizen of a democracy* should vote.

(2) In *it-is* and *there-is* **sentences,** the first two words are mere structural props, which can make the sentences

sound lame and indecisive. Sometimes, the subject of a sentence receives needed emphasis if it is introduced by *it is* or *there is* and has its predicate changed into a modifying clause:

Emphatic: It is *his competence* that we question—not his honesty.

More often, however, the rearrangement of sentence elements made necessary by *it is* or *there is* causes awkwardness:

Awkward: In 1958, *there was* a strike participated in by five thousand union members.

Improved: In 1958, five thousand union members went on strike.

S 3d   Excessive Subordination   *awk*

Avoid overburdened sentences caused by excessive subordination.

Excessive subordination causes various types of overburdened sentences. One common type *dovetails* several dependent clauses into each other thus making a subordinating connective follow another subordinating connective or a relative pronoun. The resulting **that-if, if-because, which-when constructions** are often awkward:

Awkward: I think *that if* there were less emphasis on conformity in high school, college students would be better prepared for independent thinking.

Improved: In my opinion, college students would be better prepared for independent thinking *if* there were less emphasis on conformity in high school.

Another type of excessive subordination results in **"house-that-Jack-built" sentences.** Several dependent clauses of the same type follow each other, making the sentence trail off into *a confusing succession of modifiers:*

Awkward:	When I was in Mexico City, I visited Jean, *who* was living with a Mexican girl *who* posed for the local artists, *who* are usually too poor to pay their rent, let alone the model's fee.
Improved:	When I was in Mexico City, I visited Jean. She was living with a Mexican girl *who* posed for the local artists but seldom received any money for her work. Most Mexican artists are too poor to pay their rent, let alone the model's fee.

Sometimes too many dependent clauses of the same type delay the main clause:

Awkward:	*When* a child is constantly watched *when* he is born and *while* he is a baby, the reason is that his mother wants to see whether he is developing as her books say he should.
Improved:	Some mothers constantly watch young children to see whether they are developing as the books say they should.

Seesaw sentences start with a dependent clause, proceed to the main clause, and then add a *second dependent clause* that in a confusing way qualifies the meaning of the first:

Confusing:	*Because many teen-agers marry hastily,* their marriages end in divorce, *because they are too immature to face adult responsibilities.*
Clearer:	Many teen-agers are too immature to face adult responsibilities. They marry hastily, and often their marriages end in divorce.

153

S 3e Awkward Modifiers *awk*

Keep disproportionately heavy modifiers from breaking up the pattern of a clause.

Lengthy appositives, verbal phrases, or dependent clauses sometimes separate elements that belong together:

Awkward: The pilot told his friends that he had flown Clinton Morris, *a resident of New York City sought by the government for income tax evasion,* out of the United States.

Awkward: The club treasurer, *being* the son of a father constantly *stressing* the importance of *maintaining* a proper sense of the value of money, refused to pay our expenses.

Awkward: In 1943, Independence Hall, *which had been the first building built on the campus and which had housed the administration of the college for many decades,* was torn down.

Exercises

A. Which of the following sentences seem clear and well built? Which seem awkward, overburdened, or confusing? If your instructor desires, revise the weak sentences.

1. Saturday mornings used to be my best time for studying, because I knew nothing was due the next morning (which was Sunday), until I started working.

2. From across the dinner-littered dining table, my father blinks myopically and asserts that current conflicts are no different from any other conflicts and that my dissent is no different from what his dissent used to be.

3. There are many ways in which a student who is interested in meeting a foreign student may come to know one.

4. A child's first impressions of people and places shape the course of her future life, frequently.

5. All electric appliances, far from being labor-saving devices, are new forms of work, decentralized and made available to everybody. (Marshall McLuhan)

6. Knowing the right answers is sometimes less important than asking the right questions.

7. As we left the city, we approached a range of hills which seemed like giant waves which were about to break.

8. John Milton was the first English writer who clearly and convincingly stated the idea that incompatibility is grounds for divorce, if I am not mistaken.

9. If someone is exercising his slightly off-key singing voice and a friend mockingly plugs her ears and winces in agony, the singer might well take the gesture as a personal insult if he didn't have a sense of humor.

10. As we were waiting for the doctor to see us, a boy with brown hair down to the small of his back played a flute, tears streaming down his face.

11. Various ways of living are being tested today and experimented with by youth whose dominant characteristic is the desire for flexibility.

12. In Roman comedy the heroine, who is usually a slave or courtesan, turns out to be the daughter of somebody respectable, so that the hero can marry her without loss of face. (Northrop Frye)

B. For each of the following sentences, point out the perspective created or the special effect achieved by the use of the passive.

1. The scientific war against deliciousness has been stepped up enormously in the last decade. (Philip Wylie)

2. When the portion of meat was brought down in its wooden

tub at dinnertime, it was duly divided as fairly as possible into as many parts as there were mouths.

3. I was taken up a narrow staircase to the men's dormitory, in which were eight or ten beds and four miserable wash-hand stands. (H. G. Wells)

4. More books have been written about Napoleon than about any other human being. (Aldous Huxley)

5. The stumps of harpoons are frequently found in the dead bodies of captured whales. (Herman Melville)

S 4 Repetition

Learn to make effective use of repetition and parallelism.

Unintentional, haphazard repetition can make a passage sound clumsy. Deliberate repetition can emphasize important points and give continuity to a sentence or a paragraph.

S 4a Awkward Repetition *rep*

Avoid unintentional repetition of sounds, syllables, words, or phrases.

Carelessly repeated sounds or sentence elements grate on the reader's ears.

Awkward: Commercials seldom make for entertain*ing* and re-lax*ing* listen*ing.*

Improved: Commercials seldom entertain and relax the listener.

Awkward:	Close examin*ation* of the results of the investig*ation* led to a reorganiz*ation* of the department.
Improved:	Close study of the results of the inquiry led to a re-organization of the department.
Awkward:	We listened to an account *of* the customs *of* the inhabitants *of* the village.
Improved:	We listened to an account of the villagers' customs.

Unintentional repetition is especially annoying when the similarity in sound covers up a *shift in meaning or relationship:*

My father lost his savings during the depression because he had *banked* on [better: "relied on"] the well-established reputation of our hometown *bank.*

S 4b Emphatic Repetition   *emp*

Use intentional repetition for clarity and continuity.

A writer may repeat important words and phrases for emphasis:

| Emphatic: | When I returned to State, *I studied* as I have never studied since. *I studied* before classes. *I studied* after classes. *I studied* till English, history, and zoology merged into one blurry mass of incoherent erudition. |
| Emphatic: | In my mother's world, *no one ever* shrugged his shoulders; *no one* was *ever* bored and lazy; *no one* was *ever* cynical; *no one ever* laughed.—Alfred Kazin, "The Bitter 30's," *Atlantic* |

Notice the cumulative effect of intentional repetition in the following passage from Stephen Crane's "The Open Boat":

Sentence Style

In the meantime, the oiler *rowed,* and then the correspondent *rowed,* and then the oiler *rowed.* Grey-faced and bowed forward, they mechanically, turn by turn, plied the leaden oars.

S 4c   Parallel Structure   //

> *Use parallel structure to help channel the reader's attention.*

Parallel structure pulls together related ideas through the repetition of characteristic grammatical patterns. The following passages make effective use of parallelism:

> My lack *of excitement,*
> > *of curiosity,*
> > *of surprise,*
> > *of* any sort of pronounced *interest,*
> > > began to arouse his distrust. (Joseph Conrad)

> The air *must be* pure
> > *if we are to* breathe;
> the soil *must be* arable
> > *if we are to* eat;
> the water *must be* clean
> > *if we are to* drink.

> *Our* houses *are* built *with* foreign taste;
> *our* shelves *are* garnished *with* foreign ornaments;
> > *our* opinions,
> > *our* tastes,
> > *our* faculties,
> > > *lean* and
> > > *follow*
> > > > *the* Past and
> > > > *the* Distant. (Emerson)

Remember:

(1) Parallel structure helps to *line up related ideas in a sentence;* it *draws together related ideas in a paragraph:*

Together we planned the house, *together we* built it, and *together we* watched it go up in smoke.

The people wanted to be told that when this particular enemy had been forced to unconditional surrender, they would re-enter the golden age. *This* unique *war would end* all wars. *This* last *war would make* the world safe for democracy. *This crusade would make* the whole world a democracy.—Walter Lippmann, *The Public Philosophy*

(2) Often, parallel structure helps to *line up dissimilar ideas for comparison or contrast.*

Her remarks provoked much comment, *self-righteous from her enemies, apologetic from her friends.*

Whereas *it is desirable that* the old *should treat with respect* the wishes of the young, *it is not desirable that* the young *should treat with respect* the wishes of the old.

We call the neat balancing of two direct opposites an **antithesis.** Note the antithetical style of the following passage:

India *is a poetic nation, yet it demands* new electrical plants. It *is a mystical nation, yet it wants* new roads. It *is* traditionally *a peaceful nation, yet it could,* if misled, *inflame* Asia.—James A. Michener, "Portraits for the Future," *Saturday Review*

(3) Parallel structure enables a writer to *make a series of parallel sentences build up to a* **climax.** Notice how the author of the following passage starts with fairly innocuous generalities and leads up to a specific point dear to his heart:

The future *is not for* little men with little minds. It *is not for* men without vision who fear progress. It *is not for* timid men who early were frightened by the story of Frankenstein. And it *is not for* those arch reactionaries who seek to shatter big enterprise and to force American industry back into the puny production patterns of its nineteenth-century infancy.

(On *faulty* parallelism, see G 10d.)

Exercises

A. Examine the uses of *repetition and parallelism* in the following sentences. Your instructor may ask you to use one or more of these as model sentences. For each model sentence, write one of your own that as far as possible preserves the structure of the original.

1. Warren believed in applauding politely to reward effort, generously to reward competence, and frenetically to reward genius.

2. War, assuming that one does not love it for its own sake, or does not use it as a background for some isolated moral, or does not, worst of all, believe in its shabby rationale, can only produce one of two reactions: a tear, or a scream.

3. Young people believe that by remaining individuals, by avoiding the marriage vows, by living together only as long as love lasts, they will avoid the togetherness demanded of the married, they will avoid the staleness of being taken for granted, they will avoid the boredom and responsibility that might emerge from a loveless marriage.

4. It requires enormous intelligence, innate or acquired by cultivation, to discharge the full responsibilities of managing a household; doing its endlessly repetitive work without deadening the mind; bringing up children, restraining, encouraging and helping them; being a companion and helpmeet to one's husband, helpfully and intelligently interested in his work; and being, at the same time, able to take on his duties and

responsibilities if she must, as thousands of women have had to. (Dorothy Thompson)

5. Eastern Oregon is a land of contrasts—of tortured rimrocks and gentle rolling pastures; of tormented sagebrush and velvet spreads of alfalfa fields; of the stench of sulphur springs and the honey and mead aroma of fresh-mown wild hay; of arid alkali flats and the swift fresh-water streams teeming with trout.

B. Point out any features that make for effective sentence style. Examine such features as sentence length, variety, emphasis. Point out any special or unusual effects.

1. We go to our libraries in order to read and take advantage of the experiences of others. I think we all realize that not every written word in a library is entirely true. Many different authors have here written what they think, what they have experienced, what they believe is true, and sometimes what they wish were true. Some are wrong, a few are right, and many are neither entirely wrong nor entirely right.

2. This is not a Utopian tract. Some of those who complain about the quality of our national life seem to be dreaming of a world in which everyone without exception has talent, taste, judgment and an unswerving allegiance to excellence. Such dreams are pleasant but unprofitable. The problem is to achieve some measure of excellence *in this society,* with all its beloved and exasperating clutter, with all its exciting and debilitating confusion of standards, with all the stubborn problems that won't be solved and the equally stubborn ones that might be.—John W. Gardner, *Excellence*

3. What mainly counted for me about Negro kids of my own age was that they were "bad boys." There were plenty of bad boys among the whites—this was, after all, a neighborhood with a long tradition of crime as a career open to aspiring talents— but the Negroes were *really* bad, bad in a way that beckoned to one, and made one feel inadequate. *We* all went home every day for a lunch of spinach-and-potatoes; *they* roamed around during lunch hour, munching on candy bars. In winter *we* had to wear itchy woolen hats and mittens and cumber-

some galoshes; *they* were bare-headed and loose as they pleased. *We* rarely played hookey, or got into serious trouble in school, for all our street-corner bravado; *they* were defiant, forever staying out (to do what delicious things?), forever making disturbances in class and in the halls, forever being sent to the principal and returning uncowed. But most important of all, they were *tough;* beautifully, enviably tough, not giving a damn for anyone or anything. To hell with the teacher, the truant officer, the cop; to hell with the whole of the adult world that held *us* in its grip and that we never had the courage to rebel against except sporadically and in petty ways.—Norman Podhoretz, *Doings and Undoings*

4

The Paragraph

For Quick Reference

In some kinds of writing, paragraph division is merely *arbitrary*. In a newspaper article, a paragraph break may occur after every long sentence, and after every group of two or three short ones. In much informal writing, the author starts a new paragraph as nonchalantly as he or she would pause in conversation. In other kinds of writing, paragraph division is *conventional*. In dialogue, a paragraph break conventionally signals a change from one speaker to another.

Even in an expository essay, some paragraphs are mainly helps to continuity: preview paragraphs announcing the author's intention, transitional paragraphs helping the reader move from one major section to the next. The meat of an essay, however, is a different kind of unit: the expository paragraph that *does justice to one major point*. It presents an important idea or an important step in an argument. It does not just state an idea but supports or defends it as well.

O 1 The Well-Made Paragraph

Write the kind of solid paragraph that presents and develops one key idea.

A well-written paragraph has a point. It offers supporting material that makes the reader take the point seriously. It provides the signals that help the reader see what kind of material is offered in support and in what order.

O 1a The Topic Sentence *coh*

Use a topic sentence to focus a paragraph clearly on one major point.

A **topic sentence** sums up a central idea:

Topic Sentence: Women have always been stuck with the sewing.

Topic Sentence: Some of the job areas most popular with students are pathetically small.

Topic Sentence: Loading and unloading grain from ships and barges was an arduous and dangerous business.

In a well-focused paragraph, all or most of what follows backs up such an initial statement. How many separate examples does the author of each of the following paragraphs use when he or she "follows through"?

The Paragraph

SAMPLE PARAGRAPH 1

Women have always been stuck with the sewing. The connection is there in Greek myth and legend—the Three Fates are women, and one of them, Atropos, cuts the thread of life. Ariadne used thread to save Theseus from the Labyrinth; in Homer, Penelope, famous for her patience, used weaving to put off her unwelcome suitors. Primitive Indian women chewed hides and sewed them with bone needles. American farm women, weighed down with huge families and no servants, spent hours stitching—*after* all the other household work was done. Even in their leisure time they quilted while they socialized. James Fenimore Cooper read novels to his wife in the evening while she sewed.

SAMPLE PARAGRAPH 2

Some of the job areas most popular with students are pathetically small. Only 1,000 foresters will be hired this year, although perhaps twice as many students got forestry degrees. Only 2,700 new architects will be needed to design all the buildings sprouting on the landscape, and almost twice that number graduated last year. Everyone wants to design things, but according to the Department of Labor, only about 300 industrial designers are added to the labor force during an average year. Landscape architecture is appealing, too, because it combines creativity with outdoor work, but only 600 are expected to find jobs in the field this year.

SAMPLE PARAGRAPH 3

Loading and unloading grain from ships and barges was an arduous and dangerous business. One had to walk through mounds of rye or corn up to the knees, an exercise which makes running along a sandy beach seem like a cakewalk. Grain dust used to fill the hold, making a smokescreen so thick a worker couldn't recognize a fellow worker at twenty feet. The occasional pier rats were so big from eating grain and chasing it down with the polluted Hudson they could have pulled Cinderella's carriage.

In writing or revising a theme, remember:

(1) A good topic sentence gives *unity to a rambling paragraph*. It can point out a logical connection you previously missed or ignored:

Poor: San Francisco is a city of beautiful parks and public buildings. Golden Gate Park, with its spacious lawns and graceful ponds, enjoys international fame. The city's Bohemian section has become the national headquarters for jazz-age poetry and philosophy. Every tourist must visit Fisherman's Wharf and Coit Tower. The city is famed for its cultural events and conventions.

Revised: *Tourists and convention managers are irresistibly attracted to San Francisco.* Miles of varied waterfront, spacious parks, and impressive public buildings contribute to the city's unique appearance and cosmopolitan atmosphere. Fisherman's Wharf, with its seafood smells and colorful shops, attracts sightseeing crowds. Coit Tower affords a spectacular view of bay and city. Golden Gate Park, with its spacious lawns and graceful ponds, enjoys international fame.

(2) A good topic sentence *gives clear direction* to a paragraph. Can you see how the topic sentence in each of the following examples steers the paragraph in a different direction?

The dormitory reminds me of a third-class hotel. Each room has the same set of unimaginative furnishings: the same pale red chest of drawers, the same light brown desks. . . .

The dormitory reminds me of a big office building. People who half know each other pass in the hall with impersonal friendliness. . . .

The dormitory reminds me of a prison. The study room is enclosed by windows with lines on them, giving the student a penned-in feeling. . . .

(3) In the theme or article as a whole, a good topic sentence *moves the presentation or the argument ahead* one essential step. Then the rest of the paragraph fills in, illustrates, and supports the point made. Then the next topic sentence again takes a step forward. Part of an article on

the influence of television on political campaigns might proceed like this:

> *Television continues to change the look of political conventions.* Speeches are fewer and shorter. Sweaty orators, bellowing and waving their arms for an hour or more, have yielded almost completely to TelePrompter readers, younger and brisker fellows, some of them very slick and many of them no fun. Both parties have shortened sign-waving, chanting demonstrations. . . .
>
> While many of the changes may be for the best, *there is something synthetic about this new kind of convention.* There is a lack of spontaneity, a sense of stuffy self-consciousness. There is something unreal about seeing a well-known newscaster starting across the floor to interview a delegate and getting stopped for an autograph. . . .
>
> Nevertheless, *television coverage of conventions manages to get across to us a great deal about the way our political system works.* We are still a nation of disparate parts. The conventions are the occasions that bring various coalitions together every four years to pull and haul at one another; to test old power centers and form new ones; to compromise and, yes, to raise a little hell together in a carnival atmosphere. . . .

O 1b   Relevant Detail   *dev*

Strengthen skimpy paragraphs by supplying relevant detail.

A good topic sentence pulls together a mass of closely related material. Notice how much detail has been brought together in the following paragraph. Notice how directly it *ties in* with the major point the author is trying to make about Latin American culture:

> *Latin American culture has been and is a dynamic element in the development of our own.* It has, for example, furnished more than 2000 place names to the United States postal directory.

Its languages have influenced American English, as such simple examples as "rodeo" and "vamoose" indicate. Its customs are part of our "Westerns" on television. Its housing, its music, its dances, its scenery, its ruins and its romance have been imitated and admired in the United States. One-third of the continental area of this republic was for a long period, as modern history goes, under the governance of Spanish viceroys or of Mexico. The largest single Christian church in the United States is identical with the dominant church in Latin America.—Howard Mumford Jones, "Goals for Americans," *Saturday Evening Post*

In many weak paragraphs, the supporting material remains *too thin*. In revising such paragraphs, build them up by providing additional relevant detail. Notice how the following passage becomes more authentic through the filling in of detail from the author's experience:

Thin: I like politicians. I have spent a lot of time in their company. Mostly, I have reported their doings, but on occasion I have assisted them. On the whole, they have proved better company than any other professional group I have had a chance to know well.

Authentic: I like politicians. *Ever since I started work as a city-hall reporter in New Mexico some thirty years ago,* I have spent a lot of time in their company—*in smoke-filled rooms, jails, campaign trains, shabby courthouse offices, Senate cloakrooms, and the White House itself.* Mostly I've been reporting their doings, but on occasion I have served them *as speech writer, district leader, campaign choreboy, and civil servant.* On the whole, they have proved better company than any other professional group I've had a chance to know well—*including writers, soldiers, businessmen, doctors, and academics.*—John Fischer, "Please Don't Bite the Politicians," *Harper's*

Build up relevant material in support of your topic sentence until the reader feels like saying: "Enough! I'll grant you have a point." Try the following:

(1) Practice building up detail in a **multiple-example** *paragraph*. Here is a paragraph that makes exceptionally ample use of relevant examples:

A person's touch makes what the other senses take in more real to the memory. A *wood carving* appeals to the touch with deep grooves and parts that are rough as well as parts that are smooth. The fingers can interpret the richness of *brocade* and the rough warmth of wool. An ancient *book* becomes even older when one feels the fragile pages. A *puppy* tugging wildly at a leash feels like energy. *Winter* is felt in the hastily prepared snowball and the pine boughs that are brittle in the sharp air. A child must feel a *hot stove* before it becomes a thing to avoid touching, and words become meaningful when he loses the skin from his tongue to the *cold metal pipe* he was warned about. The energy of the *sun* becomes more apparent when one focuses a magnifying glass on his fingers. A *baby chick* is something altogether new when one holds the cotton-like ball of feathers and feels its nervous heartbeat. An *oil painting* is only paint and canvas until one touches the swirls made by the artist's brush. A *rose* is only a flower until one holds it in his hands and pulls the petals from the intricate pattern. A human *voice* becomes more than sounds when one speaks with his fingers to his throat to feel the vibrations. The surface of a *rock* is only light and shadow until one feels its ridges and ripples. Touching helps one to see and hear more clearly.

(2) Give priority to supporting detail by practicing the **examples-first** *paragraph*. When you reverse the usual order from topic sentence to supporting detail, you force yourself to provide the relevant examples that in the end will add up to a well-earned generalization:

The shops of the border town are filled with many souvenirs, "piñatas," pottery, bullhorns, and "serapes," all made from cheap material and decorated in a gaudy manner which the tourist thinks is true Mexican folk art. Tourists are everywhere, haggling with the shopkeepers, eager to get something for nothing, carrying huge packages and boxes filled with the treasures bought at the many shops. Car horns blare at the people who are too entranced with the sights to watch where they are going. Raucous tunes pour from the nightclubs, open in broad daylight. Few children are seen in the town, but some boys swim in the Rio Grande and dive to retrieve the coins that tourists throw as they cross the bridge above. People come for a cheap thrill, a quick divorce, cheap liquor. *A border town is the tourist's Mexico, a gaudy caricature of the real country.*

O 1c Transition *trans*

Use transitional expressions to help your reader follow from step to step.

Transitional phrases help the reader who wants to know: "Where are you headed?" Phrases like *for instance, for example,* or *to illustrate* take the reader from a general point to a specific example. *Similarly, furthermore,* and *in addition* prepare the reader to continue the same line of thought. *However, but, on the contrary,* and *by contrast* signal that the argument is turning around, that objections or complications are about to follow.

Look at the italicized transitional expressions in the following paragraphs. In your own words, can you explain how each moves the paragraph forward one step?

Many animals are capable of emitting meaningful sounds. Hens, *for instance,* warn their chicks of impending danger. *Similarly,* dogs growl at strangers to express distrust or hostility. Most of our pets, *in fact,* have a "vocabulary" of differentiated sounds to express hunger, pain, or satisfaction.

Most of us are less tolerant than we think. *It is true that* we tend to be tolerant of things sufficiently remote, such as Buddhism or impressionist painting. *But* we lose our tempers quickly when confronted with minor irritations. My friends, *at any rate,* will rage at drivers who block their way, at acquaintances who are late for appointments, or at manufacturers of mechanisms that break down.

The fact that "intelligence" is a noun shouldn't delude us into believing that it names some single attribute we can attach a number to, like "height." *In life,* we face a variety of tasks and environments. Intelligence takes many forms: a machinist suggests a new production technique, a housewife manages in spite of inflation, a hustler helps build a huge conglomerate. *Similarly,* how intelligent a person's behavior is will vary with time. Why should we suppose that these changes are fluctuations from some fixed, basic level? *Most important,* what persons of almost any IQ can learn or do depends on what they want to do and on what kind of education and training they are given.

All the frontier industrial countries except Russia received massive waves of emigrants from Europe. They *therefore* had a more rapid population growth than their industrializing predecessors had experienced. As frontier countries with great room for expansion, *however,* they were also characterized by considerable internal migration and continuing new opportunities. *As a result* their birth rates remained comparatively high. In the decade from 1950 to 1960, with continued immigration, these countries grew in population at an average rate of 2.13 per cent a year, compared with 1.76 per cent for the rest of the world.—Kingsley Davis, "Population," *Scientific American*

O 1d   Recurrent Terms   *coh*

Use recurrent or related terms to help hold a paragraph together.

In a well-focused paragraph, the same central term and various synonyms of it may come up several times. Such **recurrent terms** show that the paragraph is focused on a major idea; they help the reader concentrate on a major point or a key issue. Notice the different ways the idea of change recurs in the following excerpt:

It is an ominous fact that in the long chain of evolution the latest link, man, has suddenly acquired alchemic powers to *alter* whatever he touches. No other species before has been able to *change* more than a tiny fraction of his habitat. Now there is but a tiny fraction that he has *left unchanged*. A bulldozer *undoes* in an hour the work of a million years.—Paul Brooks, "Canyonlands," *Atlantic*

Notice how many words and phrases in the following paragraph echo the author's central point—the Victorian tendency to *avoid* discussion of sex:

In Victorian times, when the *denial* of sexual impulses, feelings, and drives was the mode and one *would not talk* about sex in polite company, an aura of sanctifying *repulsiveness* surrounded the whole topic. Males and females dealt with each other as though neither possessed sexual organs. William James, that redoubtable crusader who was far ahead of his time on every other topic, treated sex with the *polite aversion* characteristic of the turn of the century. In the whole two volumes of his epoch-making *Principles of Psychology,* only one page is devoted to sex, at the end of which he adds, "These details are a little *unpleasant to discuss*. . . ." But William Blake's warning a century before Victorianism, that "He who desires but acts not, breeds pestilence," was amply demonstrated by the later psychotherapists. Freud, a Victorian who did look at sex, was right in his description of the morass of neurotic symptoms which resulted from *cutting off* so vital a part of the human body and the self.—Rollo May, *Love and Will*

pestilence - spreading of dangerous disease Statement: attitude towards sex in the Victorian time

---

Exercises

A. For each of the following paragraphs, state the key idea in your own words. Point out the details or examples that support it. Point out any transitional expressions and show how they

The Paragraph

help move the paragraph forward. Point out any recurrent or related terms.

1. All the evidence indicates that the population upsurge in the underdeveloped countries is not helping them to advance economically. On the contrary, it may well be interfering with their economic growth. A surplus of labor on the farms holds back the mechanization of agriculture. A rapid rise in the number of people to be maintained uses up income that might otherwise be utilized for long-term investment in education, equipment and other capital needs. To put it in concrete terms, it is difficult to give a child the basic education he needs to become an engineer when he is one of eight children of an illiterate farmer who must support the family with the produce of two acres of ground.—Kingsley Davis, "Population," *Scientific American*

2. My personal Mexican-ness eventually produced serious problems for me. Upon entering grade school I learned English rapidly and rather well, always ranking either first or second in my class; yet the hard core of me remained stubbornly Mexican. This chauvinism may have been a reaction to the constant racial prejudice we encountered on all sides. The neighborhood cops were always running us off the streets and calling us "dirty greasers," and most of our teachers frankly regarded us as totally inferior. I still remember the galling disdain of my sixth-grade teacher, whose constant mimicking of our heavily accented speech drove me to a desperate study of *Webster's Dictionary* in the hope of acquiring a vocabulary larger than hers. Sadly enough, I succeeded only too well, and for the next few years I spoke the most ridiculous high-flown rhetoric in the Denver public schools. One of my favorite words was "indubitably" and it must have driven everyone mad. I finally got rid of my accent by constantly reciting "Peter Piper picked a peck of pickled peppers" with little round pebbles in my mouth.—Enrique Hank Lopez, "Back to Bachimba," *Horizon*

3. The prestige of science was colossal. The man in the street and the woman in the kitchen, confronted on every hand with new machines and devices which they owed to the laboratory,

were ready to believe that science could accomplish almost anything; and they were being deluged with scientific information and theory. The newspapers were giving columns of space to inform (or misinform) them of the latest discoveries: a new dictum from Albert Einstein was now front-page stuff even though practically nobody could understand it. Outlines of knowledge poured from the presses to tell people about the planetesimal hypothesis and the constitution of the atom, to describe for them in unwarranted detail the daily life of the cave-man, and to acquaint them with electrons, endocrines, hormones, vitamins, reflexes, and psychoses.—Frederick Lewis Allen, *Only Yesterday*

4. What must be even more surprising is the thinness of coverage right here at home in the center of our national news, Washington. Washington has a very large press corps. The roster of the National Press Club is substantial, and the State Department auditorium is easily filled by a glamour press conference. The trouble is that most of the Washington press corps runs as a herd, concentrating on the "big" story of the day to the neglect of much else. The news services have large staffs, and a few papers priding themselves on their national news maintain bureaus ranging from a half-dozen full-time correspondents to three times that number. But most of the so-called bureaus in Washington are one-man affairs. Except for an hour of gossip at the Press Club or at one of the other informal meeting places, and for what a lonesome man picks up from his home Congressional delegation, and the steady stream of inspired handouts, the average Washington reporter never gets beneath the surface of the day's one obvious story. —Philip M. Wagner, "What Makes a Really Good Newspaper," *Harper's*

B. Write a *multiple-example* paragraph about a type of person, a type of building, or a type of art. Pack the paragraph with as many different examples of the same basic trait or for the same basic point as you can.

C. Study the following *examples-first* paragraph. Write a similar paragraph about something you have had a chance to observe on the social, political, or educational scene. Build up your examples first and then funnel them into your general point.

Black Africans sweeping the streets of Paris; Algerians and Italians working on the high-speed assembly lines of the vast Renault auto plant; Turkish waiters in the cafes of Hamburg; Portuguese laborers at the construction sites on the outskirts of Geneva; Indians and Pakistanis driving busses through the heart of London — all over Western Europe, millions of immigrants from the poorer southern end of the Continent, from North and Central Africa, from Asia Minor and the Middle East, from South Asia and the Caribbean, are doing the vital but back-breaking work that the native-born are glad to leave them, despite widespread complaints that "the foreigners are coming here to eat our bread and take our jobs . . ." As it was put by one European economist, "The immigrants increasingly play the role of a basic industrial proletariat in the West European economies, while the native-born citizens comprise the 'new working class' of technicians, managers and supervisors."

— Schofield Coryell, "New Grapes of Wrath," *Ramparts*

D. From a recent theme, select a paragraph that could be improved by use of a clear topic sentence, fuller building up of examples, and the like. Hand in both the "Before" and the "After" version.

O 2   Organizing the Paragraph

Give your paragraphs an overall pattern that the reader can follow.

You can keep your reader moving along if your paragraphs give him a sense of direction. To help you in revising a rambling paragraph, ask yourself: "Could I outline the structure of this paragraph? Does it serve some overall purpose? Is it shaped by some overall strategy?"

O 2a   The All-Purpose Paragraph   *coh*

> **Organize the typical expository paragraph by going from statement through explanation to illustration.**

A topic sentence has its strongest impact if it is brief and to the point. Often, your next step will be to explain and elaborate. You may have to explain some of your key terms; you may have to show how a process works. Then, as a third step, you provide the examples, the illustrations, that support your key point. Sometimes, as an optional fourth step, a writer reinforces the main point by *restating* it, in a "clincher sentence," at the end.

Notice how the following paragraphs vary the basic pattern of *statement—explanation—illustration.* (Here and in later examples, words and phrases that help give continuity to the paragraph have been italicized.)

SAMPLE PARAGRAPH 1

Key idea

Detailed restatement

First example

Second example

> The deep sea has its *stars,* and perhaps here and there an eerie and transient equivalent of *moonlight,* for the mysterious *phenomemon of luminescence* is displayed by perhaps half of all the fishes that live in dimly lit or darkened waters, and by many of the lower forms as well. Many fishes carry *luminous torches* that can be turned on or off at will, presumably helping them find or pursue their prey. Others have *rows of lights* over their bodies, in patterns that vary from species to species and may be a sort of recognition mark or badge by which the bearer can be known as friend or enemy. The deep-sea squid ejects a

Third example | spurt of fluid that becomes a *luminous cloud,* the counterpart of the 'ink' of his shallow-water relative.—Rachel Carson, *The Sea Around Us*

SAMPLE PARAGRAPH 2

        Where do the terms of businesese come from?

Key question

Key idea

Most, *of course,* are hand-me-downs from former generations of businessmen, *but* many are the fruit of cross-fertilization with other jargons. A business-

First set
of examples

man who castigates government bureaucrats, *for example,* is at the same time apt to be activating,

Second set
of examples

effectuating, optimizing, minimizing, and maximizing—and at all levels and echelons within the framework of broad policy areas. *Similarly,* though he is amused by the long-hairs and the social scientists, he is beginning to speak knowingly of projective techniques, social dynamics, depth interviewing, *and* sometime soon, if he keeps up at this rate, he will probably appropriate that hallmark of the sound sociological paper, "insightful." Businesese,

Restatement
of key idea

in fact, has very nearly become the great common meeting ground of the jargons.—William H. Whyte, "The Language of Business," *Fortune*

SAMPLE PARAGRAPH 3

Key idea

        Every time a man unburdens his heart to a stranger he reaffirms the *love* that unites humanity.

Explanation

To be sure, he is unpacking his *heart* with words, but at the same time he is encouraged to expect *interest* and *sympathy,* and he usually gets it. His interlocutor feels unable to impose his own standards on his confidant's behavior; for once he feels *how another man feels.* It is not always sorrow and squalor that is passed on in this way but sometimes joy and pride. I remember a truck driver telling me

Example from
personal
experience

once about his wife, how sexy and clever and loving she was, and how beautiful. He showed me a photograph of her and I blushed for guilt because I had expected something plastic and I saw a woman by trendy standards plain, fat, and ill-clad. Half the

point in reading novels and seeing plays and films
is to exercise the *faculty of sympathy* with our own
kind, so often obliterated in the multifarious controls and compulsions of actual social existence.
—Germaine Greer, *The Female Eunuch*

More general
application

SAMPLE PARAGRAPH 4

Not the least remarkable thing about Huck's
feeling for people is that his tenderness goes
along with the *assumption that his fellow men are
likely to be dangerous and wicked.* He travels in-
cognito, never telling the truth about himself and
never twice telling the same lie, for he *trusts no
one* and the lie comforts him even when it is not
necessary. He *instinctively knows* that the best
way to keep a party of men away from Jim on the
raft is to beg them to come aboard to help his
family stricken with smallpox. And if he had not
already had the *knowledge of human weakness
and stupidity* and cowardice, he would soon have
acquired it, for all his encounters forcibly teach it
to him—the insensate feud of the Graingerfords
and Shepherdsons, the invasion of the raft by the
Duke and the King, the murder of Boggs, the
lynching party, and the speech of Colonel Sher-
burn. Yet his *profound and bitter knowledge of
human depravity* never prevents him from being
a friend to man.—Lionel Trilling, *The Liberal
Imagination*

Key idea

First example

Second example

Further support
for key idea

Restatement
of key idea

O 2b   Paragraphs with a Special   *coh*
Purpose

*Make your readers see a clear pattern in
paragraphs that serve a special purpose.*

Often the organization of a paragraph is determined by
its special purpose: to describe a step in a process, to compare two related things, to choose between alternatives.

The Paragraph

Study the way a different overall purpose helps structure each of the following sample paragraphs:

(1) *Tracing a* **process** *in time:*

Beginnings

Later
developments

     The orphanage across the street is torn down, a city housing project *begins to rise* in its place, and on the marvelous vacant lot next to the old orphanage they are building a playground. Much excitement and anticipation as *Opening Day draws near.* Mayor LaGuardia himself comes to dedicate this great gesture of public benevolence. He speaks of neighborliness and borrowing cups of sugar, and of the playground he says that children of all races, colors, and creeds will learn to live together in harmony. *A week later,* some of us are swatting flies on the playground's inadequate little ball field. A gang of Negro kids, pretty much our own age, enter from the other side and order us out of the park. We refuse, proudly and indignantly, with superb masculine fervor. There is a fight, they win, and we retreat, half whimpering, half with bravado. My first nauseating experience of cowardice. And my first appalled realization that there are people in the world who do not seem to be afraid of anything, who act as though they have nothing to lose. *Thereafter* the playground becomes a battleground, sometimes quiet, sometimes the scene of athletic competition between Them and Us. But rocks are thrown as often as baseballs. *Gradually* we abandon the place and use the streets instead. The streets are safer, though we do not admit this to ourselves. We are not, after all, sissies—that most dreaded

End result

epithet of an American boyhood.—Norman Podhoretz, *Doings and Undoings*

(2) *Examining* **cause and effect:**

Key idea

     Europeans with time-honored experience in the technique of painlessly extracting cash from foreigners' pockets have correctly gauged that Americans

Cause
(with specific
examples)

Effect
(with specific
examples)

like to travel abroad provided they don't really have to leave home. *They've seen* the U.S. armed forces and U.S. oil companies spend millions to give their personnel the illusion of living in a European or African suburbia filled with shopping centers, post exchanges, movie houses, ice-cream parlors, juke boxes, and American-style parking lots. *Smart promoters now give* the American abroad exactly what he wants. Hotel rooms are furnished to please him, meal hours drastically advanced to suit the American habit of eating dinner at 6 P.M., arrangements made to satisfy the Americans' affection for crowds, action, and noise.—Joseph Wechsberg, "The American Abroad," *Atlantic*

(3) *Working out a* **comparison or contrast:**

Key idea
(linked to
preceding step in
discussion)

First subtopic
(situation in
Alger's books)

Second subtopic
(contrasting
situation today)

Just as Alger's view of money as something to be made and kept no longer generally operates, [neither] does his view of how it should be given away. There is a great deal of "charity" in Alger, but *it is always man-to-man, even palm-to-palm.* It is a gesture in the tradition of the New Testament, a retail transaction between two individuals, spiritual in essence, monetary in form. The adjective that comes first to mind when we think of it is "Christian." *The adjective that comes first to mind when we think of charity today is "organized."* Via drives, community chests, red feathers, we can give more away more quickly. At the same time the primitive-Christian heart of the process, man-to-man giving, is weakened. Warmheartedness is communized.—Clifton Fadiman, "Party of One," *Holiday*

(4) *Choosing among* **alternatives:**

History shows that wars between cities, states, and geographic regions cease once the

First alternative
examined and
rejected

Second alternative
presented and
supported

originally independent units have amalgamated under the leadership of a single government with the power of making and enforcing laws that are binding upon individuals. *One might reason on this basis that* if all of the industrialized and semi-industrialized regions of the world were to federate under a common government, the probability of another war would be greatly decreased. It seems likely that this conclusion would be valid if the resultant federation were as complete as was the federation formed by the original thirteen colonies in America. *On the other hand,* it is extremely unlikely that such a highly centralized federation could come into existence at the present time; nationalistic feelings of individual men and groups of men, and conflicts of economic interests, are too strong to permit rapid transition. *Also,* those nations which have high per capita reserves of resources and high per capita production would be most reluctant to delegate their sovereignties to higher authority and to abandon the economic barriers that now exist.—Harrison Brown, *The Challenge of Man's Future*

(5) *Tracing an* analogy:

Detailed
analogy

Ecstasy is beyond pleasure. Ordinarily, one thinks of the rainbow spectrum of light as a band having red at one end and violet at the other, thus not seeing that violet is the mixture of red and blue. The spectrum could therefore be displayed as a ring or concentric circles instead of a band, but its eye-striking central circle would be where pale, bright yellow comes nearest to white light. This would represent ecstasy. But it can be approached in two ways, starting from violet: through the blues and greens of pleasure or the reds and oranges of pain. *This explains why* ecstasy can be achieved in battle, by ascetic self-torture

Detailed
application

and through the many variations of sadomasochistic sexuality. This we call the left-hand, or negative, approach. The right-hand, or positive, approach is through activities that are loving and life-affirming.
—Alan Watts, "The Future of Ecstasy"

O 2c   Paragraphs with a Special Strategy   *coh*

Experiment with strategies that channel the reader's attention.

Like a larger composition, a paragraph can employ strategies designed to capture the reader's attention, to hold his interest, to keep his mind from wandering. Try some of the following:

(1) *Anticipate the questions of the curious reader.* In presenting information, especially, avoid the effect of merely presenting miscellaneous facts. The following paragraph might have been put together to answer questions somewhat in the order an interested reader would ask them:

What evidence?

Comets strew debris behind them in interplanetary space. *Some of it is seen* from the earth as the zodiacal light, which is visible as a glow in the eastern sky before sunrise and in the western sky after sunset. (It is brightest in the Tropics.) Much of the zodiacal light near the plane of the earth's orbit is sunlight scattered by fine dust left behind by comets. Under ideal observing conditions cometary dust *also appears* as the Gegenschein, or counterglow: a faint luminous patch in the night sky in a direction opposite that of the sun. Comets need to *contribute about 10 tons of dust per second* to the inner solar system in order to maintain this level of illumination. Over a period of several thousand years *the particles are*

Where else observed?

How produced?

What becomes of it?

gradually broken down by collisions with other particles, or are blown away by solar radiation. —Fred L. Whipple, "The Nature of Comets," *Scientific American*

(2) *Make the reader follow you through the steps in your investigation.* Create suspense by making the reader look at the data first. Then work out the conclusions that your facts suggest. Such a paragraph follows an **inductive order:**

Detailed report of experiment

Psychologists studying race prejudice have many times made an interesting experiment. They seat a few people in a row, show a picture to the first in line, and ask him to whisper a description of it in a few words to a second who will whisper the information to the third, and so on. The picture is of a policeman and a badly dressed, uncouth Negro. The policeman is holding a knife in his hand; the Negro is unarmed. Almost never is the description transmitted to more than two or three individuals in succession, before the knife has passed from the hand of the policeman and is now being held

Interpretation of experiment

in a threatening manner, by the Negro! *In other words,* the picture is transformed until it fits the preexisting concept in the mind, which is that an open knife is far more likely to be

General application of findings

held by a Negro than a policeman. *This sort of unconscious alteration* of what is perceived, to make it accord with what is already believed, is universal and is one of the most important of all the facts with which communication has to deal.—Bruce Bliven, *Preview for Tomorrow*

(3) *Arrange material in a* **climactic order.** Go from the unimportant to the important, from the optional to the essential:

Random
impressions

Crucial
detail

The morning sun was streaming through the crevices of the canvas when the man awoke. A warm glow pervaded the whole atmosphere of the marquee, and a single big blue fly buzzed musically round and round it. Besides the buzz of the fly there was not a sound. He looked about—at the benches—at the table supported by trestles—at his basket of tools—at the stove where the furmity had been boiled—at the empty basins—at some shed grains of wheat—at the corks which dotted the grassy floor. Among the odds and ends he discerned a little shining object, and picked it up. *It was his wife's ring.*—Thomas Hardy, *The Mayor of Casterbridge*

Exercises

A. How were the following paragraphs put together? Chart the purposes or the strategies that helped shape each paragraph.

1. Animals are always realists. They have intelligence in varying degrees—chickens are stupid, elephants are said to be very clever—but, bright or foolish, animals react only to reality. They may be fooled by appearance, by pictures or reflections, but once they know them as such, they promptly lose interest. Distance and darkness and silence are not fearful to them, filled with voices or forms, or invisible presences. Sheep in the pasture do not seem to fear phantom sheep beyond the fence, mice don't look for mouse goblins in the clock, birds do not worship a divine thunderbird.—Susanne K. Langer, "The Prince of Creation," *Fortune*

2. In many simple societies, the "institutionalized ways" of controlling marriage run to diverse schemes and devices. Often they include special living quarters designed to make it easy for marriageable girls to attract a husband: the Bontok people of the Philippines keep their girls in a special house, called

the *olag,* where lovers call, sex play is free, and marriage is supposed to result. The Ekoi of Nigeria, who like their women fat, send them away to be specially fattened for marriage. Other peoples, such as the Yao of central Africa and the aborigines of the Canary Islands, send their daughters away to "convents" where old women teach them the special skills and mysteries that a young wife needs to know.—John Finley Scott, "Sororities and the Husband Game," Trans-*action*

3. Immigration, exile, the tides of the Atlantic, the killing breath of famine, the murderous streets of Belfast had brought our parents to New York. We were to be the children of the second chance, living proof that a man can start over in his life and make something valuable out of that effort. But most of the time that second chance had become warped by some grasping obsession with property. We began to visit friends who kept china closets filled with dishes that you were supposed to look at and admire but never sully with the fruits of the earth. People bought cars and two-family houses, and the dime-a-week insurance man vanished somewhere, and nobody needed credit at the corner grocery store anymore. The coal stove gave way to steam heat.—Pete Hamill, "Notes on the New Irish," *New York*

4. When films first broke on the world, let's say with the full-length, full-scale achievement of D. W. Griffith, *The Birth of a Nation,* one of its most persuasive and hitherto unexperienced powers lay in the absolute reality of the moving image. The camera is a scientific instrument, not a paintbrush: its special virtues are accuracy and actuality. Thus, when Griffith organized a pan-shot which began with a mother and child huddled in terror on a mountain and then moved slowly to a raging battle on the plain beneath, we were left breathless by a juxtaposition in scale—from the individual to the group, from the passive to the active—that was, quite literally, taking place before our eyes. Our belief in the medium had begun with actual railroad trains roaring down actual tracks right at us, with actual ocean waves breaking somewhere near our feet. Griffith moved from simple documentation to high imagination, from fact to fiction, from present to past; and he took us with him because he used his camera as a faithful

recorder of something that was really and truly going on: he did not abandon his camera's ability to state visual facts. —Walter Kerr, "What Good Is Television?" *Horizon*

5. It was never learning I associated with that school: only the necessity to succeed, to get ahead of the others in the daily struggle to "make a good impression" on our teachers, who grimly, wearily, and often with ill-concealed distaste watched against our relapsing into the natural savagery they expected of Brownsville boys. The white, cool, thinly ruled record book sat over us from their desks all day long, and had remorselessly entered into it each day—in blue ink if we had passed, in red ink if we had not—our attendance, our conduct, our "effort," our merits and demerits; and to the last possible decimal point in calculation, our standing in an unending series of "tests" —surprise tests, daily tests, weekly tests, formal midterm tests, final tests. They never stopped trying to dig out of us whatever small morsel of fact we had managed to get down the night before. We had to prove that we were really alert, ready for anything, always in the race. That white thinly ruled record book figured in my mind as the judgment seat; the very thinness and remote blue lightness of its lines instantly showed its cold authority over me; so much space had been left on each page, columns and columns in which to note down everything about us, implacably and forever.—Alfred Kazin, *A Walker in the City*

B. Study the following student-written paragraphs and describe the way they are organized. Then write your own set of paragraphs using the following "starter sentences:

"Advertising is full of_____."
"We often forget that there are two kinds of _____."
"My classes always possessed at least one _____."

1. Advertising is full of indoctrination that helps keep women in their place. Women are to be soft for men, smell good for men, and cook for them and their families. Billboards lining the streets and highways picture faultless figures, clinging panty-hose, and phony makeup: perfect females, each strand

of hair faithfully in place, with a roll of paper towels or bottle of dishwashing liquid in their hands. Magazines are filled with ads which imply that females should try to be pleasing for men: "The fragrance which can shake your world . . . and his."

2. We often forget that there are two basic kinds of crime. By taking action against crime, we hope to soothe a basic paranoia of our society. We fear being stolen from, or cheated. Also we fear death or personal injury. These are the crimes involving two parties, a criminal and a victim. But our society also reacts to someone offending against our personal morality. Because of this we have laws against homosexuality, drunkenness, obscene publications, and lately, the usage of narcotics. These crimes involve only one party, the "criminal." We thus have two quite different kinds of criminal behavior: the crimes involving a victim, versus the crimes without victims.

3. My classes always possessed at least one uncompromising conservative with very forceful opinions, so that it created a right-wing atmosphere from which my ears never rested. For example, one girl was a strong-headed Republican, a dedicated Mormon, and was teetering on the edge of John Birchism. She had a great reverence for the flag and her country, but hated certain peoples that existed in her great America— blacks, Mexicans, Jews, and so on. She was a staunch supporter of white supremacy, with the school whitened beyond salvation to her pleasure. Her heroes were men like Richard Nixon, George Wallace, and Ronald Reagan, while she detested even hearing the names of people like Martin Luther King or Robert Kennedy.

5

The Whole Theme

For Quick Reference

The finished theme is the result of a process. Ideally, the process of composition moves through five overlapping stages:

(1) You *explore* your subject. You gather material; you mobilize your resources.

(2) You bring your subject into *focus*. You zero in on a key question or a major point. You limit yourself to what you can handle in detail.

(3) You *organize* your material. You sort things out and put them in order. You work out some overall strategy that suits your material and that fits your purpose.

(4) You write your *first draft*. You try to make sure that your ideas come through clearly, that they catch and hold the attention of your reader.

(5) You *revise* your paper as necessary. You fill in missing links, or reshuffle parts that seem out of order. You proofread your final draft for spelling and punctuation and the like.

O 3 Gathering Material *dev*

Take time to work up your subject.

No one can draw water from an empty well. No one can write a paper from an empty mind. Take time for *pre-writing*—work up a rich fund of materials to draw on when you put the actual paper together.

Suppose you are going to write a paper about welfare, or about the "welfare problem." Your first question should be: "What do I know?" What do you know that could serve as food for thought on this topic? Explore avenues like the following:

(1) "Where has welfare or the welfare problem touched *my own experience?*" Here are some ways welfare might have touched the lives of your family, friends, acquaintances:

- Elderly relatives were concerned about the passage of Medicare legislation. What were they worried about? What did they say?

- A neighbor is always complaining about people on welfare who are driving a sports car or spending their days on the beach.

- A friend told you about his problems in trying to collect unemployment insurance.

- A friend of the family lost his job and tried to stay "off welfare."

Do these different situations have anything in common? What did you learn from them about how welfare works? Would you go back to any of these people to learn more?

(2) "What role does welfare play in current news and in *current controversy?*" When is the last time you read a newspaper report about investigations of alleged welfare chiseling? When is the last time you listened to a political candidate who seemed to be running against the people on the welfare rolls? When is the last time you heard someone advance some tangible ideas on how to deal with poverty? What groups and individuals in our society seem to care?

(3) "What *reading* have I done that would provide some background for current discussion of welfare and poverty?" In a book like Charles Dickens' *Hard Times,* we see impoverished workers put in long hours in the sweatshops of the nineteenth century. In Upton Sinclair's *The Jungle* we see workers without job security of any kind, working in filth and mortal danger on the job. In John Steinbeck's *Grapes of Wrath,* we see the small farmers uprooted by an economy out of control, people willing to work but with no place to go. Books such as these vividly re-create the *conditions* that led to much of the welfare legislation with which we are familiar: minimum wage laws, child labor laws, unemployment insurance, social security.

Obviously, the kind and extent of your preliminary exploration will vary for different assignments. Usually you will be able to draw on one or more of the following sources of material:

- Current *observation*—close first-hand study of scenes, people, objects, events.

- Past *experience*—the memory bank of everything you have experienced and read.

- Informed *opinion*—the views of others who have studied the same subject.

- Scholarly *research*—the systematic sifting of evidence from records, documents, and other printed sources.

- Critical *reading*—poems, novels, plays.

Exercises

A. Assume you have become interested in how our society treats *the handicapped*. Bring together from your own experience and observation everything you can remember about people who were handicapped. Keep writing—just get down on paper any details and incidents as they come to mind. (Leave any sorting out for some future time when you might want to draw on this preliminary collection of material.)

B. Assume you have been asked to write about a *vanishing institution:* the farm horse, street cars, the passenger train, the corner grocery, the railroad station, or the like. Write down all you can remember about your experiences with it. Start from your earliest childhood memories. Write as fast and as much as you can.

C. Assume you have been asked to join in a discussion of *colonialism*. Write down anything you remember about books and movies that show the white man in a colonial situation. Bring in as much authentic detail as you can. Write as fast and as much as possible. Leave any editorializing or sorting out for later.

O 4   Bringing Things into Focus

Learn how to bring a big subject under control.

In practice, we do not write about birds in general, or about welfare as a large umbrella topic. We write because some part of our general subject is not well known, and we want to fill the gap. We write because an issue has come up, and we want to take a stand. We write because something has gone wrong, and we want something to be done.

Our reader wants to know: "What are you trying to accomplish? What are you trying to say? What do you want us to do?" This kind of question helps us bring a paper into focus. It helps us pull things together. The more clearly focused a paper, the better the chance that our point will sink in, or that our information will be put to use. To bring your subject into focus

- narrow down the *area* to be covered;

- close in on one limited *question* to be answered;

- use your paper to support *one central point.*

O 4a   Limiting the Subject   *coh*

Limit the area to be covered.

No one could write a paper on "Education in America." A writer interested in American education may restrict this field according to *kind:* academic, physical, religious. He may restrict it according to *area:* a state, a town, the nation's capital, Indian reservations in Arizona. He may limit himself to a particular *level:* grade school, high school, college. He may limit his discussion to a certain *type of student:* gifted, retarded, emotionally disturbed. A manageable topic might look like this:

Space-age science at Washington High

"Released time" and the Winchester Public Schools: No time for God

Talking typewriters for the retarded

Home economics for boys

195

Stagnant schools and the migrant child
How to succeed in a military academy

Each large subject can be split up into several medium-sized subjects. Each of these in turn will yield limited subjects narrow enough to serve as topics for short papers:

General Area: Conflict Between the Generations

Intermediate: Conflict over Drugs
Different Attitudes Toward Sex
Different Definitions of Success
Different Attitudes Toward Progress
Changing Views of Marriage
What Happened to Patriotism
Youth and the Military
Religion Old and New

Limited: ("Success" topic further broken down)

What Young People Look for in a Job
Competition vs. "Working with People"
The Good Things that Money Can't Buy
Making Do vs. Compulsory Consumption
Staying Close to the Earth

What would you include in a list of limited topics for one of the *other* medium-sized subjects in the above list?

O 4b Choosing a Key Question *coh*

Formulate a key question that your paper will answer.

The more *specific* the key question you choose, the more likely your paper is to have a clear focus. "How do crime comics shape their readers' attitudes?" is a very *general* question. Crime comics could affect the reader's attitude toward many things: police work, violence, minority groups, criminals, courts. Try to point your question at a more limited issue:

- Is it true that crime comics equate ugliness with depravity, thus encouraging the reader to judge by appearances?
- Is it true that heroes look white, Anglo-Saxon, and Protestant, while villains look Latin, for instance, or Oriental?
- Is it true that in the crime comics people are either all good or all bad?
- Do crime comics reveal the political sympathies of their authors?

A *pointed* question is more likely to produce a focused paper than a question that is merely exploratory. Avoid questions like "What are some of the causes of adolescent crime?" The "What-are-some" kind of question often leads to a paper in which many different things are *mentioned* but few of them studied in detail. Substitute a "What-is-the-most" or "What-is-the-best" kind of question: "What is the most serious obstacle to communication between a teenager and his or her parents?" "What are three key features shared by successful television comedians?"

O 4c   Formulating a Thesis   *coh*

State one major point, and drive it home.

We scatter the attention of an audience by saying a little something about many different points. We make an impact by concentrating on one major point and supporting it as fully as we can. For example, the writer of a travel article could get our attention by claiming that people in Eastern Europe are fascinated by everything American. The writer could then devote the rest of the article to providing many striking examples. We call the central idea that the rest of the presentation supports the **thesis**. The thesis is the assertion, generalization, or claim that is backed up by examples, evidence, statistics.

Writing that first states a thesis and then supports it has many uses. We use it, for instance, when we

- defend a *generalization* in an essay exam;
- call for *action* in a letter to the editor;
- make good a *promoter's claim* in an advertising brochure;
- establish someone's aptitude for a job, in a letter of *recommendation;*
- defend a political candidate against a rival's *charge*.

Whenever possible, state your thesis in a *single* **thesis sentence:**

Topic: Urban Redevelopment

Thesis: Redeveloped neighborhoods lack the varied life of the grown neighborhoods they replace.

Topic: Life in Suburbia

Thesis: Living in the suburbs does not prevent people from developing a sense of community.

Make sure your thesis is a *clear statement of a limited point*. The thesis should not merely map out the general territory but focus on a limited issue:

Too vague:	A modern suburb is a good place to live.
Focused more clearly:	Modern suburbs have kept alive the American traditions of being a good neighbor.
Too vague:	Today's children are spoiled.
Focused more clearly:	Grade school teachers lack the means of disciplining their students.

O 4d   Supporting Your Thesis   *dev*

Fill in the material that will support your thesis.

When you formulate a thesis, you commit yourself. You take a stand. When you support your thesis, you follow through. You deliver the goods.

In the following excerpt, from Gordon Parks' *A Choice of Weapons,* the first sentence serves as a thesis; and each of the three paragraphs of the excerpt takes up one incident that bears out the point made by the thesis:

Thesis

When I was eleven, I became possessed of an exaggerated fear of death. It started one quiet summer afternoon with an explosion in the alley behind our house.

First incident

I jumped from under a shade tree and tailed Poppa toward the scene. Black smoke billowed skyward, a large hole gaped in the wall of our barn. . . .

Second incident

Then once, with two fields, I had swum along the bottom of the muddy Marmaton River, trying to locate the body of a Negro man. We had been promised fifty cents apiece by the same white policeman who had shot him while he was in the water trying to escape arrest. . . .

Third incident

One night at the Empress Theater, I sat alone in the peanut gallery watching a motion picture, *The Phantom of the Opera.* When the curious heroine, against Lon Chaney's warning, snatched away his mask, and the skull of death filled the screen, I screamed out loud. . . .

A good thesis sentence serves as a *program* for the paper as a whole. It helps you decide what to include and what to keep out. It helps you decide what is **relevant.** Suppose your thesis reads as follows:

Thesis — Nineteenth-century American fiction is often a man's world.

The reader is likely to say: "Let's take a look—maybe you are right." You then provide striking familiar examples:

First example — In Mark Twain's *Huck Finn,* the aunt is left behind, and the story revolves around the boy, his father, and Jim, the runaway slave. . . .

Second example — In Melville's *Moby Dick,* we follow Ishmael and the all-male crew of the whaling ship in pursuit of the White Whale. . . .

Third example — In Cooper's Leatherstocking novels, we move in a frontier world of hunters and scouts and braves. . . .

Exercises

A. Suppose you wanted to write a paper relevant to a general topic of current concern. How much narrowing would you have to do before you reach the level where people can see actual effects on their own lives? Or where they could get their own hands dirty trying to do something about the problem? Note how the following general topics have been scaled down:

Very General:	How Technology Runs Our Lives
Less General:	The Spread of Automation The Motorized Society The Proliferation of Gadgets
Specific:	The Automated Assembly Line Your Checking Account and the Computer How Appliances Put the Housewife to Work
Very General:	Improving the Quality of Life
Less General:	Cleaning Up the Environment Solving Chronic Unemployment Transportation Fit for Human Beings
Specific:	Bottles vs. Cans: A Problem in Ecology Plastics that Decompose The Psychology of Litterbugs

Provide a similar set of intermediate and specific topics for two of the following general subjects:

The Plight of the City

The Future of Marriage

Educational Opportunities for Minorities

Jobs for the Class of 1984

Freedom of the Press

Protecting the Consumer

B. Assume you are preparing five pointed questions for an *interview* with one of the following: a college president, a police chief, a black minister, a White House aide, a diplomat from a country currently in the news. Formulate questions *limited* enough to steer the interview away from vague generalities. The class as a whole may want to choose the two or three sets of questions most likely to produce significant, detailed responses.

C. Study the following example of a thesis-and-support paper. How, and how well, did the girl who wrote it support her thesis? How relevant is the material she provides?

The Whole Theme

SUCCESS IS (IS NOT) HAVING A GOOD JOB

Thesis

Parents view success in terms of security and a good job, but today's youth value people more than things. Parents want and expect their children to succeed. Parents believe in what the future should be, while the young look at the present and do not think that far ahead in their lives.

Support (first example)

A girl from a family I know is in a situation that illustrates this point. Her parents want her to marry a boy who has a good job and makes good money. She is twenty-two and going to school at the moment. She has known a boy for about a year now, and she wants to marry him. But he is only an auto mechanic. When she first started dating him, her parents objected because he was not good enough for her. They kept telling her how she wouldn't be able to have all the things she was used to in life. They told her she wouldn't be able to go to fancy places to eat or have a nice car to sit in. She handled the situation by just disregarding what her parents told her.

She didn't care what the boy's background was, or if he had a good job. Her parents tried unsuccessfully to influence her feelings about him. They were pointing out his bad qualities. They told her he was poor and lazy (because he didn't finish college). His hair was too long. She went through many arguments with her parents. Finally she gave up trying to defend her ideals. It is difficult for her to talk to her parents about anything, because they always bring up the subject of her friend. She gets frustrated because her parents are always mimicking him.

(Second example)

My own situation fits into this general picture. My parents think that I should study hard and get a good job. They are constantly reminding me. As far back as grammar school, they were pouring all this into my head. When I used to get allowances on Sundays, they would always say, "Study hard so you'll get a good job in the future."

My parents emphasized education so much that it was coming out of our ears. All the children had to complete four years of college. There was no chance of anyone dropping out. I remember one semester in junior college, I was carrying twelve units. My father asked me how many units I was carrying. When I told him, he really got upset. He began to make a big thing out of it. He kept asking why I was carrying so few units. I tried to explain to him that at the beginning twelve units was an average load, but he didn't agree. I finally gave up. I let him continue lecturing me, but my mind had stopped listening.

When the next semester came, he again asked me how many units I was carrying. I was reliving in my mind what we had gone through the semester before in those two weeks. When I answered his question, he called the school to check up on me. My mind was going through the stages of losing respect for him for not trusting me. I was at the point where I was losing total interest in education. Today I can no longer and do not wish to discuss school with my parents.

(Third example) My girlfriend has a problem with her parents regarding marriage. She is the eldest child in the family. Her mother and father want her to marry someone who is in a profession—a doctor, or a pharmacist. She was about to get married a year ago to a pre-medical student, but something happened. Her mother told her she had made a mistake in not marrying the boy. Her mother even told her to try and get back together with him. He was a medical student and would be able to give her security. She is now in this constant battle with her mother about getting married.

There is indeed a generation gap between the young and their parents on the topic of success.

D. Of the thesis sentences presented in the following brief passages, select the three that come closest to your own views. For each one, jot down briefly what *supporting material* you could supply from your own experience and reading to back up the point made.

1. *Students profit as much (or more) from a summer of work, travel, or reading as from additional coursework in summer*

sessions. Though such experiences are less systematic than academic learning, they are educational in the sense that they broaden the student's perspective.

2. *The public schools do not fully practice the constitutional principle of separation of church and state.* Students, whether of Christian, Jewish, or agnostic parents, participate in Christmas plays and Easter pageants, and sing religious songs.

3. *Teen-age fads and fashions have increasing influence on the adult world.* Teen-age styles set the pace for much advertising and strongly influence adult fashions and even hair styles.

4. *The population of the typical big city is declining in income and social status.* The unskilled and the less educated remain, while the middle class moves out to the suburbs to find living space and better schools for the children.

5. *Fear of violence restricts the activities of many Americans.* People stay away from public parks; older people are afraid to venture out into the streets.

6. *Minority groups are becoming proud of their separate heritage.* Americans who used to feel like second-class citizens are asserting their separate identity.

O 5   Getting Organized

Present your material in a clear and consistent sequence.

When we present material in a paper, we have to make sure that the readers can find the way. We organize the material in some overall pattern that will make sense to them. Four familiar kinds of themes illustrate patterns of organization that help us give shape and direction to a piece of writing.

O 5a   Process

coh

Present essential steps in the right order.

Describing the process of papermaking, we trace the necessary steps that turn wood chips first into pulp, then into a paper web, and finally into sheets of paper. Describing the process of radio transmitting, we follow the newscaster's voice through microphone and transmitter to the receiving set and the listener's ear. What we learn from the process theme has many applications. We apply it when we

- explain a *scientific* process:
  how energy of motion converts into electricity
  how sediments build up on the ocean floor
  how a translation machine scans a sentence

- give *directions:*
  how to plant a lawn
  how to make wine from your own grapes
  how to make pottery

- trace a *historical* chain of events:
  how nomads became villagers
  how the railroad transformed rural America

The following instructions will help you write better process themes:

(1) *Pay attention to detail.* No one can make a machine work, or produce an enameled vase, who does not have a concern for the *little* things that add up to the whole. Take in details like those in the following paragraph:

A black and white garden spider dropped down from one of the higher branches of the tree. He picked a flimsy, forked twig, covered with large drops of water from the rain, and swung in on it like a toy glider coming in for a landing. As he caught hold of it, it sagged under his weight, and several large water drops slid off to the ground below. The spider sat on the twig until it ceased vibrating. Then he carefully moved to the end of one of the forks. He first walked rather fast, but halfway down the twig fork he slipped and turned upside down. He tried to right himself but failed, so he moved along the twig upside down, fighting both the vibrations of the twig and the large water drops. When the spider reached the end of the twig fork, he carefully fastened a silver thread to the end of the fork. Then he slowly righted himself on the twig. He proceeded to crouch in a peculiar position, somewhat like a sprinter set in his starting blocks. With a mighty leap, he jumped toward another twig fork, but he missed it. He swung down below the twig and hung by his silver thread until the vibrations and his swinging stopped. He climbed up the thread and repeated the maneuver, and again he failed. The third time he jumped, he caught the other twig and proceeded to fasten his silver thread to it. Running back between the two forks the spider began to build his web.

(2) *Concentrate on what is essential.* At a given stage of the process, ask yourself: "What is needed to make the work proceed? What, if left out, would prevent my reader from producing the desired result?" Note the grimly businesslike fashion in which the author of the following passage makes us see "how it works":

The sergeant turned to the captain, saluted and placed himself immediately behind that officer, who in turn moved apart one pace. These movements left the condemned man and the sergeant standing on the two ends of the same plank, which spanned three of the crossties of the bridge. The end upon which the civilian stood almost, but not quite, reached a fourth. This plank had been held in place by the weight of the captain; it was now held by that of the sergeant. At a signal from the former the latter would step aside, the plank would tilt and the condemned man go down between two ties.—Ambrose Bierce, "An Occurrence at Owl Creek Bridge"

(3) *Relate the new and technical to what is familiar.*
How is the process you describe similar to something the
reader knows? The following short process theme uses extended **analogy** to make us understand the process of vision:

The eye operates like a simple box camera. Such a camera
has four essential parts: a shutter, a lens, a chamber or box, and
a sensitized plate or film. The shutter's job is to allow light to
pass through the lens. The lens is a circular piece of glass with
curved faces to concentrate the light upon the plate or film. After
being concentrated by the lens, a beam of light must pass through
the chamber to reach the sensitized plate. The sensitized plate or
film then receives an impression of the projected image.

The four corresponding parts of the eye are the iris, the lens,
the vitreous body, and the retina. The iris is a muscular dia-
phragm which can close or dilate to regulate the passage of light
to the lens. The lens is composed of a semi-solid, crystalline sub-
stance. Like the lens of the camera, the lens of the eye serves to
concentrate and focus light. The vitreous body is a large area
between the lens and the retina. It is void of any material save a
transparent liquid. The retina, through its rods and cones, receives an impression of the projected image.

In the camera, a beam of light passing through the shutter
strikes the lens. It is then focused and projected through the
chamber to the rear wall of the camera. There, a sensitized plate
or film registers an impression of the image carried by the beam
of light. In the eye, a beam of light passing through the iris hits
the lens. The lens focuses the beam and projects it through the
vitreous body to the rear wall of the eye. There, the retina receives an impression of the image carried on this beam of light.
From the retina, a stimulus is then flashed to the brain through
the optic nerve.

(4) *Break up the whole sequence into major divisions,
or emphasize the most significant steps.* An "and-then" sequence becomes confusing, because it gives equal emphasis
to many parts, events, or operations. Suppose your paper
follows the assembly line in an automobile factory: the

basic parts of the body are welded together; the doors are hung; the body shells are dipped into a chemical solution; they are spray-painted; they are dried in ovens; electrical wiring is laid; door locks and other mechanisms are installed; glass is installed; interior lining is installed; and so on. Try to break up the body's progress into three major stages:

    I. Building the body shell
   II. Painting the body
  III. Outfitting the painted shell

Could you set up three or four major stages for one or more of the following?

Repainting the House
Setting up Camp
Courting—the Old-Fashioned Way
Putting in a Lawn
Putting in a Concrete (Sidewalk) (Driveway) (Wall)

O 5b   Classification   *coh*

Sort out your material into plausible categories.

When we classify things, we group them together on the basis of what they have in common. No two people are exactly alike. Yet we constantly sort them out according to features they share: extrovert and introvert; single, married, and divorced; joiners and loners; upper class, upper middle class, lower middle class, lower class.

Classification is the most common way of organizing the material for a piece of writing. Here is a collection of material for a paper about a person:

SUBJECT: Last semester's psychology teacher

(1) had a loud, clear voice
(2) told some interesting stories about students helped by psychology
(3) came to class late several times
(4) explained difficult words
(5) wasn't sarcastic toward students
(6) wore colorful neckties
(7) walked with a limp
(8) had been an exchange teacher in France
(9) outlined subject clearly
(10) spaced assignments well
(11) talked over test I did poorly on
(12) served in the Army Signal Corps

What goes with what? Here are four possible categories:

  I. *Teaching methods:* (2) relevant anecdotes, (4) explanation of terms, (9) clear outline, (10) spacing of assignments, and perhaps (1) effective speech habits

 II. *Attitude toward students:* (5) absence of sarcasm, (11) assistance after class

III. *Personal traits:* (6) sporty clothes, (7) limp, (3) lack of punctuality

 IV. *Background:* (8) teaching experience abroad, (12) service in Signal Corps

A student concerned about his success in school would probably conclude that categories I, II, and IV are most significant. A second look at III might suggest an effective strategy for the paper as a whole: an unpromising first impression, belied by the teacher's effectiveness. The outline of the finished paper might look like this:

    I. Unpromising external characteristics
   II. Effectiveness as a teacher
       A. Interesting background
       B. Effective presentation of subject
       C. Positive attitude toward students
  III. Lesson learned
      ("Don't judge a teacher by his ties.")

Here are some other subjects with material sorted out into major categories:

SUBJECT: Types of comic strips
    I. Righteous crime fighters (Dick Tracy, Robin Malone)
   II. Comic stereotypes (Dennis the Menace, Blondie, Bugs Bunny)
  III. Social satire (L'il Abner, Doonesbury)
  IV. Amusing human foibles (Peanuts, Pogo)

SUBJECT: Types of high school teachers
    I. The *authoritarian* personality (strict discipline, one-way teaching, heavy assignments, severe grading)
   II. The *journeyman* teacher (reliance on the textbook, moderate assignments, "don't-rock-the-boat" attitude)
  III. The students' *friend* (chummy attitude, many bull sessions, unusual projects, fraternizing outside of school)

Remember the following advice when setting up such major categories:

(1) *Let the subject of your paper help you determine appropriate categories.* Writing about campus social life, you might divide students into Greeks, co-op dwellers, and independents. Writing about "cultural" subjects for vocational students, you might divide them into nursing majors, engineering majors, police majors, and so on.

(2) *Avoid a confusing mixture of criteria.* It does not make sense to divide students into graduates of local high schools, disadvantaged students, and Catholics. It *does* make sense to sort them out according to geographical origin (local, rest of the state, out of state, foreign), *or* according to belief (Catholics, Protestants, Jews, agnostics), *or* according to social and economic background.

O 5c   Comparison and Contrast   *coh*

Show connections between things normally considered separately.

The immediate need for comparison and contrast arises when we are faced with a choice. We often compare and contrast to justify a *preference.* To justify our preference for a lackluster incumbent over a more dynamic challenger, we may compare their records on a number of crucial points. More basically, comparison and contrast helps us *notice* things we previously took for granted. We learn to identify a style of architecture by noting the features it shares with other styles and those features that set it apart. We are more vividly aware of the American way of doing things after we spend a year in Mexico or in France.

To make possible fruitful comparison and contrast, the author must *line up* the material so that one thing throws light upon the other. Here are the two basic ways of organizing the comparison-and-contrast paper:

(1) *The author discusses two things together—feature by feature, point by point.* A **point-by-point comparison** takes up one feature of, say, the Volkswagen, and then immediately asks: "Now what does this look like for the Ford?" A typical outline would look like this:

The Whole Theme

   I. Economy
      A. Initial cost (data for both cars)
      B. Cost of operation (data for both cars)
      C. Resale value (data for both cars)
  II. Comfort and convenience
      A. Space for passengers and luggage (data for both cars)
      B. Maneuverability (data for both cars)
 III. Performance
      A. Acceleration and speed (data for both cars)
      B. Durability (data for both cars)

(2) *The author discusses two things separately but takes up the same points in the same order.* Such a **parallel-order comparison** gives a coherent picture of each of the two things being compared, while at the same time helping the reader see the connections between the two. In the following portrait of two types of baseball fans, the same three points are taken up both times in the identical order: I. absorption in the game; II. attitude toward fellow fans; III. interest in the players.

Thesis	The true baseball fan is found in the bleachers, not in the grandstand.
Point 1	The man in the bleachers *forgets himself in the game.* When he gets excited . . .
Point 2	He is apt to *turn to a total stranger,* tap him on the shoulder, and say, "Ain't that boy Aaron the berries!" . . .
Point 3	Though his seat is farthest from the diamond and he cannot see the batters' faces, he *recognizes each one* of them as they come up. . . .
Transition	The man in the grandstand looks at the game differently. . . .

Point 1	He never quite *gives himself up to the game.* He never cuts loose with a wild yell. . . .
Point 2	If he is sitting among people who are strangers to him, he *treats them like strangers.* . . .
Point 3	He has to refer to his scorecard to get the *names of the players.* . . .

O 5d   Argument   *coh*

Follow the order of a logical argument.

A well-organized argument takes the reader along step by step to the desired conclusion. Here are some familiar kinds:

(1) The logical coherence of the paper may derive from **cause-and-effect** relationships. The following outline might represent an essay by a teacher concerned about students' lack of interest in poetry:

I. *First step:* The author states the central concern:
Children like poetry; they make up jingles and keep chanting them to each other; they listen avidly to poems about little pigs and clever cats. Most college freshmen, on the other hand, are either indifferent or hostile toward poetry, both traditional and modern.

II. *Second step:* The author asks and answers the obvious question: Why?
Poetry is often presented to students as something special and solemn; memorizing and reciting make many students regard it as drudgery; prose paraphrase necessarily emphasizes the most prosaic aspect of poetry.

III. *Third step:* The author suggests remedies at least partly implied in the diagnosis:
Teachers of poetry should emphasize oral reading; they should cater to their students' interest in song and story by including ballads and narrative poetry; they should

213

encourage discussion and writing rather than make poetry the subject of objective tests.

(2) A second kind of argument leads to the desired conclusion through *qualification of* or *attack upon a familiar idea*. Such a **"yes, but"** paper takes the readers first onto common ground but then invites them to *move on* from there:

   I. *First step:* A familiar idea is confirmed:
   It is true that many required courses do not help to prepare the student for his professional career (detailed illustrations).
  II. *Second step:* A qualification or objection is stated:
   But a responsible citizen must be able to recognize competence and quackery in fields other than his own (detailed illustrations).
 III. *Third step:* A balanced conclusion is drawn:
   Therefore, a student needs required courses that give him a basic understanding of some important disciplines outside his own field.

In a "pro-and-con" paper, the *yes* and the *but* carry about equal weight. When the resulting paper clearly plays two *opposed* ideas off against each other, it mirrors the **dialectic** process:

   I. *Thesis:* It is true that modern industrial society makes for unprecedented interdependence among its citizens.
  II. *Antithesis:* But such interdependence is an essential condition of mass production and mass consumption.
 III. *Synthesis:* Interdependence is the price modern society pays for a high standard of living.

(3) A third logical pattern *presents examples, case histories, or evidence and then draws a general conclusion.*

Such **inductive order** is especially effective when a writer has to overcome prejudice or distrust:

    I. *First step:* Data are presented:

       Carlotta Brink, heroine of *Vengeance Is Mine,*

       A. is rude to her servants (examples)

       B. insults tradespeople (examples)

       C. attempts to put other people in the wrong (examples)

       D. is unconcerned about her husband's business problems (examples)

       E. scolds her children without provocation (examples)

   II. *Second step:* The conclusion is drawn:

       Carlotta is inconsiderate and unkind.

(4) In many papers we apply common assumptions to specific instances. Here is a rough outline of a **deductive argument,** which *draws conclusions from premises previously established* or *applies generalizations to specific examples:*

    I. A college should develop in its students a sense for spiritual values (elaboration and support).

   II. Architecture gives tangible expression to such values as dignity and permanence (elaboration and support).

  III. The buildings facing the traditional Inner Quad of the college exhibit several of these qualities (elaboration and support).

  IV. Of the modern classroom buildings on this campus, few suggest a sense of tradition, a sense of style, a feeling of dignity (elaboration and support).

   V. Therefore, the buildings surrounding the Inner Quad should not be torn down to make room for additional "cell block" structures.

Exercises

Process

A. Identify the ten or twelve *essential steps* in a complicated process that is well known to you from first-hand observation or experience. Try to group the various steps into several major stages. Use the following outline form to report your findings.

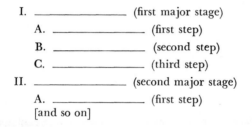

```
 I. _____ (first major stage)
    A. _____ (first step)
    B. _____ (second step)
    C. _____ (third step)
II. _____ (second major stage)
    A. _____ (first step)
    [and so on]
```

B. Assume you are giving your reader instructions for a complicated task. Write a paragraph describing *in full detail* one essential step. Try to include everything that the reader would have to know and do to produce the right results.

C. In one sentence each, explain the six most essential *technical terms* that you would need in tracing one of the following processes: generating electricity, pollination, the life cycle of a butterfly, transmission of a visual image by television, the making of sugar, preparing a French (Spanish, Italian, Mexican, Chinese) dish.

Classification

D. The following "interest inventory" was adapted from a student paper. How would you *classify* the items in order to present them in a plausible sequence? Prepare a brief outline showing how you have sorted them out.

1. contact sports
2. coffee dates
3. religious retreats
4. taking a girl to the movies
5. work for worldwide disarmament
6. long hikes
7. beach barbecues
8. vacation trips
9. fellowship meetings
10. swimming
11. social work
12. student government

E. A student paper listed the following points as guidelines for parents. How would you sort these points out into *major categories?* Prepare an outline reflecting what you would consider the most plausible classification.

1. Parents should avoid swearing or vulgarity.
2. Parents should not contradict each other in the presence of their children.
3. Parents should provide encouragement when children do something constructive.
4. Punishment should be impartial when there are several children.
5. Parents should not shower their children with gifts.
6. One parent should not overrule the other in matters of discipline.
7. Parents should show affection, whether by a pat on the back or a good word.
8. Parents should respect children as individuals, letting them develop their own likes and dislikes.
9. Parents should not be overprotective.
10. Children should be allowed to learn from their own mistakes.

11. Parents should refrain from quarreling in the presence of their children.

12. Parents should teach good manners by example.

13. Parents should allow their children to choose their own friends.

14. Parents should not give vent to their frustrations or irritations by punishing their children.

15. Parents should not take notice of a child only when it does something wrong.

F. What is your favorite reading matter? Have you ever sorted it out into recurrent types? Choose one of the following: science fiction, detective novels, Western novels, historical novels, nineteenth-century British fiction, current American short stories, biographies, autobiographies, books on travel or exploration. Sort the books you have read in this major category out into a few major types. For each, write a short paragraph indicating the major features that examples of the type have in common.

Comparison and Contrast

G. Of the following topics, choose the one that seems most promising for fruitful comparison and contrast. Write *two* rough outlines—one for a point-by-point comparison, the other for a parallel-order comparison. Choose one: your high school campus and your present college campus, two successful television comedians with different styles, old-style and "adult" Western movies, a student hang-out and an expensive restaurant.

H. Write a rough outline for a comparison and contrast of *two major characters* from imaginative literature. Choose the central figures of two Shakespeare plays, two nineteenth-century British novels, or two modern American novels. Make it *either* a point-by-point or a parallel-order comparison, and be prepared to defend your choice.

I. Write a rough outline for a comparison and contrast of *two sets of attitudes,* of two distinct positions, on some major aspect of education: discipline in high school, sex education, supervision of the private lives of college students. Use either a point-by-point or a parallel-order comparison and be prepared to defend your choice.

Argument

J. Have you recently become strongly aware of two different or opposed views on a familiar problem or current issue? Use your outline to line up the *pros and cons* and to lead up to your own conclusion. Possible topics:

> The use of violence for political ends
> Legal control of the ownership and sales of guns
> Freeway construction in urban or scenic areas
> The future of atomic energy

K. Write an outline for an *inductively organized* paper on a subject of your choice. Present the evidence first; then draw your conclusion.

L. Write an outline for a paper in which you present a *specific, limited proposal* for the reform of high school or college education. Show how your proposal derives from basic assumptions about the nature or purposes of education. Try to make each major point in your outline a necessary step in your argument.

O 6   Beginnings and Endings

Learn how to enlist your readers' attention and how to leave them with a strong final impression.

The experienced writer increasingly thinks about his or her audience as a paper begins to take shape. How can we attract and hold our readers' attention? How can we make clear to them what we are trying to do? How can we leave them with a strong final impression?

O 6a   Titles   *coh*

Use your title to attract the reader without promising more than you are going to deliver.

A good title is specific enough to stake out a limited area, honest enough to prevent later disappointment, and striking enough to compete with other claims on the reader's time. It often has a dramatic or humorous touch:

> At Last Lincoln Found a General
> The Crime of Punishment
> Second Things First
> On Becoming Human

Bad titles tend to be vague, colorless, sprawling, or deceptive. Here are some weak titles followed by a choice of possible improvements:

Before: Business Success

After: Selling the Brooklyn Bridge
Where the Customer Is King
Red Ink, Black Ink

Before: Qualities of a Future Spouse

After: What Makes Eligible Men Eligible
Breadwinner or Prince Charming?
A Girl like Your Mother

Before: Juvenile Delinquency

After: My Stay at Juvenile Hall
The Boy from a Good Family
A Hopeless Case

O 6b   Introductions   *coh*

Use your introduction to attract the reader but also to do important groundwork for the paper.

An effective introduction creates interest; it hooks the reader into the essay or story. It sketches out the territory to be covered, often by narrowing down a more general subject. It sets the tone for the rest of the essay. Above all, it *heads straight for the central idea* to be developed in the rest of the paper.

You will seldom write a paper requiring more than *one short introductory paragraph.* Here are some typical examples:

(1) The writer may attract the reader's attention by relating the subject to a *topical event or a current controversy:*

Russian, Anyone?

On August 12 . . . the Soviet government announced the construction of Russia's first. . . . Though Russian scientific journals had published detailed accounts of . . . , the lack of qualified translators had kept American scientists unaware of the Russians' rapid progress in this field. . . .

(2) The writer may make the reader take a *new look at a familiar situation:*

The Life of Stress

A lot of sympathy is being wasted on executives for leading lives so full of stress and strain that it impairs their health. Actually, their subordinates suffer more from high blood pressure and artery disease. These surprising findings . . .—*Time*

(3) The writer may approach a general subject *from a personal angle,* showing personal interest in or qualifications for the subject:

The Whole Theme

It Takes Four to Start a War

A few months ago a freak thunderstorm hit the city that sent a lightning bolt crashing to the ground a few blocks from my apartment. The sound jolted me in terror from my sleep. My body responded with a dose of adrenalin and sweat and a galloping heart. I crossed my fingers because I was sure it was nuclear war. I am not often conscious of this fear, but I suspect my subconscious dwells on it, for I am of that generation that was herded into the halls of elementary schools to lean against ceramic tile walls and tuck our heads between our knees. . . .

(4) The writer may use *a dramatic case* to lead us into a discussion of a more general problem or situation:

No Exit

Neal is twenty and has been on heroin since that day he remembers so well, his fifteenth birthday, when someone on his block took him to the Embassy Hotel in Manhattan and invited him to buy a fix. "Henry, my friend, was always fooling around with the goof balls, and now he had found something even better. I tried it and liked it." Of all the drug problems afflicting the world, heroin is the most deadly and the one that most seriously affects American young people. . . .

(5) An *initial quotation* may serve as the keynote for the rest of the paper:

Who Is Hamlet?

"It is a commonplace that the character of Hamlet holds up the mirror to his critics."[1] Shakespeare's Hamlet has been aptly described as the sphinx of the Western world, with each critic giving his own subjective answer to the riddle it proposes. . . .

(6) *Striking facts or statistics* may dramatize the issue to be discussed:

Monolingualism Is Obsolete

Last year, only one out of ten American high school graduates had studied a foreign language. In spite of the publicity recently given to the teaching of foreign languages in primary and secondary schools . . .

(7) A *striking contrast* may heighten the point to be made:

American Children Are Spoiled

Not too many decades ago, young children were early taught the difference between what they were, and were not, allowed to do. Today, many American parents treat their children as if they could do no wrong. The most obvious manifestation of this change . . .

(8) A *provocative statement* may challenge a familiar belief or ideal:

Freedom Is Impossible

Freedom in society is impossible. When the desires of two people do not agree, both cannot be satisfied. Who is going to be free to realize his desire—the man who wants to walk down the street shouting and singing, or his neighbor who seeks peace and quiet? The man who wants to build a new highway, or the one who wants to retain the unspoiled natural beauty of the land? . . .

(9) An *amusing anecdote* may convey an important idea:

Medical Journalism—With and Without Upbeat

As a veteran writer of medical and psychological articles for the mass-circulation "slicks," I have a fellow feeling for the violinist who rebelled after having been with an orchestra for thirty years. One day, so the story goes, he sat with his hands folded during rehearsal, and when the conductor rapped on the podium with his baton and demanded furiously, "Why aren't you playing?" replied, with a melancholy sigh, "Because I don't like music." Sometimes I feel like sitting at my typewriter with my hands folded. I don't like popularization. It has gone too far. The little learning—with illustrations—which the magazines have been pouring into a thirsty public has become a dangerous thing. . . .—Edith M. Stern, *Saturday Review*

Some common ways of introducing a theme are usually *ineffective:*

- a *repetition,* often verbatim, *of the assignment.*

- a *colorless summarizing statement:* "There are many qualities that the average college graduate looks for in a job. Most of them probably consider the following most important. . . ."

- an *unsupported claim to interest:* "Migratory birds are a fascinating subject. Ever since I was a little child I have been interested in the migration of birds. Studying them has proved a wonderful hobby. . . ."

- *complaints or apologies:* "I find it hard to discuss prejudice in a paper of 500 words. Prejudice is a vast subject. . . ."

O 6c   Conclusions   *coh*

> **Use your conclusion to tie together different parts of your paper and reinforce its central message.**

Avoid conclusions that are merely a lame restatement of points already clear. Try making your conclusion fulfill an expectation created earlier in your paper. For instance, make it give a direct answer to a question asked in your title or introduction or tie it in with a key incident treated early in the paper.

Here are some examples of effective conclusions:

(1) A *final anecdote* that reinforces the central idea:

. . . Only once did I ever hear of an official football speech which met with my entire approval. It was made by a Harvard captain. His team had lost to Yale but by a smaller score than was expected. It had been a fast and interesting game. At the dinner when the team broke training the captain said, "We lost to Yale but I think we had a satisfactory season. We have had fun out of football and it seems to me that ought to be the very best reason for playing the game."

A shocked silence followed his remarks. He was never invited to come to Cambridge to assist in the coaching of any future Harvard eleven. His heresy was profound. He had practically intimated that being defeated was less than tragic.—Heywood Broun, "A Study in Sportsmanship," *Harper's*

(2) A strong *final quotation:*

. . . The drug epidemic seems to be the shadow of an end-of-century plague. It is part of a larger set of social problems that medical advances have done little to solve. As Horace Sutton has said, "Way ahead materially, we have done poorly in combating social diseases. It is a branch of medical science in which no Nobel prizes are given."

(3) A *forecast or warning* based on facts developed in the paper:

. . . In education we have not yet acquired that kind of will. But we need to acquire it, and we have no time to lose. We must acquire it in this decade. For if, in the crucial years which are coming, our people remain as unprepared as they are for their responsibilities and their mission, they may not be equal to the challenge, and if they do not succeed, they may never have a second chance to try.—Walter Lippmann, "The Shortage in Education," *Atlantic*

(4) A suggestion for *remedial action:*

. . . If the leading citizens in a community would make it a point to visit their state prison, talk with the warden, then return to their communities with a better understanding of actual down-to-earth prison problems, they would have taken one of the most important and most effective steps toward a solution of our crime problem.—Erle Stanley Gardner, "Parole and the Prisons—An Opportunity Wasted," *Atlantic*

(5) A *return from the specific to the general,* relating the findings of the paper to a general trend:

. . . Inge's family plays constitute a kind of aesthetic isolationism upon which the world of outside—the world of moral choice, decision, and social pressures—never impinges. Although he has endowed the commonplace with some depth, it is not enough to engage serious attention. William Inge is yet another example of Broadway's reluctance or inability to deal intelligently with the American world at large.—Robert Brustein, "The Men-Taming Women of William Inge," *Harper's*

Here are some examples of *ineffective* conclusions:

- the *platitude:* "This problem deserves the serious attention of every right-thinking American."

- the *silver lining:* "When things look their grimmest, a turn for the better is usually not far away."

- the *panacea:* "The restoration of proper discipline in the nation's schools will make juvenile delinquency a thing of the past."

- the *conclusion raising problems* that weaken or distract from the point of the paper: "Of course, a small car has obvious disadvantages for a family with numerous children or for the traveler in need of luggage space."

Exercises

A. Study the following *book titles* and rank the three best titles in order of their effectiveness. Explain what makes them effective. What kind of a book does each make you expect?

1. *George Washington, Man and Monument*
2. *Freedom in the Modern World*
3. *The City in History*
4. *The American Way of War*
5. *The Inner City Mother Goose*
6. *Number: The Language of Science*
7. *Lost Worlds of Africa*
8. *The Feminine Mystique*
9. *The Naked Ape*
10. *The Second Sex*

B. Look through recent issues of general-circulation *magazines* to find five articles whose titles you consider exceptionally effective. Defend your choices.

C. Describe the approach chosen in each of the following introductions. Comment on the effectiveness of both *introduction and title*. Do they make the reader want to go on reading? Do they seem to lead clearly and directly into a specific subject? What kind of paper would you expect in each case?

The Whole Theme

1.

Prison Reform: A Must

By now, just about all of us are aware of the requests and demands by numerous organizations and groups, as well as individuals, for prison reform. Many people are somewhat skeptical of this trend as just being part of the movement to change nearly all of society. I was already convinced that prison wasn't a whole lot of fun, but also felt that the testimony of cons and ex-cons was biased, if not altogether lies. Being somewhat of an optimist, I felt that the whole world wasn't bad. But after doing only a minimal amount of research into the subject, I have decided that much of what is heard is true and there is a real need for such a reform of the prison system.

2.

The New Illiteracy

We hear much about the reawakening interest in the humanities, the new appreciation of the generalness in the liberal arts, the growing dissatisfaction with overspecialization. Maybe so. But these signs are minute, I suggest, [compared with] those coming from the other direction. I offer the proposition that the trends that have been working against the humanities are likely to increase, not decrease, in the decade ahead. . . .—William H. Whyte, Jr., *Saturday Review*

3.

Mary Had a Little Delinquent

In today's world, the worst kind of juvenile delinquent is not the one who has become a public blotch on the good name of society, or who has been blasted to fame in a newspaper headline. More frightening is a silent, sneaking kind of young rebel. Normal enough in looks, this person creeps through our culture until suddenly—POW—his disrespect for authority is revealed. The delinquent of this second variety with whom I am most intimately acquainted is—*me!* I am very good at being bad.

4.

"I Didn't Bring Anyone Here, and I Can't Send Anybody Home"

When I recently went back to the great yellow prison at San Quentin, it was, in a sense, to make good on a debt incurred twenty years ago. I'd started my career as a prison teacher with a good liberal's prejudice in favor of prisoners and against their guards. When I left, about five years later, I wasn't so sure of myself, for I'd met more than one prisoner who fully deserved to be locked up and more than one guard who turned out to be a decent human being.

The debt I'm talking about, then, was an obligation to report as truly as I could about the prison guard—or, as he's officially known in California, the correctional officer. . . .—Kenneth Lamott, *Saturday Review*

5.

The Bent and Blunted Free Lance

In the chivalry of the thirteenth century, an important figure was the free lance, an independent knight who sold his fighting skill to the highest bidder and, so legend says, tilted his bold weapon in defense of the helpless against all sorts of dragons and outrages. So far in the twentieth century an important adjunct to communication has been the free-lance writer who has made a living, and a considerable social impact, with his pen. . . .—Hartzell Spence, *Saturday Review*

D. Examine the introduction or "lead" in three current articles from different general-interest magazines. Write a well-developed paragraph about each one. Describe the approach followed and evaluate its effectiveness.

E. Describe the function and estimate the probable effectiveness of the following conclusions:

1. (A paper describing the game of badminton)
   . . . Badminton can be very exciting. If you are ever looking for a good time I suggest that you try this game. I know from experience that it can really be a lot of fun.

2. (A paper trying to demonstrate the futility of censoring comic books)
   . . . the parents can do most to counteract the comic-book habit. If they read to their children from good books, if they teach their children to treat good books as treasured possessions, if they make it a habit to talk about good books in the home, the positive attraction of good literature may prove more effective than censorship possibly can.

3. (A paper discussing several examples of "tolerance")
   . . . We thus conclude that by "tolerance" we mean allowing beliefs and actions of which we do not wholly approve. Since many of us approve wholeheartedly of only very few things, life without tolerance would be truly intolerable.

4. (A paper on race prejudice)
   . . . What can the individual do to combat racial prejudice? This question is very hard to answer, because nobody can predict the future.

5. (A paper on the democratic process)
   . . . The benefits society derives from the democratic process are often unspectacular, and slow in coming. Its weaknesses and disadvantages are often glaringly evident. By its very nature, democracy, in order to survive, must give its enemies the right to be heard and to pursue their goals. As Chesterton has said, "The world will never be safe for democracy—it is a dangerous trade."

O 7   Continuity and Transition

Learn how to take your reader along from point to point.

A paper has continuity when it takes the reader along. Good writing has a pied-piper effect. It is accompanied in the reader's mind by a running commentary somewhat like the following: "This I have to hear." "Now I can see where you are headed." "That's what I *thought* you were leading up to." "Yes, I see."

O 7a Key Sentences

coh

Use emphatic key sentences that serve as guideposts to the reader.

A topic sentence becomes a guide to the intention of a paragraph (see O 1a) . A **thesis sentence** gives direction to the paper as a whole. From paragraph to paragraph, and even within a paragraph, the most basic method of moving a paper along is to make a key statement that calls for an explanation, to make an assertion that calls for proof.

Study the following excerpted version of an article that is exceptionally deliberate and clear-cut in its organizational scheme. Can you see how the key sentences the author formulates in response to his four major questions help the reader follow him step by step?

What are the students like? They come from all sorts of backgrounds. . . .
Only one thing they are certain to have in common: they are roughly in the same age group. . . .
Why do they come to college? They come because it is assumed that they will come, because almost everyone they know does. . . .
A second and related reason why students come is to make good contacts. . . .
Many come simply to learn to make a living. . . .
To have fun is still another motive. . . .
There are students who actually come because they want to learn. . . .
What happens to students in college? It is the students' first

meeting, most likely, with a national and perhaps international group of men and women of their own age. . . .

Furthermore, college is the students' first encounter with live intellectuals. . . .

Students are surprised, too, at their first meeting with really violent political opinion of all possible varieties. . . .

It is in college, too, that the sharp bitter sting of failure is first experienced to any appreciable extent. . . .

What does the student learn? On the simplest level he has acquired a considerable amount of information. . . .

He will also have learned to question. . . .—James K. Feibleman, "What Happens in College," *Saturday Review*

O 7b   Synonyms and Recurrent Terms   *coh*

Use key terms and their synonyms to focus the reader's attention.

In a paper on academic freedom, terms and phrases like "freedom," "liberty," "independent thought," "free inquiry," "responsible choice," "absence of interference," and "self-government" show that the writer is never straying far from the central issue. The echo effect of such synonyms reassures the reader that he or she is not expected to take unexplained sudden jumps.

In the following excerpt, can you find all the words and phrases that in one way or another echo the idea of *work?*

What elements of the national character are attributable to this long-time agrarian environment? First and foremost is the habit of work. For the colonial farmer ceaseless striving constituted the price of survival. . . .

The tradition of toil so begun found new sustenance as settlers opened up the boundless stretches of the interior. "In the free States," wrote Harriet Martineau in 1837, "labour is more really and heartily honoured. . . ."

One source of Northern antagonism to the system of human bondage was the fear that it was jeopardizing this basic tenet of the American creed. "Wherever labor is mainly performed by slaves," Daniel Webster told the United States Senate, "it is regarded as . . ."

Probably no legacy from our farmer forebears has entered more deeply into the national psychology. If an American has no purposeful work on hand . . .

This worship of work has made it difficult for Americans to learn how to play. As Poor Richard saw it, "Leisure is . . ."

The first mitigations of the daily grind took the form of hunting, fishing, barnraisings and logrollings—activities that had no social stigma because they contributed to the basic needs of living. . . .

The importance attached to useful work had the further effect of helping to make "this new man" indifferent to aesthetic considerations. . . .—Arthur M. Schlesinger, *Paths to the Present*

O 7c   Patterns of Expectation   *coh*

Use a consistent overall pattern to guide the reader's expectations.

If a writer sets up a clear-cut overall pattern, the reader is ready for the next step before it comes. Suppose an author is examining the causes of war. He takes up *minor* contributing causes first, as if to get them out of the way. He gradually moves on to major ones. The reader will be ready for a final central or crucial cause coming as the **climax** of the article or the book.

Here are some familiar patterns that can help guide the expectations of a reader:

- **Enumeration:** Lining major points up in a numerical sequence makes for a formal, systematic presentation. In the following discussion of language, the key points gain force from marching across the page in a 1–2–3 order:

> There are *five simple facts* about language in general which we must grasp before we can understand a specific language or pass judgment on a particular usage. . . .
> *In the first place,* language is basically speech. . . .
> *In the second place,* language is personal. . . .
> *The third fact* about language is that it changes. . . .
> *The fourth great fact* about language . . . is that its users are, in one way or another, isolated. . . .
> *The fifth great fact* about language is that it is a historical growth of a specific kind. . . .—Donald J. Lloyd, "Snobs, Slobs, and the English Language," *The American Scholar*

- **From Problem to Solution:** Can you see the logical pattern that helps move forward the following student paper?

Problem
> In any family, there is a network of antagonistic desires. A young girl might want to practice her violin, while her brother insists that the noise interferes with his studying. . . .

Solution
First
alternative
> These situations must be solved or managed. If one parent dictates without consideration of the others, the family will be run in an authoritarian manner. Women used to bend to the wishes of an authoritarian husband. . . .

Second
alternative
> If no authority figure guides and directs these daily decisions, the individuals in the family must create some method of living together. . . .

- **Study of Alternatives:** Systematic study of *different* possible choices or different possible causes accounts for the purposeful forward movement of much successful professional writing. Look at the following example:

Continuity and Transition

Thesis	The diversity of higher education in the United States is unprecedented. . . .
First problem is taken up; one alternative is considered	Consider the *question of size.* The small campus offers . . .
Second alternative is considered	Others feel hemmed in by these very qualities. They welcome the *comparative anonymity and impersonality* of the big university. . . .
Second problem is taken up; first alternative is considered	Another familiar question is whether the student should go to a *college next door, in the next city, or a thousand miles away.* By living at home . . .
Second alternative is considered	Balanced against this, there are considerable advantages to a youngster in *seeing and living in an unfamiliar region* of the country. . . .
Alternatives are weighed	But this question too must be decided in terms of the individual. . . .
Third problem is taken up; first alternative is considered	*Co-education* poses still another problem. Those who favor it argue . . .
Second alternative is considered	Others believe that *young men and women* will work better if . . .
Alternatives are weighed	There is no pat answer. It might be healthy for one youngster . . .
Fourth problem is taken up	The so-called *"prestige"* colleges and *universities* present a special problem. . . .— John W. Gardner, "How to Choose a College, If Any," *Harper's*

O 7d   Transitions   *trans*

Use transitional phrases to help the reader move smoothly from one point to the next.

In a well-written paper, the reader can see how the writer moves from point to point. But the connection is seldom as obvious as the writer thinks. Transitional phrases are directional signals that help the reader move along without stumbling.

Here are common transitional phrases:

Addition:	too, also, furthermore, similarly, moreover
Illustration:	for example, for instance
Paraphrase or Summary:	that is, in other words, in short, to conclude, to sum up
Logical Conclusion:	so, therefore, thus, accordingly, consequently, as a result, hence
Contrast or Objection:	but, however, nevertheless, on the other hand, conversely, on the contrary
Concession:	granted that . . . , no doubt, to be sure, it is true that . . .
Reiteration:	indeed, in fact

Point out all transitional expressions in the following passage. In your own words, what kind of signal does each give the reader?

It is seldom hard to construct conspiracy theories of history in retrospect. Distinguished Southern historians, for example, worked diligently for many years to demonstrate that President Lincoln had deliberately tricked the South into the Civil War, that after the innocent Confederates fired on Fort Sumter, Lincoln rubbed his hands with glee and used the incident to justify mobilizing Union troops. Similarly, Franklin D. Roosevelt was attacked in immense detail by as distinguished an American historian as Charles A. Beard for instigating the Japanese assault on Pearl Harbor. Although these studies had a lunatic logic, they suffer from one overwhelming liability: They are not true. Lincoln did not want war. Roosevelt did—but with the Nazis, not the Japanese. In fact, if Hitler had not gone completely off his rails and declared war on the United States, we might well have gone roaring off into the Pacific in 1942 and left Europe to its fate.—John P. Roche, "The Pentagon Papers and Historical Hindsight," *The New Leader*

Note: Avoid transitions that merely add without showing why. Shun expressions like "Another interesting point is . . ." or "We might also take a look at . . ." These make it sound as though the writer asked: "What else can I say?" They make the reader feel that what follows is at best optional and at worst mere padding.

O 7e   Outlines   *coh*

Use outlines to help you work out and strengthen the organization of a piece of writing.

Outlines help you visualize the structure of a paper; they help you confront and solve problems of organization. The more clearly you have outlined a paper in your own mind, the better your reader will be able to follow.

(1) Construct a *working outline* by jotting down major points in a tentative order. To be useful in *writing* a paper, an outline should be informal and flexible. A working outline resembles an architect's preliminary sketches rather than the finished blueprint. When jotting down a working outline, the writer is in effect saying: "Let's see what it would look like on paper."

Suppose a writer wants to discuss an important common element in books that have enjoyed a tremendous vogue with adolescents. He might first jot down titles as they come to mind:

Catcher in the Rye
Goethe's *Young Werther*
Catch-22
The Prophet

The Whole Theme

> *The Stranger*
> *Lord of the Flies*

To arrange these titles in a plausible order, he might decide to start with the *classic* example: Goethe's *Werther,* the book that "invented adolescence." He would then discuss outstanding *recent* examples, taking them up roughly in the order in which they became popular. Finally, he would discuss in detail a *personal* example—a book that meant a great deal to him as an adolescent. The working outline might look like this:

> classic example: Goethe's *Werther*
> recent examples:
>> *Catcher in the Rye*
>> *The Stranger*
>> *Lord of the Flies*
>> *Catch-22*
>
> my own favorite:
>> *Slaughterhouse Five*

(2) Use the *final outline* as a final check on organization and as a guide to the reader. Your instructor may require you to submit a final outline with any paper presenting a substantial argument or organizing a substantial body of material. Two major forms are common:

- The **topic outline** is most useful for quick reference. It presents, in logical order, the topics and subtopics that a paper covers. Like other outlines, it is often preceded by a thesis sentence summarizing the central idea of the paper. Here is an example:

Sororities and the Single Girl

Thesis   The social activities of a sorority are designed to help girls conclude desirable middle-class marriages.

I. Keeping girls away from undesirable men

    A. Dating arrangements with fraternities

    B. Busy social calendar discouraging independent dating

II. Husband-hunting opportunities

III. Emphasis on formal courtship rather than casual dating

    A. "Pinnings" as formal ceremonies

    B. The role of pinnings and engagements in sorority "news"

- In a **sentence outline,** the writer sums up, in one complete sentence each, what he has to say on each topic and subtopic. The sentence outline thus forces him to think through the material more thoroughly than does the topic outline, which merely indicates the ground to be covered. A sentence outline might look like this:

Main Street Isn't Pennsylvania Avenue

Thesis   A successful business career alone does not qualify an executive for government work.

  I. Prominent business people have often occupied high positions in the federal government.

  II. Business people often have qualifications that government officials tend to lack.

    A. They are in close contact with the general public.

    B. They have thorough training in organizational problems.

      1. They are trained in administrative efficiency.

      2. They are cost-conscious.

  III. But business executives often lack preparation for other aspects of government work.

    A. They tend to lack the experience necessary for dealing with people from foreign cultures.

      1. They may alienate foreign diplomats.

      2. They tend to ignore public opinion abroad.

B. They have had little experience with the delays inherent in democratic processes.

  IV. The personal qualifications of the individual executive
are more important than business background.

Check your finished outlines against the following suggestions:

(1) *Avoid single subdivisions.* If there is a subdivision
A, there should be a subdivision *B.* If there is a section
numbered *1,* there should be a section numbered *2.* If a
section covers only one major point or one major step,
leave it undivided.

(2) *Avoid a long sequence of parallel elements,* such
as *I—X, A—F, or 1—8.* Try to split the sequence into two
or three major groups.

(3) *Use parallel grammatical structure* for headings
of the same rank in order to emphasize their logical relation. For instance, if *A 1* reads "To revive the student's interest." *A 2* and *A 3* should also be worded as infinitives:
"To promote the student's participation"; "To develop the
student's independent judgment."

(4) In a topic outline, *make each topic specific and informative.* In a sentence outline, make each subdivision a
complete sentence. *Make each sentence sum up an idea*
rather than merely indicate a topic.

Exercises

A. Read the following passage from Henry Steele Commager's *The American Mind.* Study it as an example of a passage
clearly focused on a central topic, and supporting a clearly stated
thesis. Answer the questions that follow it.

The temptation to experiment was deeply ingrained in the American character and fortified by American experience. America itself had been the greatest of experiments, one renewed by each generation of pioneers, and where every community was a gamble and an opportunity; the American was a gambler and an opportunist. He had few local attachments, pulled up stakes without compunction, and settled easily into new communities; where few regions or professions were overcrowded and every newcomer added to the wealth and the drawing power, he was sure of a welcome.

He was always ready to do old things in new ways, or for that matter, to do things which had not been done before. Except in law, tradition and precedent discouraged him, and the novel was a challenge. Pioneering had put a premium upon ingenuity and handiness, and where each man turned readily to farming, building, and trading, it seemed natural that he should turn with equal readiness to preaching, lawing, or doctoring, or combine these with other trades and professions.

The distrust of the expert, rationalized into a democratic axiom during the Jacksonian era, was deeply ingrained in the American character and persisted long after its original justification had passed. With opportunism went inventiveness, which was similarly invited by circumstances. Americans, who recorded at the Patent Office in Washington more inventions than were recorded in all the Old World nations together, likewise found more new roads to Heaven than had ever before been imagined, while their schools multiplied the seven liberal arts tenfold. Denominationalism and the inflated curriculum were not so much monuments to theological or secular learning as to the passion for experiment and inventiveness, and to an amiable tolerance.

1. How many words can you find in this passage that all echo or repeat the idea of "experiment"? Find all the synonyms or near-synonyms of this central term.

2. How many major instances of applications of the major thesis can you identify? Describe in your own words four or five *major kinds* of experiment that this passage maps out.

3. Select *one* of the major kinds of experiment mentioned here. Write a paragraph in which you fill in specific examples from your own reading or observation. Use a variety of transitional expressions. (Underline them in your finished paragraph.)

B. In each of the following pairs of sentences, a transitional word or phrase has been left out. Fill in a transition that will help the reader move smoothly from the first sentence to the second.

1. There are many special schools which should be considered by the young person who is not going on to college. The boy who wishes to be an X-ray technician and the girl who wishes to be a practical nurse, _____, will find many schools at which they may receive training.

2. Apprenticeship systems are still operating in every industry and offer wide opportunities for ambitious youngsters. They must be warned, _____, that in some of the older crafts entry is jealously guarded.

3. The home environment is the largest single factor determining the grade school youngster's "scholastic aptitude." _____, how well he learns in school depends on what he has learned at home.

4. Rennie was lazy, self-indulgent, spoiled. _____ _____, he did remarkably well in his favorite subjects.

5. The basic promise that American society has always held out to its citizens is equality of opportunity. The typical substandard big-city school, _____, is profoundly un-American.

6. Black athletes are not as pampered as some white sports fans seem to think. _____ the outstanding black athlete enjoys many privileges, but when a black and a white man are equally well qualified, coaches are likely to give preference to the latter.

7. The European system of education very early separates youngsters permanently on the basis of ability. The American system, _____, is designed to make possible numerous second chances.

8. In many Latin American countries, more young men study to be lawyers than are needed in their country. _____ _____, in many underdeveloped countries more young men study to be engineers than a preindustrial society could support.

9. A highly specialized skill limits a person's job opportunities. It _____ makes the specialist a potential victim of technological unemployment.

10. Our leaders are fond of the phrase "the free world." In actual fact, _____, societies that foster political freedom are the exception rather than the rule.

C. Prepare a rough outline of each of the following student papers. Are they hard to outline, or easy? How would you describe the overall pattern of each paper? What has each writer done to help the reader follow?

My Friend, My Enemy

Mimi is practically my best friend. On the outside, she is a loud-talking, big-mouthed, obnoxious girl. At a party, her only aim seems to be fun, with no feelings about anyone else. During the course of a conversation, she tells all she knows about her friends and their personal lives, never leaving out a detail or personal remark. Though Mimi is my best friend, her utter disregard for other people's feelings also makes her my worst enemy.

After seeing Mimi once, you won't forget her. She has a wild mop of short blond hair, which is combed once a day. Her big blue eyes are continually covered by a pair of heavy, coke-bottle lens glasses. She weighs well over her quota, a fact she explains by saying "there's more of me to love" and "I was thin once, but I wasn't as jolly." Her clothes are in the casual range of tennis shoes, big sweaters, and skirts.

What's ticking inside her head? Most noticeable is a bad, bad temper. She has the idea that no man is good enough to be his brother's keeper. This is her basic philosophy: If she decides to swear or dress sloppily, it's her business and nobody else's. Her temper makes her rage at people who make noise while she sleeps and at such things as a dirty bathroom basin. Usually her rage is a short atomic blast, but it never has a fallout of grudges. After waking, Mimi speaks to no one for at least two hours. She simply glares at any bystander.

A greater sense of humor never was found in one human being. In high school she called herself "Sherman" because she was as big as a tank. Everyone loved and hated her at the same time. Some people claimed that she sold beer and wine from her hall locker and made stencils of the teachers' signatures. When she was sent to the dean, she presented her ideas on how to improve the school honor code.

The parties Mimi goes to are never boring. She cuts everyone to pieces, including—and especially—me. At one time, she told everyone that I mixed my make-up in a huge vat and spread it on with a spatula. She is always talking to my friends and warning them about my numerous shortcomings.

Mimi lives across the hall in our boarding house. There she can sit for hours with a piece of clay or even a cigarette box and create small things for her enjoyment. Her jolly laugh is heard around the house when small things amuse her.

Few people understand what provokes Mimi, and they resent her carefree attitude. When I see her sitting like a fat little baby on the floor reading the college daily or a letter from home, enjoying every word like a piece of candy, I would like to hug her. However, as she slowly reveals my life to all present, I would like to kill her.

To many people, Mimi is just another coed. But to me she is a villain, the Medusa, Eleanor Roosevelt, Jerry Lewis, and Jack the Ripper, with a heart as big as a statue, all rolled into one fat, fun-loving, childlike package.

No More Favors, Please

Many times in a conversation I have heard it said that "a boss's son has it made." I doubt whether a person who makes that statement has ever worked for his father. At any rate, during the four years that I worked for my father's water softener firm, I was not treated nearly as well as were the other employees.

With them my father was generous and tolerant. They

received $2.50 an hour or $100.00 for their standard forty-hour week. And if Jerry or Fred helped to sell a new water softener to one of our customers, he was awarded a $20.00 commission. Whenever Jerry asked for a little time off to go fishing, my father promptly granted his request. And once Fred got two days off to take a trip to Chicago, and Dad didn't even dock his pay. If Jack and Kenny botched an installation job, my father would reprove them in a kindly tone and explain how they could have avoided the mistake. Once Kenny failed to tighten a packing nut on a valve, and the water leaked all over the customer's floor. Father sent over a man to clean up the mess and just told Kenny to be more careful next time. On another occasion Jack and Kenny dropped a softener down a customer's stairs, ruining the softener and damaging several steps. When they reported the incident to him with worried and anxious looks, Father calmed their fears and told them his insurance would cover the loss. If one of his men became involved in a dispute with a customer over a repair bill, it was his employee, and not the customer, who was always right.

But where I was concerned, my father was a close-fisted and harsh employer. My weekly paycheck was an unvarying fifty dollars, whether I worked forty hours or fifty-five, and the occasional salary raises the other employees enjoyed were never extended to me. I rarely received a commission on the sales I made; my father would either say that he couldn't afford to pay me any extra just then, or else that I wasn't really entitled to the money. If I wanted to take part in some school activity or go on a beach party with some friends, my father would not only refuse to give me time off, but he would often find extra jobs that would force me to work overtime. My mistakes called forth only anger from my father, never understanding. If anything went wrong with one of the company trucks while I was driving, he always assumed I had been driving like my "hot rod friends." If a customer complained about my service or her bill, my father bawled me out for giving him and his business a bad name. Once when I forgot to reduce the water pressure in the back-wash machine and caused about twenty dollars worth of mineral to be washed down the drain, he spent half an afternoon sarcastically analyzing my mistake and showing me, in minute detail, how my carelessness had "cut into the profits for the year." Insurance never covered *my* accidents; their cost was deducted from my salary, "to teach me to be more careful."

I don't know whether my father was so harsh with me because he didn't want to appear to be favoring me; but I do know that his constant criticism convinced me that the role of boss's son is a role I don't want to play for a lifetime.

A Change of Places

I lived in a neighborhood that respectable white people like to think does not exist. Ninety percent of its people were poor Negroes. The rest, like me, were poor whites. I was a minority. All my friends were black, as were my enemies. I lived by their standards, and, consequently, I felt the pains of being different. Whenever we played games, my name was not Dick, but "Milky," or "Sugar," or that old standby "Whitey." If a new club was formed in the neighborhood, I was always left out because I couldn't be trusted with any secrets. If I made a new friend and he asked me to come play at his house, I had to prepare myself for that same chilling, motherly line, 'You can't have any friends in, Georgie, because your father is sleeping, and you'd better come in anyway because it's time to eat." Whenever I got into a fight with another kid, I knew that there would be no help from any of my friends, because I was white and they were black, and the bonds of color were much stronger than the ties of friendship. I had to stand alone.

My soul was not that of a young child, in those days. As a matter of survival, I had encased myself in a callus of bitter acceptance. Smiles became a strange, bewildering phenomenon to the muscles of my face. The usual childhood tears were never able to find an escape route through my eyes. Crying is not allowed when one is a minority, for one doesn't show his feelings, or else his weaknesses may be exposed. And so I existed, very cold and all alone.

But my father, unlike the other fathers in that neighborhood, was able to increase his income enough to take us out and into a new environment. Left behind were those cluttered streets and crowded apartment buildings, and those cold black faces. I soon found myself in a new world, a world of front lawns, and pastel-colored toilet bowls, and two-car garages. As for the people, they were not black, as I had expected them to be, but white like me. For a while then, I was happy. But then a Negro family moved into our neighborhood, and they had a boy my age. He was a raisin in a sugar bowl, and he knew it. He was cold and lonely as I had been, and I remembered that awful feeling that I had left behind.

Theme Topics

Thesis and Support

1. Write a paper in which you support as fully as you can *one limited statement* about one of the following areas:

   - toys as a reflection of American society;
   - the role of women in current American movies;
   - images of childhood in American advertising;
   - the image of the Indian in American westerns;
   - the treatment of conflict or violence in science fiction;
   - guidance from teachers and counselors concerning jobs for girls;
   - teachers' attitudes towards children from Spanish-speaking backgrounds.

Process

2. Assume that your reader is a high school graduate with little detailed knowledge of science or engineering. Describe the *process* underlying one of the following: the operation of a television set, jet engine, or computer; the life cycle of a

butterfly or frog; the manufacture of paper, sugar, or other product that goes through numerous stages in the production process.

3. Write *instructions* that will help your readers perform a difficult task well. Choose one requiring a skill that you have acquired but that is not generally shared. Preferably the task to be performed should require loving care: the preparation of an unusual and difficult dish; the grafting of a bush or tree; the grooming of a horse.

Classification

4. Write a paper in which you divide *a group of people* into three or four major categories. For instance, you might classify children as leaders, followers, and loners; or teachers as authoritarian, chummy, and withdrawn. Make sure to establish categories that reflect your own experience and that you can fill in with graphic detail.

5. Have you found that one of the following labels covers *different things*? Classify them, setting up several major categories and describing them as fully as you can. Choose one of the following:

- crime comics
- war movies
- commercials
- college courses
- comedians
- radicals
- fads

Comparison and Contrast

6. Compare and contrast two fairly complicated pieces of *equipment or machinery* designed for basically the same job. For instance, compare and contrast an ordinary car motor with a diesel or jet engine. Or compare and contrast two

related forms of *music or dance:* the polka and the waltz, dixieland and progressive jazz, gospel and blues.

7. Compare and contrast one of the following: current men's fashions and women's fashions, girls' talk and boys' talk, men's and women's ways of dealing with children, behavior of boys (or girls) among themselves and in a mixed group.

Argument

8. Write a paper in which you examine the pros and cons in order to lead the reader to a balanced conclusion. Choose a topic for which you can identify *two strong opposing views.* For instance, should the primary goal of higher education be the creation of an élite equipped to understand and deal with the complex issues of our time? Or should higher education aim at providing the best possible education for everyone?

9. We are often told that a whole generation of boys took as a model the Horatio Alger hero, who made his way to fame and fortune through self-reliance, honesty, and hard work. Do young people today find any such *culture hero* in what they read or watch? Can you identify a recurrent type that might serve as a model or ideal for large numbers of young people? Use the *inductive approach* in presenting your findings.

10. Argue as fully as you can your position on one of the following issues. Try to make your reader see as fully as you can the steps by which your argument proceeds.

    a. Should a newspaper represent the opinions of its journalists, its publishers, its advertisers, or its public?

    b. Should a college make it a policy to bar undesirable or controversial speakers?

    c. Should college professors be allowed to bring their own political views into the classroom?

    d. Is there ever any justification for censorship?

6
Mechanics and Spelling

For Quick Reference

M 1   Manuscript Mechanics

Submit neat and competently prepared copy.

Whenever you hand in a theme or a report, the outward appearance of your manuscript is the first thing to strike your reader. A good first impression is likely to put the reader in a receptive mood.

M 1a   Penmanship and Typing   *ms*

Make sure all copy, whether handwritten or typed, is neat and legible.

To produce legible handwritten copy, use composition paper of standard size, preferably ruled in *wide lines,* and a reliable pen. Prune your writing of flourishes; avoid excessive slanting or excessive crowding. Unconventional handwriting is much more likely to annoy than it is to impress the reader.

To prepare typewritten copy, use unlined paper of standard size. Onionskin paper or semitransparent sheets are for carbon copies. *Double-space* all material except block quotations and footnotes. Leave two spaces after a period or other end punctuation; use two hyphens—with no space on either side—to make a dash.

Proofread all typewritten copy carefully. *Last-minute corrections* are permissible on the final copy, provided they look neat and are few in number.

(1) Draw a line through words and phrases that you want to omit; *do not use parentheses or square brackets for this purpose:*

> He started the complaints to which we had become accustomed ~~to~~.

(2) To correct a word, draw a line through it and insert the corrected word in the space immediately above; avoid crossing out or inserting individual letters:

> A girl working in an office has to stay calm,
>   collected
> cool, and ~~collective~~.

(3) To add a missing word, insert a caret (∧) and write the word immediately above:

>   not
> Thou shalt ∧ steal.

M 1b   Titles of Themes   *MS*

Use standard form for the titles of your themes.

Titles of themes follow the rules for the capitalization of words in titles of publications (see SP 6b). Do *not* underline or put in quotation marks the title that you assign to one of your own themes. Use a question mark or an exclamation mark after it where appropriate, but do *not* use a period even if your title is a complete sentence:

Chivalry Is Dead
Is Chivalry Dead?
Chivalry Is Dead!

M 1c   Spacing and Syllabication   *div*

Observe conventional spacing and syllabication.

Whether your papers are handwritten or typed, leave adequate margins. An inch and a half on the left and at the top, and an inch on the right and at the bottom are about standard. Indent the first lines of paragraphs, about an inch in longhand or five spaces in typed copy. To make a last-minute change in the paragraphing of a paper, insert the symbol ¶ to indicate an additional paragraph break. Insert *"no* ¶*"* in the margin to indicate that an existing paragraph break should be ignored.

An uneven right margin is preferable to the practice of dividing words at the end of every second or third line. Dictionaries generally use centered dots to indicate where a word may conventionally be divided *(com·pli·ment)*. A few generally observed practices are worth remembering:

(1) Setting off single letters saves little or no space and tends to confuse the reader. Do not divide words like *about, alone,* and *enough* or like *many* and *via.* Similarly, do not set off the ending *-ed* in words like *complained* or *renewed.*

(2) Hyphenated words become confusing when divided at any point other than at the original hyphen. Do

Mechanics and Spelling

not break up the *American* in "un-American" or the *sister* in "sister-in-law."

(3) Do not divide the last word on a page.

M 1d   Italics   *ital*

> **Use italics to set off special words and phrases from the rest of a sentence.**

Italics (or slanted type) are indicated in the handwritten or typed manuscript by underlining.

(1) Italics identify *technical terms* and words borrowed from *foreign languages*. (See P 6e.)

(2) Italics *emphasize* or call special attention to part of a sentence:

> The judge told me to apologize *in person* to everyone who had sat down in the freshly painted pews.

> The company is not liable for accidents caused by the negligence of employees or *by mechanical defects*.

(3) Italics set off the *title of a publication* from the text in which it is cited. Italicize titles of periodicals and of works published as separate units. Use **quotation marks** to set off titles of articles, chapters, songs, or poems that are merely a part of a complete publication:

> In *El Laberinto de la Soledad,* Octavio Paz describes the Mexican character.

> The old songs like "The Jolly Ploughboy" and "The Green Glens of Antrim" gave way to "Galway Bay" and "I'll Take You Home Again, Kathleen."

M 2 Abbreviations and Numbers

Avoid the overuse of abbreviations in ordinary prose.

Abbreviations save time and space. Here as in other matters, however, formal written English discourages excessive short cuts.

M 2a Abbreviations

ab

Spell out inappropriate abbreviations.

Some abbreviations are *generally appropriate* in expository writing:

(1) Before or after names, the titles *Mr., Mrs., Dr., St.* (*Saint*); the abbreviations *Jr.* and *Sr.;* degrees like *M.D.* and *Ph.D.* (Mr. John J. Smith, Jr.; Dr. Alfred Joyce or Alfred Joyce, M.D.). Use *Prof.* only before the *full* name: Prof. James F. Jones.

(2) Before or after numerals, the abbreviations *No.,* A.D. and B.C., A.M. and P.M., and the symbol $ (in 1066 A.D.; at 5:30 A.M.; $275).

(3) Initials standing for the names of agencies, organizations, business firms, technical processes, chemical compounds, and the like, when the full name is awkward or unfamiliar: *AFL-CIO, FBI, CIA, IBM, UNICEF, PTA, FM radio.*

(4) Some common Latin abbreviations; *e.g.* (for example), *etc.* (and so on), *i.e.* (that is). However, the mod-

ern tendency is to prefer the corresponding English expressions.

Other abbreviations are appropriate only in addresses, newspaper reports, technical reports, and other special contexts. Most of these have to be *written in full* in ordinary expository prose:

- With a few exceptions, names of countries, states, streets, and the like, are spelled out in ordinary writing: *United States; Schenectady, New York; Union Street.* (Exceptions: *USSR; Washington, D.C.*)

- The ampersand ("&") and abbreviations like *Inc.* and *Bros.* occur in ordinary writing only in references to organizations that employ those abbreviations in their official titles: *Smith & Company, Inc.* Spell out % and ¢.

- In ordinary expository prose, *lb.* (pound), *oz.* (ounce), *ft.* (foot), and *in.* (inch) are usually spelled out. Some units of measurement are more unwieldy and are abbreviated, provided they are used with figures: *45 mph, 1500 rpm.*

M 2b   Numbers   *ab*

> *Use figures in accordance with standard practice.*

In ordinary expository prose, the use of figures is to some extent restricted. They are generally appropriate in references to the day of the month (*May 13*), the year (*1917*), street numbers (*1014 Union Avenue*), and page numbers (*Chapter 7, page 18*). For other uses of numbers, the following conventions are widely observed:

(1) Numbers from one to ten, and *round numbers* requiring no more than two words, are usually spelled out: *three dollars a seat, five hundred years later, ten thousand copies.*

(2) Figures are used for *exact sums, technical measurements, decimals, and percentages,* as well as for references to time using A.M. or P.M.: *$7.22; 500,673 inhabitants; 57 percent; 2:30 P.M.*

(3) Figures are avoided at the beginning of a sentence: "Fifteen out of 28 replied . . ." or "When questioned, 15 out of 28 replied. . . ." Except in special situations like this one, changes from figures to words (and vice versa) in a series of numbers are generally avoided.

(4) When spelled out, *compound numbers* from 21 to 99 are hyphenated: *twenty-five, one hundred and forty-six.*

Exercise

Rewrite the following passage, using abbreviations and numerals in accordance with standard practice:

Mister Geo. Brown had resided at Eighteen N. Washington St. since Feb. nineteen-hundred and forty-four. Though he weighed only one hundred and twenty-six lbs. and measured little more than 5 ft., he was an ardent devotee of the rugged life. He did his exercises every A.M. and refused to send for the Dr. when he had a cold. 3 yrs. after he moved here from Chicago, Ill., the Boys Scouts of America made him an hon-.

Mechanics and Spelling

orary member, & he soon became known in scout circles for the many $ he contributed to the Boy Scout movement. One Sat. afternoon B. forgot to spell out the amount on a check for one-hundred and twenty-five dollars intended for a bldg. drive and payable to the B. S. of A. The treasurer, Bernard Simpson of Arlington, Va., wrote in 2 additional figures, spelled out the changed amount, and left the U.S. after withdrawing B.'s life savings of twelve-thousand five-hundred and fifty dollars from the local bank. "Ah," said Geo. when he found 2$ and 36 cts. left in his account, "if I had only spelled out the No.'s and abbrev.!"

SP 1   Spelling Problems

Improve your spelling by developing good spelling habits.

Merely looking up misspelled words has little long-range effect. The following procedure has a good chance of producing favorable results:

- *Find out which words you tend to misspell.* Make a list of all spelling errors pointed out to you in your themes, quizzes, and exams. Work your way through a list of common spelling demons (such as the one printed under SP 3) and copy those that you have found troublesome in your own writing.

- *Put in twenty minutes three times a week over a period of time.* Unless you work on your spelling regularly, you will make little progress. You cannot unlearn in two or three hours the spelling habits that you developed over many years.

- *Work out a definite routine and stick to it.* At each sitting, take up a group of perhaps ten or twenty spelling words. If you are a "visualizer," place your spelling words before you in clear, legible handwriting. Try putting them on a set of small note cards that you can carry around with you. Run your eyes over each word until you can see both the individual letters and the whole word at the same time. If you learn primarily by ear, read each word aloud. Then spell each letter individually: *Receive*—R-E-C-E-I-V-E. If you learn best when you can bring your nerves and muscles into play, try writing each word in large letters. Trace it over several times.

- *Make use of memory devices like the following:*

MAC got ACquainted.
ALL RIGHT means ALL is RIGHT.
There's an INNING in begINNING.
Don't beLIEve LIEs.
There's a CRITIC in CRITICism.
There's IRON in the envIRONment.
Men who GOVERN are a GOVERNment.
PERhaps he will give a PERfect PERformance.
There's a COG in reCOGnition.
There's a VILLA in VILLAin.

SP 1a   Spelling and Pronunciation   *sp*

Watch for differences between the spoken and the written word.

Some words become spelling problems because the gap between spelling and pronunciation is unusually wide:

(1) Watch for *silent consonants*. Insert the silent consonants in "condem*n*," "de*b*t," "dou*b*t," "foreign," "mor*t*-gage," and "sovereign."

(2) Watch for *vowels occurring in unstressed positions*. *A, e,* and *i* become indistinguishable in the endings *-ate* and *-ite*, *-able* and *-ible*, *-ance* and *-ence*, *-ant* and *-ent*. You can sometimes choose the right ending by associating the word with a closely related one: *definite* (fin*i*sh, def*i*nition) ; *separate* (sep*a*ration) ; *ultimate* (ultim*a*tum) ; *indispensable* (dispens*a*ry) . For many other words no such crutches are available. Watch out for the following:

a: accept*able*, accept*ance*, advis*able*, attend*ance*, attend*ant*, brilli*ant*, perform*ance*

e: consist*ent*, excell*ence*, excell*ent*, exist*ence*, experi*ence*, independ*ent*, persist*ent*, tend*ency*

i: irresist*ible*, plaus*ible*, poss*ible*, suscept*ible*

(3) Watch for *sounds not pronounced* in much nonstandard or informal speech:

accident*a*lly, can*d*idate, Feb*r*uary, gove*r*nment, lib*r*ary, prob*a*bly, quan*t*ity

(4) In unstressed positions, words like *have, can,* or *will* tend to appear in shortened forms. Do not substitute *of* for *have* in combinations like *could have been, might have been, should have been.*

SP 1b   Variant Forms   *sp*

Watch for different forms of the same word.

Some words are confusing because they appear in a variety of forms. Especially confusing are different spellings in variant forms of the *same root word:* "till" but "until," "four" and "fourteen" but "forty," "forward" but "foremost," "nine" and "ninety" but "ninth."

(1) Watch out for spelling differences in pairs of words representing different parts of speech:

> absorb—absorption, advise (v.)—advice (n.), conscience—conscientious, courteous—courtesy, curious—curiosity, dissent—dissension, generous—generosity, genius—ingenious, proceed—procedure, pronounce—pronunciation, renounce—renunciation

(2) Sometimes a confusing change in spelling accompanies a *change in the grammatical form* of the same word. For instance, you "choose" and "lead" in the present, but you "chose" and "led" in the past. Some plural forms cause spelling difficulties: one *man* but several *men,* one *woman* but several *women.* Remember these especially:

Singular:	hero	Negro	potato	tomato	wife
Plural:	heroes	Negroes	potatoes	tomatoes	wives
Singular:	freshman	postman	life	veto	calf
Plural:	freshmen	postmen	lives	vetoes	calves

(3) Be sure to add the *-ed* for *past tense* or *past participle* in words like the following:

> He *used* to come.
> She was supposed to write.
> They were prejudiced (biased).

Note: Your dictionary lists the correct spelling of plural forms that are difficult or unusual. Sometimes it lists two acceptable forms: *buffalos* or *buffaloes, scarfs* or *scarves.*

Mechanics and Spelling

SP 1c   Confusing Pairs   *sp*

Watch for words that sound similar or alike.

Some words need attention because they sound similar but differ in spelling or in meaning. Here is a partial list of these:

Accept:	to *acc*ept a bribe; to find something *acc*eptable; to make an *acc*eptance speech
Except:	everyone *exc*ept Judy; to make an *exc*eption; to *exc*ept (exempt, exclude) present company
Capital:	unused capit*a*l; modern capit*a*lism; the capit*a*l of France; capit*a*l letters
Capitol:	the cupola of the Capit*o*l; remodeling the façade of the Capit*o*l
Cite:	*c*ited for bravery; to *c*ite many different authorities; a *c*itation for reckless driving
Site:	the *s*ite of the new high school (where it is *sit*uated or located)
Council:	the members of the city coun*c*il; Coun*c*ilor Brown
Counsel:	the coun*s*eling staff of the college; camp coun*s*elors
Desert:	he lost his way in the de*s*ert; he de*s*erted his family; he got his just de*s*erts
Dessert:	the dinner did not include a de*ss*ert
Effect:	to *e*ffect (produce, bring about) a change; immediate *e*ffects; an *e*ffective speech
Affect:	it *a*ffected (had an influence on) his grade; he spoke with an *a*ffected (artificial) British accent
Loose:	lo*os*e and fast; lo*os*en your grip
Lose:	win or lo*s*e; a bad lo*s*er
Personal:	a perso*na*l appeal; speak to him perso*na*lly
Personnel:	a perso*nne*l bureau; hire additional perso*nne*l
Presents:	visitors bearing presen*ts*

Presence:	your presen*ce* is requested; presen*ce* of mind
Principal:	his princip*al* (main) argument; the princip*al* of the school
Principle:	princi*ples* (rules, standards) of conduct; the princi*ples* of economics
Quiet:	be qu*iet*; a qu*iet* neighborhood
Quite:	qu*ite* so; not qu*ite*
Than:	bigger th*an* life; more trouble th*an* it is worth
Then:	now and th*en*; until th*en*
There:	here and th*ere*; th*ere* you are; no one was th*ere*
Their:	they lost th*eir* appetite; mental ills and th*eir* cure
To:	go *to* bed; cut *to* pieces; easy *to* do; hard *to* deny
Too:	*too* good to be true; bring your children, *too*
Whether:	*whe*ther good or bad
Weather:	bad *wea*ther; to *wea*ther the storm

Exercises

A. In available dictionaries, check the status of simplified spellings like trave*l*ed, thr*u*, an*e*sthetic, th*o*, catalo*g*, or any others you have encountered.

B. Insert the missing letter in each of the following words: accept___nce, attend___nce, brilli___nt, consist___ncy, defin___te, excell___nt, exist___nce, experi___nce, independ___nt, indispens___ble, occurr___nce, irresist___ble, perform___nce, persist___nt, separ___te, tend___ncy.

C. Look up the plural of *cargo, Eskimo, hoof, mosquito, motto, piano, solo, soprano, wharf, zero.*

Mechanics and Spelling

D. After the number of each sentence, write down the choice that fits the context.

1. Pierre *accepted/excepted* our invitation.

2. The injury *effected/affected* her hearing.

3. The *presence/presents* of heavily armed troops quieted the crowd.

4. The angry teachers shouted down the surprised *principle/principal*.

5. The new rules applied to all *personal/personnel*.

6. He loved the town, but staying *their/there* had become impossible.

7. She cherished the *quiet/quite* moments after the children had left for school.

8. Seymour was *too/to* short-tempered to work in public relations.

9. Anything was better *then/than* going back down the mountain.

10. Three members of the city *council/counsel* had resigned.

SP 2   Spelling Rules

Let a few simple spelling rules help you with common errors.

The purpose of spelling rules is *not* to make English spelling appear more regular than it is but to help you memorize words that follow a common pattern. Spelling rules provide a key to a group of words that you would otherwise have to study individually.

SP 2a   *I* Before *E*

Put i *before* e *except after* c.

Identical sounds are often spelled differently in different words. For instance, *ie* and *ei* often stand for the same sound. If you sort out the words in question, you get the following:

ie: achieve, believe, chief, grief, niece, piece (of pie), relieve
cei: ceiling, conceited, conceive, perceive, receive, receipt

In the second group of words, the *ei* is regularly preceded by *c.* In other words, it is *i* before *e* except after *c.* About half a dozen words do not fit into this pattern:

ei: either, leisure, neither, seize, weird
cie: financier, species

SP 2b   Doubled Consonant   *sp*

Double *a single final consonant before an* added vowel.

In many words a *single final consonant* is doubled before an ending (or **suffix**) that begins with a vowel: *-ed, -er, -est, -ing.* Doubling occurs under the following conditions:

(1) The vowel preceding the final consonant *must be a single vowel.* It cannot be a "long" or double vowel **(diphthong)** indicated in writing by combinations like *oa, ea, ee,* and *ou* or by a silent final *e* (k*i*te, h*o*pe, h*a*te). Note the differences in pronunciation and in spelling in the following pairs:

Mechanics and Spelling

bar—barred	bare—bared
bat—batted	boat—boating
hop—hopping	hope—hoping
plan—planned	plane—planed
red—redder	read—reading
scrap—scrapped	scrape—scraped
slip—slipped	sleep—sleeping
stop—stopped	stoop—stooped

(2) The last syllable before the suffix *must be the one stressed in pronunciation.* Sometimes a shift in stress will be reflected in a difference in the spelling of different forms of the same word. Compare the following groups:

admit, admitted, admittance	edit, edited, editing
forget, forgetting, forgettable	benefit, benefited
begin, beginning, beginner	harden, hardened
overlap, overlapping	prohibit, prohibited, prohibitive
regret, regretted, regrettable	develop, developing
prefer, preferred, preferring	preference, preferable
refer, referred, referring	reference

SP 2c   Y as a Vowel   *sp*

Change y to ie before s.

Y is sometimes used *as a consonant* (year, youth), sometimes *as a vowel* (my, dry; hurry, study). As a single final vowel, it changes to *ie* before *s,* to *i* before all other endings except *-ing.*

ie: family—families, fly—flies, study—studies, try—tries, quantity—quantities *i:* beauty—beautiful, bury—burial, busy—business, copy—copied, dry—drier, lively—livelihood, noisy—noisily

y: burying, copying, studying, trying, worrying

When it follows another vowel, *y* is usually preserved: *delays, joys, played, valleys.* A few common exceptions are *day—daily, gay—gaily, lay—laid, pay—paid, say—said.*

SP 2d   Final *E*   *sp*

Drop the final silent e before an added vowel.

A silent *e* at the end of a word is dropped before an ending that *begins with a vowel;* it is preserved before an ending that begins with a consonant:

bore	boring	boredom
hate	hating	hateful
like	liking, likable	likely
love	loving, lovable	lovely

The following words do *not* fit into this pattern: *argue—argument, due—duly, dye—dyeing* (as against *die—dying*), *mile—mileage, true—truly, whole—wholly.*

Note: A final *e* may signal the difference in pronunciation between the final consonants in *rag* and *rage* or in *aspic* and *notice.* Such a final *e* is preserved not only before a consonant but also before *a* or *o:*

ge: advantage—advantageous, change—changeable, courage—courageous, outrage—outrageous

ce: notice—noticeable, peace—peaceable

Exercises

A. Insert *ei* or *ie:* ach__vement, bel__ver, dec__tful, f__ld, inconc__vable, misch__f, perc__ve, rec__ving, rel__f, s__ze, w__rd, y__ld.

B. Select the appropriate word in each of the numbered pairs: *(1) bared/ (2) barred* from office; his *(3) bating/ (4) batting* average; *(5) caned/ (6) canned* meat; *(7) biding/ (8) bidding* their time; *(9) hoping/ (10) hopping* for the best; *(11) pined/ (12) pinned* to the mat; a *(13) well-planed/ (14) well-planned* outing; *(15) robed/ (16) robbed* in white; a boy *(17) spiting/ (18) spitting* his parents; *(19) taped/ (20) tapped* him on the shoulder.

C. Combine the following words with the suggested endings: accompany__ed, advantage__ous, argue__ing, benefit__ed, carry__s, come__ing, confide__ing, differ__ing, excite__able, friendly__ness, lively__hood, occur__ing, prefer__ed, remit__ance, sad__er, satisfy__ed, shine__ing, sole__ly, study__ing, tragedy__s, try__s, use__ing, valley__s, whole__ly, write__ing.

SP 3   Words Often Misspelled   *sp*

Watch for words frequently misspelled.

The following are among the words most frequently misspelled in student writing. Take up a group of twenty or twenty-five at a time:

Words Often Misspelled

absence	analysis	beneficial
abundance	analyze	benefited
accessible	annual	boundaries
accidentally	anticipate	breath
acclaim	anxiety	brilliant
accommodate	apologize	Britain
accompanied	apology	buses
accomplish	apparatus	business
accumulate	apparent	calendar
accurately	appearance	candidate
accuses	applies	career
accustom	applying	careless
achievement	appreciate	carrying
acknowledgment	approach	category
acquaintance	appropriate	ceiling
acquire	approximately	cemetery
acquitted	area	challenge
across	argue	changeable
actuality	arguing	character
address	argument	characteristic
adequate	arising	chief
admit	arrangement	choose
adolescence	article	chose
advantageous	artistically	clothes
advertisement	ascend	coarse
afraid	assent	column
against	athlete	comfortable
aggravate	athletic	comfortably
aggressive	attendance	coming
alleviate	audience	commission
allotted	authority	committed
allowed	balance	committee
all right	basically	companies
already	basis	competition
altar	beauty	competitive
altogether	becoming	completely
always	before	comprehension
amateur	beginning	conceivable
among	belief	conceive
amount	believe	concentrate

Mechanics and Spelling

condemn
confident
confidential
conscience
conscientious
conscious
considerably
consistent
continually
continuous
control
controlled
convenience
convenient
coolly
courageous
course
courteous
criticism
criticize
cruelty
curiosity
curriculum
dealt
deceit
deceive
decision
definite
definitely
definition
dependent
describe
description
desirability
desirable
despair
desperate
destruction
devastate
develop

development
device
difference
different
difficult
dilemma
dining
disappear
disappearance
disappoint
disastrous
discipline
disease
disgusted
dissatisfaction
dissatisfied
doesn't
dominant
due
during
ecstasy
efficiency
efficient
eighth
eliminate
embarrass
embarrassment
eminent
emphasize
endeavor
enforce
enough
entertain
environment
equipped
erroneous
especially
etc.
exaggerate
excellent

exceptionally
exercise
exhaust
exhilarate
existence
experience
explanation
extraordinary
extremely
familiar
families
fascinate
finally
financial
financier
foreign
forward
friend
fulfill
fundamentally
further
gaiety
generally
genius
government
governor
grammar
guaranteed
guidance
happily
happiness
height
heroes
heroine
hindrance
hopeful
huge
humorous
hundred
hurriedly

Words Often Misspelled

hypocrisy	meant	persuade
hypocrite	medieval	pertain
ignorant	merely	phase
imaginary	mileage	phenomenon
imagination	miniature	philosophy
immediately	minute	physical
immensely	mischievous	piece
incidentally	muscle	pleasant
indefinite	mysterious	possess
independent	naïve	possession
indispensable	necessarily	possible
inevitable	necessary	practical
influence	ninety	precede
ingenious	noticeable	prejudice
intellectual	obstacle	prepare
intelligence	occasion	prevalent
interest	occasionally	privilege
interpret	occurred	probably
interrupt	occurrence	procedure
involve	omit	proceed
irrelevant	operate	professor
irresistible	opinion	prominent
itself	opponent	propaganda
jealous	opportunity	prophecy
knowledge	optimism	psychology
laboratory	original	pursue
laid	paid	quantity
leisure	parallel	really
likelihood	paralysis	recommend
literature	paralyze	regard
livelihood	particularly	relief
loneliness	passed	relieve
losing	past	religion
magnificence	peace	repetition
maintain	peculiar	representative
maintenance	perceive	resource
manageable	perform	response
manufacturer	performance	rhythm
marriage	permanent	ridiculous
mathematics	persistent	roommate

Mechanics and Spelling

safety	strength	tragedy
satisfactorily	stretch	transferred
schedule	strictly	tries
seize	studying	undoubtedly
sense	subtle	unnecessary
separate	succeed	useful
sergeant	successful	using
shining	summarize	various
significance	surprise	vengeance
similar	temperament	villain
sincerely	tendency	weird
sophomore	therefore	writing
speech	thorough	
sponsor	together	

SP 4   The Apostrophe

Use the apostrophe for contractions and possessives.

The **apostrophe** has no exact equivalent in speech and is therefore easily omitted or misplaced.

SP 4a   Contractions   *ap*

Use the apostrophe in informal contracted forms.

Use the apostrophe to show that one or more letters have been omitted (*I'll* go now; *I'm* too tired; *we're* almost ready). It appears most frequently in contractions using a shortened form of *not: haven't, can't, wouldn't, won't, isn't.* Take care not to misspell *doesn't,* which is a shortened form of *"does* not."

Remember: *It's,* meaning "it is," differs from *its,* meaning "of it" or "belonging to it." *Who's* meaning "who is," differs from *whose,* which means "of whom" or "of which." *They're* means "they are" and differs from both *there* and *their:*

> *It's* time to give the cat *its* milk.
> *Who's* to say *whose* fault it is?
> If *their* lights are turned off, *they're* not *there.*

Note: Contractions are characteristic of informal conversation. Avoid them in formal reports, research papers, and letters of application. Some readers approve of contractions only in distinctly informal writing.

SP 4b   Possessives

Use the apostrophe for the possessive of nouns.

The **possessive** is usually produced by adding an apostrophe plus *s* to the plain form of a noun: *my sister's purse, Mr. Smith's garage, the student's notebook.* Often the possessive shows where something belongs, or who owns an article. But it also shows many other relationships: *the boy's friends, the firemen's ball, a man's world, the child's innocence, the children's capers, the general's dismissal.* Possessives occur in many familiar expressions: *an hour's drive, the day's news, a moment's notice, a dollar's worth, tonight's paper.*

Note the following variations:

(1) Sometimes the plain form of a noun already ends in *s.* The possessive is then formed by adding an apostrophe

Mechanics and Spelling

only. This applies especially to plural forms. Compare the following pairs:

the Turk's wives (one Turk) the Turks' wives (several Turks)

a week's pay two weeks' pay

Names of individuals do not always follow this rule. The writer may or may not add a second *s*, depending on whether he would expect an extra syllable in pronunciation: *Mr. Jones' car—Mr. Jones's car; Dolores' hair—Dolores's hair; Charles Dickens' first novel—Charles Dickens's first novel*.

(2) The apostrophe is *not* used in the *possessive forms of personal pronouns*. No apostrophe appears in *his, hers, its, ours, yours,* or *theirs*. It does appear, however, in the possessive forms of such indefinite pronouns as *one* (one's friends), *everyone* (to everyone's surprise), *someone* (at someone's suggestion; also, at someone else's house).

SP 4c Plurals of Letters and Symbols *ap*

Use the apostrophe in special situations.

Use the apostrophe to separate the plural *s* from the name of a letter or a symbol or from a word named as a word (two large 7's; if's and but's):

Those great big beautiful A's so avidly sought, those little miserly C's so often found, were meant for another time and another student body.—Oscar Handlin, "Are the Colleges Killing Education?" *Atlantic*

Exercise

Check for appropriate use of the apostrophe in choosing between the spellings in each of the following pairs.

1. When the mother and the father respect each *(1) other's/ (2) others'* opinions, children learn to live harmoniously by following their *(3) elders/ (4) elders'* example.

2. Since the *(5) chairmans/ (6) chairman's* resignation, the *(7) members/ (8) member's* have been speculating about *(9) whose/ (10) who's* going to succeed him.

3. *(11) Mrs. Beattys/ (12) Mrs. Beatty's* husband still sends her *(13) flowers/ (14) flower's* on *(15) Valentines/ (16) Valentine's* Day.

4. We were all overjoyed when my *(17) sister's/ (18) sisters'* baby took *(19) its/ (20) it's* first faltering steps.

5. A *(21) student's/ (22) students'* lack of interest is not always the *(23) teachers/ (24) teacher's* fault.

6. *(25) Its/ (26) It's* the *(27) parents/ (28) parents'* responsibility to provide for their *(29) children's/ (30) childrens'* religious education.

7. *(31) Lets/ (32) Let's* borrow *(33) someones/ (34) someone's* car and go for an *(35) hour's/ (36) hours'* drive.

8. *(37) Charles/ (38) Charles's* father murmured audibly that the assembled *(39) relatives/ (40) relative's* had consumed at least ten *(41) dollars/ (42) dollars'* worth of food.

SP 5 The Hyphen

Use the hyphen where required by current practice.

Use of the **hyphen** is the least uniform and the least stable feature of English spelling. In doubtful cases, the most recent edition of a reputable dictionary is the best available guide.

SP 5a Compound Words

Know which compound words require a hyphen.

Treatment varies for words habitually used together as a single expression. Some compound words are clearly distinguished from ordinary combinations by differences in both writing and pronunciation: *black bird* (black BIRD) but *blackbird* (BLACKbird), *dark room* (dark ROOM) but *darkroom* (DARKroom). Such unmistakable compounds are *bellboy, bridesmaid, headache, highway, newsstand, summertime,* and *stepmother.* In many similar compounds, however, the parts are conventionally kept separate: *commander in chief, goose flesh, high school, labor union, second cousin.* Still other compound words conventionally require a hyphen:

able-bodied, bull's-eye, cave-in, great-grandfather, merry-go-round, mother-in-law.

Note: Be sure to spell *today, tomorrow, nevertheless,* and *nowadays* as single words. Be sure *not* to spell as single words *all right, a lot* (a lot of time), *be able,* and *no one.*

SP 5b   Prefixes   *hyp*

Know which prefixes require a hyphen.

Many hyphenated compounds consist of a prefix and the word it precedes:

(1) *All-, ex-* (in the sense of "former"), *quasi-, self-,* and sometimes *co-* require a hyphen: *all-knowing, ex-husband, quasi-judicial, self-contained, co-author.*

(2) All prefixes require a hyphen before words beginning with a capital letter: *all-American, anti-American, pro-American, un-American.*

(3) Often a hyphen prevents the meeting of two identical vowels: *anti-intellectual, semi-independent.*

Note: Sometimes a hyphen distinguishes an unfamiliar use of a prefix from a familiar one: *recover—re-cover* (make a new cover), *recreation—re-creation* (creating again or anew).

SP 5c   Group Modifiers   *hyp*

Use the hyphen with group modifiers.

Several words may temporarily combine as a modifier preceding a noun. They are then usually joined to each other by hyphens: *a flying-saucer hat, a middle-of-the-road policy, a question-and-answer period, a step-by-step account, a devil-may-care attitude.* No hyphens are used when the same combinations serve some other function in a sentence: *tend toward the middle of the road; explain a process step by step.*

Note: No hyphen is used when a modifier preceding a noun is in turn modified by an adverb ending in *-ly: a fast-*

rising executive, a well-balanced account; but *a rapidly growing city, a carefully documented study.*

Exercise

Insert hyphens or combine elements where appropriate.

1. The prospective son in law listened self consciously to Mother's praise of the bride to be.

2. Those who denounced the parking privileges for out of town students were obviously not from out of town.

3. Both pro British and anti British Arabs were united in their contempt for ex king Farouk.

4. The anti intellectual local news paper had called our candidate an absent minded ex professor and a tool of the labor unions; never the less he was elected.

5. Now a days few self respecting candidates conduct old fashioned campaigns taking them into out of the way places.

6. Mr. Andrews and his co author have written a well documented account of the un democratic procedures followed by quasi judicial agencies.

SP 6   Capitals

Capitalize words as required by standard practice.

Although practice varies on minor points, certain conventions of capitalization are widely observed.

SP 6a   Proper Names   *cap*

Capitalize proper names.

Proper names are always capitalized. Capitalize the names of persons, places, regions, historical periods, ships, days of the week, months (but not seasons), organizations, religions: *James, Brazil, the Middle Ages, S.S. Independence, Sunday, February, Buddhism.* Capitalize words derived from proper names: *English grammar, French pastry, German beer, Parisian fashions, Christian charity, Marxist ideas.*

Note the following:

(1) In some words the proper name involved has been lost sight of, and a lower-case letter is used: *guinea pig, india rubber, pasteurized milk.*

(2) The same word may serve as a general term but also as a proper name for one person, institution, or place:

democratic (many institutions)	Democratic (name of the party)
orthodox (many attitudes)	Orthodox (name of the church)
history (general subject)	History 31 (specific course)
west (general direction)	Middle West (specific area)
my mother (common relationship)	Mother (name of the person)

(3) The general term for a title, a family relationship, an institution, or a geographical feature is capitalized when it combines with a proper name: *Major Brown, Aunt Augusta, Sergeant Barnacle, Campbell High School, Indiana University, Tennessee Valley Authority, Medora Heights, Lake Erie.* Some titles refer to only one person and can take

the place of the person's name: *the Pope, the Queen* (of England), *the President* (of the United States).

SP 6b Titles of Publications

cap

Capitalize major words in titles.

A capital letter marks the first and all major words in the title of a book, other publication, or work of art. The only words not counting as major are articles (*a, an,* and *the*), prepositions (*at, in, on, of, from, with*), and connectives (*and, but, if, when*). Prepositions and connectives are usually capitalized when they have five or more letters. Observe these conventions in writing the titles of a theme:

> Goalie Without a Mask
> Travels with a Friend Through Suburbia
> How to Lose Friends and Become a Public Enemy

The same conventions apply to titles of publications cited in a sentence:

Several generations of Americans read *Sink or Swim, Phil the Fiddler, Mark the Match Boy,* and *From Canal Boy to President,* records of achievement which rewarded personal goodness with happiness and goods.—Saul Bellow, "The Writer as Moralist," *Atlantic*

Exercise

Assume you are working as an editor of a newsmagazine. Which of the words in the following sentences should be capital-

ized? After the number of each sentence, write down and capitalize all such words.

1. A yale graduate, baird worked at chase manhattan and smith
   barney & co.

2. Pistol shots crackled in dearborn, the detroit suburb that is
   home to the ford motor company's sprawling river rouge
   plant.

3. Last october, a huge and very ugly statue of sir winston
   churchill was unveiled in parliament square, london.

4. As he was helped aboard, egyptian mohammed aly clutched a
   small blue-bound koran that had been given to him by the
   arab mayor of hebron.

5. The sprawling city of canton, 110 miles by rail from hong
   kong, has for centuries been china's principal gathering place
   for asian and european traders.

6. The american tourist cashing her traveler's check at tokyo's
   hotel okura got a bundle of good news.

7. Last week 3,500 delegates met in manhattan to celebrate the
   centennial of the union of american hebrew congregations,
   founded in cincinnati by rabbi isaac wise in 1873.

8. At columbia and barnard, at atlanta's morehouse college and
   the university of virginia, economics was suddenly the subject to take.

9. In january, the university of oregon announced a new course
   called "can man survive?"

10. Like other newspapers, the new york journal-american had
    learned the art of catering to the irish catholics.

7

Punctuation

For Quick Reference

When we speak, we do more than put the right words together in the right order. We pause at the right times, raise our voices for emphasis. To the structures and forms of the written sentence, speech adds **intonation:** differences in timing, pitch, and stress that make our words mean what we want them to mean. When writing, we use punctuation marks for similar purposes.

Punctuation marks may separate groups of words from each other. They may establish different kinds of connection between them. For instance, punctuation may show two closely related groups of words to be a general statement followed by detailed explanation:

> The room was full of noisy men: ranchers, merchants, and lawyers.

It may show them to be an important statement followed by incidental additional information:

> Richard inherited his uncle's estate, which had been in the family since 1632.

The following chapter surveys the relations within a sentence (and between sentences) that are conventionally signaled by punctuation.

P 1   End Punctuation

> *Use end punctuation to put a stop to an utterance that is grammatically complete.*

Utterances terminated by end punctuation may have to become part of a narrative or argument before their full

PUNCTUATION MARKS
Reference Chart

meaning becomes clear. They do not need anything before them or after them to be complete as far as *grammatical structure* is concerned.

P 1a   Exclamations and Questions   *!/?/*

> *Indicate exclamations and questions by adding the appropriate marks.*

Use the exclamation mark to give an utterance *unusual emphasis*. Such utterances range from a groan, curse, or shout to an order or a command. The **exclamation mark** can signal excitement, insistence, surprise, indignation, or fear:

> Ouch!
> Silence! Get up! Close the book!
> He loves me!
> And this man wants to be President!

Use the question mark whenever an utterance is worded *as request for information*. Whenever you raise your voice inquiringly at the end of something you say, you should terminate the written equivalent with a **question mark** (*He sent you a check?*). Not all questions, however, are marked by intonation.

> Who are you?
> What did he want?

Do not forget to use question marks at the end of questions that are long or involved:

How is the student who enters college as a freshman supposed to find her way through the maze of instructions and regulations printed in small print in the college catalog?

P 1b Sentences and Sentence Fragments   *frag*

Use the period at the end of a simple statement.

In formal writing, the units separated by **periods** are grammatically self-contained; they are complete sentences. Guard against using a period to set off a unit that is not a complete sentence but merely a **sentence fragment.** Guard against omitting the period between two complete sentences, thus producing a **fused sentence:**

Complete: He is gone. *He left for Alaska.*

Fragment: He left yesterday. *For Alaska.*

Fused: You won't find him *he left for Alaska.*

It used to be thought that sentence fragments result from a breakdown in grammar or in logic. Actually, most fragments merely transfer to the written page patterns that are acceptable in speech but *unconventional* in writing. The type of sentence fragment most common in student writing results when an afterthought is added to the main statement. After making a statement (*I left home*), a writer may add an explanation (*To go to college*). He may make a statement (*These are my relatives*) and add a comment (*A fine group of people*).

Grammatically, such fragments are of several common types:

Appositives: A great man. My history teacher. Carts loaded with fruit.

Adjectives, Adverbs:	Beautiful in the morning sun. Carelessly as usual.
Prepositional Phrases:	For the last time. With great trepidation. On behalf of the management.
Verbals, Verbal Phrases:	Leaving the car behind. Other things being equal.
Dependent Clauses:	Because I did not study. Though nobody replied. Which came far too late.

Do the following to eliminate sentence fragments:

(1) Many fragments can be joined to the main statement either *without any punctuation* at all (*I left home to go to college*) or by a comma (*These are my relatives, a fine group of people*). Whenever a fragment is pointed out to you, try first to connect it with the main idea in such a way that the sentence flows smoothly, without interruption. (See P 2–4 for situations where a comma would be required.)

Fragment:	Be sure to be there. *At seven o'clock.*
Revised:	Be sure to be there *at seven o'clock.*
Fragment:	He bought a used car. *In spite of my warnings.*
Revised:	He bought a used car *in spite of my warnings.*

(2) To show a *definite break in thought,* use a **dash** instead of a period. (See also P 5a.)

These are my relatives—*a motley crew.*

He would close his eyes and talk into the dictaphone—*a strange way to write an English theme.*

(3) To link *an explanatory afterthought to* the preceding statement, use a colon or a common transitional ex-

pression. The **colon** serves to introduce a *list or description* of something that has already been mentioned in a more general way:

> We have two excellent players this year: *Phil and Tom.*
>
> She served an old-fashioned breakfast: *fishballs, brown bread, and baked beans.*
>
> Your friend lacks an essential quality: *tact.*

Explanations or examples added to a complete statement are often introduced by expressions like *especially, such as, namely,* or *for example.* When they introduce material that is not a complete sentence, these expressions are usually preceded by a **comma:**

> He took several courses in the humanities, *such as French Literature and Elementary Logic.*
>
> Plato and Aristotle wrote in the same language, *namely Greek.*

In formal usage, another comma often keeps *namely, for example, for instance,* and *that is* separate from what they introduce:

> Professor Miller objected to my system of punctuating, for example, my use of dashes.

(4) If the fragment cannot become part of the preceding statement, you may have to develop the material it contains into *a complete sentence:*

Fragment: He appealed to a higher court. *Being a futile effort.*
Revised: He appealed to a higher court. *The effort was futile.*

P 1c Permissible Nonsentences

frag

Recognize intentional fragments used for special effects.

Permissible fragments are common in speech and are used in writing for special effects. Experienced writers use permissible fragments, better called **nonsentences,** for special purposes. The following examples illustrate the most common of these:

(1) *Common transitional expressions:*

So much for past developments. *Now for* a look at our present problems.

(2) *Answers to questions,* suggesting the give-and-take of conversation or the rhetorical question-and-answer technique of the orator:

What did we gain? *Nothing.*

(3) *Descriptive passages,* especially when designed to give a static, pictorial effect:

We stood in the hot dry night air at one in the morning, waiting for a train at an Arizona station. *Nothing but the purple arc of sky and at the end of the platform the silhouette of a cottonwood tree lapped by a hot breeze. The stars big as sunflowers.*—Alistair Cooke, *One Man's America*

(4) In narrative, *passages suggesting random, disconnected thought:*

Fifty dollars to Dorothy's piano teacher. His sister. Another plain girl. She might as well learn how to play the piano.—Irwin Shaw, "Main Currents of American Thought"

There he is: the brother. *Image of him. Haunting face.*—James Joyce, *Ulysses*

(5) Afterthoughts deliberately delayed for *ironic effect:*

Man is the only animal that blushes. *Or needs to.* (Mark Twain)

Many teachers discourage their students from experimenting with such incomplete sentences.

Exercises

A. In which of the following passages is the second unit a sentence fragment? Write *frag* after the number of each such passage. In which of the following passages is the second unit a complete separate sentence? Write *S* for satisfactory after the number.

1. I was standing in the orchestra pit. Looking up at the scarred stage.
2. Christmas time in prison is a sad time. Grimy walls like any other time of the year.
3. The cry for law and order has changed nothing. Crimes are still as gruesome and numerous as before.
4. Americans were considered materialists. Interested only in money.
5. The story begins like a typical short story. A story about a small town having a drawing once a year.
6. The smart students bragged about their grades. The athletic stars treated other people as inferiors.

7. A regulation target resembles an upside-down saucer. Measuring no more than five inches in diameter.

8. She simply could not satisfy anybody's standards. Not those of her superiors and not those of her co-workers.

9. The ocean has always beckoned to man. Daring him to risk all to sail the seas.

10. Felipe has never washed a dish in his life. He does not mind cooking.

11. Men once had clearly defined roles. Hunting and fishing.

12. We made our way to the station in a blizzard. Only to find the train already gone.

13. One woman was a female jockey. The other woman interviewed was a commercial pilot.

14. The supposedly kidnapped youngster was sitting next to the shed. Happy as a bird.

15. They were studying the marvels of Indian architecture. Such as Aztec pyramids and Mayan temples.

B. How would you revise punctuation in each of the following?

1. We tried a new sales technique. With good results.

2. What good does it do to kill a person for taking someone else's life.

3. He was attacking his favorite target. Public money for private schools.

4. American schools are neglecting the major languages of the modern world. Especially Russian and Chinese.

5. When will people realize that the resources of this planet are not inexhaustible.

6. Her favorite authors were always experimenting with impossible new ideas. For example, robots with human emotions.

7. In the old sentimental stories, the desperate unwed mother would leave her child on soneone's doorstep. In a wicker basket.

8. The prime suspect had spent the evening conducting a symphony orchestra. A perfect alibi.

9. He began to consider the unthinkable. Turning himself in.

10. She left school after two years. To take over her father's business.

P 2 Linking Punctuation

Use commas or semicolons as required when several clauses combine in a larger sentence.

Several short statements may combine to become part of a larger sentence. We call each "sub-sentence" in the new combined sentence a **clause.** Independent clauses are still self-contained. They could easily be separated again by a period. However, dependent clauses have been linked in a more permanent way. They would sound incomplete if separated from the main clause. (See P 3a for noun clauses. See P 3b for relative clauses.)

P 2a Comma Splice CS

Use the semicolon between complete sentences that are closely related.

A **semicolon** may replace the period between two complete sentences. Often two statements go together as related pieces of information, develop the same mood or point of view, or line up related ideas for contrast. When a semicolon replaces the period between two such statements, the first word of the second statement is *not* capitalized:

Sunshine was everywhere; orchards were in bloom.

Some librarians circulate books; others hoard them.

The Queen is not allowed to wear a crown; nothing less than a halo will suffice.—Kingsley Martin, "Strange Interlude," *Atlantic*

Do not use a comma alone to join two clauses. Notice that there is no grammatical link between the two clauses in each of the above pairs. The clauses remain "independent." A **comma splice** runs on from one independent clause to the next with only a comma to keep them apart:

Comma Splice:	The doctor looked worn, he had stayed up all night.
Revised:	The doctor looked worn; he had stayed up all night.

Note the following exceptions to the traditional rule against the comma splice:

(1) Commas may appear between the independent clauses in a sentence composed of *three or more parallel clauses.* Note that the clauses in the following examples are closely related in meaning and similar in structure:

Be brief, be blunt, be gone.

Students in India demonstrate against the use of English, Vietnamese reformers protest against the use of French, young Israelis have no use for the languages once spoken by their parents.

(2) Some of the best modern writers use the comma between *two* clauses when the logical connection or similarity in structure is especially close. For instance, there may be a close *cause-and-effect* relationship, or a *carefully balanced contrast:*

The fire was dead, the ship was gone.—William Golding, *Lord of the Flies*

Rage cannot be hidden, it can only be dissembled.—James Baldwin, *Notes of a Native Son*

Today Kleist gives pleasure, most of Goethe is a classroom bore.—Susan Sontag, *Against Interpretation*

Conservative teachers and editors consider this practice careless or, at best, informal.

Note: Never merely juxtapose two independent clauses without any punctuation. A **fused sentence** results when two such clauses are simply run together without a connective:

Fused: I am not sick or anything I just like to sit in a chair and think.

Revised: I am not sick; I just like to sit in a chair and think.

P 2b   Coordinating Connectives   ,/

Use a comma when a "coordinator" links two clauses.

Coordinating connectives typically require a comma. *And, but, for, or, nor, so,* and *yet* link two clauses without making the one more important than the other. They are typically preceded by a **comma:**

The bell finally rang, *and* George rushed out of the room.
She saw me, *but* she did not recognize me.
We went inside, *for* it had started to rain.
You had better apologize, *or* she will not speak to you again.

Notice the reversal of subject and verb after *nor:*

We cannot through the courts force parents to be kind, *nor can we force* men to be wise by the pressure of committees.—Dan Lacy, "Obscenity and Censorship," *The Christian Century*

Do not use the comma with these connectives when they merely join two words or two phrases (came in *and* sat down, tired *but* happy, for cash *or* on credit) .

Notice the following variations:

(1) *And, but,* and *or* are often used without a comma *when the clauses they join are short. Yet* and *so* are often used with a **semicolon:**

> The wind was blowing *and* the water was cold.
>
> The critics praised Oliver's work; *yet* no one bought his paintings.

(2) Any coordinating connective may be used with a semicolon, especially if the connective joins *clauses that already contain commas* or that are unusually long:

> Previously the river has always been accompanied by mountains near or far; *but* they lay generally parallel to its course. Now in the Big Bend the river encounters mountains in a new and extraordinary way; *for* they lie, chain after chain of them, directly across its way.—Paul Horgan, "Pages from a Rio Grande Notebook," *New York Times Book Review*

Note: Coordinating connectives leave the clauses they join self-sufficient or independent grammatically. Thus, the clauses they connect may still be kept separate from each other by a **period:**

> I called your office twice. *But* nobody answered. *So* I left without you.

P 2c   Adverbial Connectives   ; /

Use a semicolon with adverbial connectives.

Adverbial connectives are *therefore, consequently, hence, accordingly, moreover, furthermore, besides, however, nevertheless, indeed,* and *in fact.* The two statements they join are often linked by a **semicolon** rather than by a period. A period, nevertheless, would still be possible and acceptable.

> Business was improving; *therefore,* we changed our plans.
>
> Business was improving. *Therefore,* we changed our plans.
>
> The hall was nearly empty; *nevertheless,* the curtain rose on time.
>
> The hall was nearly empty. *Nevertheless,* the curtain rose on time.

Notice the following points:

(1) If a comma replaces the semicolon, the sentence turns into a comma splice:

Comma Splice: French Canadians insist on preserving their language, therefore federal employees are being taught French.

Revised: French Canadians insist on preserving their language; therefore, federal employees are being taught French.

(2) The adverbial connective need not be placed at the point where the first statement ends and the second begins. The *semicolon appears at the point where the two statements join,* regardless of the position of the connective:

> Attendance is compulsory; *therefore,* the students have no choice.

Attendance is compulsory; the students, *therefore,* have no choice.

Attendance is compulsory; the students have no choice, *therefore.*

You can use this possible shift in position to identify members of this group. They share their freedom of movement with adverbs (and are therefore called *"adverbial* connectives" or "connective *adverbs")* .

(3) Adverbial connectives are often *set off from the rest of the second statement* by **commas,** as in the examples already given. You then have to make sure that there is a punctuation mark both before and after the connective:

Formal: The food, *however,* was impossible.

Note: Informal and journalistic writing tend toward **open punctuation,** using fewer commas than formal writing does. Accordingly, the authors of popular books and magazine articles tend not to separate adverbial connectives from the rest of a clause.

P 2d   Subordinating Connectives $\mathcal{P}$

Use commas or no punctuation as required with "subordinators."

Subordinating connectives normally introduce adverbial clauses, which tell us something about the circumstances of the action or event described in the main part of the sentence. *When, whenever, while, before, after, since, until, as long as,* and *where* introduce information about time and place. *Because, if, provided,* and *unless* introduce reasons or conditions.

An *if* or a *because* changes a self-sufficient, independent clause into a **dependent clause,** which normally cannot stand by itself. "If I were a boy" does not become a complete sentence until you answer the question "If you were a boy, then what?" Beware of dependent clauses added to a main statement as an afterthought:

Fragment: He failed the test. *Because he did not study.*

Revised: He failed the test *because he did not study.*

Observe the following guidelines:

(1) *Do not separate restrictive adverbial clauses from the rest of the sentence.* Adverbial clauses usually restrict or qualify in a significant way the meaning of the clause to which they are joined. Suppose a father tells his son, "I'll raise your allowance *after I strike oil.*" Without the proviso about striking oil, the sentence would sound like an immediate promise of more money. With the proviso, it means that the son will get more money only by a remote chance. When they *follow* the main clause, such **restrictive** clauses are not set off by punctuation:

> I consulted my notes *before I spoke.*
> Do not sign anything *until you hear from me.*
> We cannot keep you on the team *unless you improve.*

Occasionally, the *time, place, or condition for an action or event is already indicated in the main clause.* In that case, the dependent clause may merely *elaborate* on the information already given. Such dependent clauses are called **nonrestrictive.** They are separated from the main clause by a **comma:**

> Bats were well developed *as far back as the Eocene, when man's ancestors were still in the trees.*

He was born *in California, where one can pick oranges during the Christmas holidays.*

(2) *Though, although,* and *whereas* usually introduce nonrestrictive material and as a result require a **comma.** Rather than adding essential qualification, these words establish a *contrast* between the statements they connect.

I like the work, *though the salary is low.*

Her friend wore a sports shirt and slacks, *whereas the other men wore tuxedos.*

Combinations like *whether or not* and *no matter how* indicate that the main statement is true *regardless* of possibilities mentioned in the dependent clause:

We are canceling the lease, *whether you like it or not.*
She will never forgive you, *no matter what you do.*

Some subordinating connectives introduce either restrictive or nonrestrictive material, depending on the meaning of the sentence:

Why are you going to town?
I am going to town *because I want to do some shopping.*
(The reason for your trip is the essential part of the sentence.)

What are you going to do?
I am going to town, because I want to do some shopping.
(The reason for your trip is added, nonrestrictive explanation.)

(3) *Set off an adverbial clause that precedes the main clause.* With a subordinating connective, you can reverse the order of the two statements which it joins. After an

introductory adverbial clause, a **comma** normally indicates where the main clause starts:

> Vote for me *if you trust me.*
> *If you trust me,* vote for me.
>
> I drove more slowly *after I noticed the police car.*
> *After I noticed the police car,* I drove more slowly.

Note: Some connectives belong to different groups of connectives depending on their meaning in the sentence. *However* is normally an adverbial connective and requires a semicolon. It sometimes takes the place of the subordinating connective *no matter* how and requires a comma:

> I cannot please him; *however, I am trying hard.*
> I cannot please him, *however hard I try.*

Though, normally a subordinating connective, is often used in informal English as an adverbial connective placed in the middle or at the end of a clause:

> I felt entitled to more freedom; *my parents, though, didn't agree with me.*

Exercises

A. Each of the following sentences consists of two independent clauses. In each case, the two clauses simply stand next to each other, without a connective. Write down the last word of the first clause and the first word of the second, with a semicolon to join them.

Example: Despair is a living death we are physically alive but
spiritually dead. (Answer) death; we

1. A pawnshop is on the ground floor above it is a hotel.

2. The old man has stepped out of the lobby he's walking down the street.

3. It must be the lunch hour I see secretaries everywhere eating their sandwiches.

4. People were shouting ridiculous commands everyone with a flashlight began directing traffic.

5. The building has two stories there are two big display windows on the ground floor.

6. My sister pranced into the room she started to tease me.

7. Poverty is a major problem in our world it is found in every city in the United States.

8. The church is usually completely quiet a few people come in to pray.

9. John wasn't going to school anymore he was a photographer.

10. Her hair was very neat every strand was in place.

11. I entered the office it was a very modern one with plants around the room.

12. We were once urged to buy and spend urgent messages to conserve are now coming at us from all directions.

13. This job was the most important thing in his life it was his chance to make it into the big time.

14. We fished in the stream until midnight it was illegal really to fish after dark.

15. She had just come out of the movie theater her face showed her satisfaction.

B. What kind of connective links the two clauses in each of the following sentences? What punctuation, if any, should there be between the two clauses? After the number of the sentence, write *C* for comma, *S* for semicolon, or *No* for no punctuation.

Punctuation

1. Her father doesn't pressure her about getting married _____ in fact, he wants her to finish college first.

2. He wasn't a big-time photographer _____ but he had enough work to keep up his studio.

3. Her false eyelashes were very long _____ and her lips were painted a bright red.

4. Before we knew it _____ the party was over.

5. Some store clerks had the disgusting habit of waiting on whites before blacks _____ no matter how long the blacks had been waiting for service.

6. Man could not survive on other planets _____ unless he created an artificial earthlike atmosphere.

7. Lawmakers must rid the country of crime _____ before it reaches epidemic proportions.

8. My father fought with Pancho Villa _____ he was, in fact, the only private in Villa's army.

9. My friends were the sons of captains or colonels _____ though a few fathers were admittedly mere sergeants and corporals.

10. Jobs were scarce and insecure _____ so my parents left town.

11. Many Spanish-speaking Americans call themselves Mexican-Americans _____ some parts of New Spain, however, were never a part of Mexico.

12. The whole crowd in the theater cheered _____ when the cavalry came to the rescue at the end of the movie.

13. When meteors hit the surface _____ they form craters like those made by volcanoes.

14. My parents never became thoroughly Americanized _____ but they had also become strangers in their native land.

15. Space exploration is incredibly expensive _____ therefore only a few of the richest nations take part.

C. Explain the use of punctuation marks in the following passage. Which adverbial clauses are *restrictive*? Which are *non-restrictive*?

English and French were widely used in Africa until most African nations became independent. Now these countries are trying to assert their linguistic independence, although their people often speak several mutually incomprehensible native tongues. After the Belgians left the Congo, names like Leopoldville and Stanleyville disappeared. Swahili could become an official language in much of East Africa if linguistic minorities were willing to accept it. Similar developments accompanied the passing of colonialism in the Far East, where Batavia turned into Jakarta many years ago. A Malaysian city recently changed its name from Jesselton to Kinabalu, because Jesselton had been named for a British empire-builder.

P 3 Punctuating Modifiers

*Distinguish between modifiers set off by
commas and those requiring no punctuation.*

Often nouns and verbs are accompanied by further material that develops, embroiders, or modifies the meaning they convey. Such material is punctuated in accordance with its function and importance in the sentence.

P 3a Unnecessary Commas   *no,*

*Unless other material intervenes, do not use
punctuation between basic elements of a sentence.*

Do not put a comma between a subject and its verb, between verb and complement, or between the two or three basic elements and the various phrases added to the sentence to describe circumstances, reasons, or conditions:

Andrea	studies	her textbooks	in bed.
Gaston	had been	a mess sergeant	during the war.
Jones	left	his wife	to shoot elephants.

The rule against punctuation breaking up the basic sentence pattern applies even when the place of the subject or complement is taken by a *clause within a clause*. Such clauses, which appear in positions frequently occupied by nouns, are called **noun clauses.** They become *part* of another clause and should not be confused with clauses which are *joined* to another clause:

Noun (subject):	*The writer* knew your name.
Noun Clause:	*Whoever wrote it* knew your name.
Noun (object):	John announced *his plans.*
Noun Clause:	John announced *that he would retire.*

P 3b   Restrictive and Nonrestrictive $\mathcal{P}$

Do not separate restrictive modifiers from what they modify; set off nonrestrictive modifiers by commas.

This convention applies especially to modifiers inserted after a noun (or noun equivalent). Such modifiers become an essential part of the main statement if *used for the purpose of identification*. In that case, they are **restrictive.** They narrow down a general term like *student* to help the reader single out one particular student, or type of student. Restrictive modifiers are *not* set off:

(*Which* student studied the book?)
The student *wearing the red hunting cap* studied the book.

(*Which* man took the money?)
The man *dressed in the pink shirt* took it.

(*What kind* of course appeals to you?)
Courses *that require hard work* appeal to me.

Often a modifier merely gives your reader *further information* about something on which he or she has already focused. It is **nonrestrictive.** Nonrestrictive material is set off from the rest of the sentence by a **comma,** or by a comma both before and after if it occurs in the middle of the sentence:

> The student studied his book.
> (*What else* about him?)
> > The student, *a freshman,* studied his book.
> > The student, *looking weary,* studied his book.
> > The student, *who had little time,* studied his book.
>
> I talked to my lawyer.
> (*What else* about this person?)
> > I talked to my lawyer, *a well-known Boston attorney.*
> > I talked to my lawyer, *who is very impatient.*

Note the following points:

(1) **Dashes** occasionally set off a nonrestrictive *modifier that contains internal punctuation* and that would not be clearly marked without them:

> His lawyer—*a gruff, stubborn, impatient man*—stalked out of the hall.

(2) A *proper name* is usually adequate identification, and a modifier following the name is set off by commas:

Mr. Smith, *my history teacher,* dismissed his class early.

In 1942, she joined the Actors' Theater, *a repertory company with strong political views.*

But occasionally a *restrictive* modifier is needed to help the reader distinguish between several people of the same name:

I find it hard to distinguish between Holmes *the author* and Holmes *the Supreme Court justice.*

(3) **Adjective clauses** modify a noun (or noun equivalent) and usually begin with *who, which,* or *that.* Clauses beginning with *when, where,* and *why* are also adjective clauses if they are used to modify a noun. Adjective clauses, like other modifiers, may be *either restrictive or nonrestrictive:*

Restrictive: According to my sister Irene, all boys *who carry briefcases* are "brains."

Nonrestrictive: Teachers, *who have become more militant over the years,* are no longer satisfied with genteel poverty.

But note that two types of adjective clauses are *always* restrictive: those beginning with *that,* and those from which the pronoun or connective has been omitted:

The book *that you sent me* was exciting reading.

Most of the things [*that*] *I like to eat* are fattening.

She wrote a long passionate letter to the man [*whom*] *she loves.*

P 3c   Sentence Modifiers   ,/

Set sentence modifiers off by commas.

Modifiers may modify sentence elements other than nouns. They may also modify the sentence as a whole rather than any part of it.

(1) *Verbals and verbal phrases modifying a verb* may be either restrictive or nonrestrictive. Notice the **comma** indicating the difference:

Restrictive: He always came into the office *carrying a shirt box full of letters under his arm.*

Nonrestrictive: Deadline newspaper writing is rapid because it cheats, *depending heavily on clichés and stock phrases.*

Always set off *verbal phrases modifying the sentence as a whole:*

To tell you the truth, I don't even recall his name.

The business outlook being rosy, he invested his savings in highly speculative stocks.

Our new manager has done rather well, *considering her lack of experience.*

(2) If a *sentence is introduced by a long or substantial modifying phrase,* a **comma** usually indicates where the main sentence starts:

After an unusually solemn Sunday dinner, Father called me into his study.

Like all newspapermen of good faith, Mencken had long fumed at the low estate of the journalistic rank and file. —Philip M. Wagner, "Mencken Remembered," *The American Scholar*

311

Set off *introductory verbals and verbal phrases* even when they are short:

> *Smiling, she* dropped the match into the gas tank.
> *To start the motor,* turn the ignition key.

(3) Expressions like *after all, of course, unfortunately, on the whole, as a rule,* and *certainly* often do not modify any one part of a sentence but establish a connection between one sentence and another. Depending on the amount of emphasis you would give such a modifier when reading, you can make it stand out from the rest of the sentence by a **comma:**

> *After all,* we are in business primarily for profit.
> *On the other hand,* the records may never be found.
> You will submit the usual reports, *of course.*

Sentence modifiers that are set off require *two* commas if they do not come first or last in the sentence:

> We do not, *as a rule,* solicit applications.
> A great many things, *to be sure,* could be said for him.

Exercise

Check the following sentences for conventional punctuation of modifiers. After the number of each sentence, put *S* for satisfactory, *U* for unsatisfactory. Be prepared to explain why the satisfactory sentences were punctuated the way they were.

1. Faced with sympathy or kindness, we reply with reserve. (Octavio Paz)

2. A young woman in California failed to "come down" after ingesting STP, a powerful hallucinogen.

3. My father who taught in both high school and college gave me pointers on academic success.

4. Looking straight ahead you see a body of polluted water the Monongahela River.

5. Overdoses of the hardest drug, heroin, killed some 900 people in New York City alone.

6. Joe apparently not having any customers was sitting in his own barber chair and smoking a cigar.

7. For Chinese-speaking children in American schools, English used to be the only approved language of instruction.

8. A person who leases a car still has to pay for repairs and maintenance.

9. On the main island of Britain, the Welsh, whose own Gaelic tongue is radically different from English, are now mostly bilingual.

10. Having swallowed enough water to last me all summer I decided to leave water skiing alone.

11. A good example of our neglect of public health problems, is the lack of therapy for the mentally ill.

12. Spain, which once experienced a strong Arab influence, has a history of repressing its women.

13. People, who have grown up in Latin American countries, stand closer to each other in conversation than North Americans.

14. Owen Nielsen, my godfather, was a passionate man who would often shout at his family at the dinner table.

15. Everyone, who is physically able, should have some exercise each day.

P 4 Coordination

Use the comma (and sometimes other marks) when several elements of the same kind appear together.

P 4a Series   ,/

Use commas to separate three or more items of the same kind in a series.

The most common pattern separates the elements from each other by **commas,** with the last comma followed by a connective tying the whole group together:

After dinner, we *talked, laughed, and sang.*

In the late spring the hills in the provinces of *Denizli, Isparta, and Afyon* (which means opium in Turkish) are bright with *red, white, and brown* poppies.

This basic, *A, B, and C* pattern can be expanded to accommodate any number of elements:

The government tries to *stifle* the growth of the poppy at its source, *cut* the flow, *spread* a protective net around the land, and finally *seize* the shipments that have gotten through.

Notice the following variations:

(1) Occasionally, you will want to arrange in a series *groups of words that already contain commas.* To prevent misreading, use **semicolons** instead of additional commas to indicate the major breaks:

Three persons were mentioned in her will: *John, her brother; Martin, her nephew;* and *Helen, her faithful nurse.*

(2) The *last comma* in a series is often left out, even in formal writing. (Most teachers, however, insist on its use.)

Then amid the silence, he *took* off his hat, *laid* it on the table and *stood* up.—James Joyce, "Ivy Day in the Committee Room"

(3) For variety or special effect, a writer may use *commas only,* leaving out the connective:

The idea was to pool all the needs of all those who had in one way or another been bested by their environment—*the crippled, the sick, the hungry, the ragged.*—John Lear, "The Business of Giving," *Saturday Review*

P 4b   Coordinate Adjectives   ,/

Separate coordinate adjectives by a comma.

Two adjectives describing different qualities of the same noun may be coordinated by a **comma** rather than by *and.* They are then called coordinate adjectives. Notice a characteristic break in speech:

a *black* and *shaggy* dog	a *black, shaggy* dog
a *starved* and *exhausted* stranger	a *starved, exhausted* stranger
a *grand* and *awe-inspiring* sunset	a *grand, awe-inspiring* sunset

Not every sequence of adjectives falls into this pattern. Often an adjective combines with a noun to indicate a type of person or object (a *public* servant, a *short* story, a *black* market). An adjective preceding such a combination modifies the combination *as a whole* and should not be separated from it by a comma. Use the comma only if you could use *and* instead.

> a *secretive* public servant (not "secretive *and* public")
> a *long* short story (not "long *and* short")
> a *lively* black market (not "lively *and* black")

P 4c   Dates and Addresses   ,/

> **Use commas with dates, addresses, page references, and similar information that has three or four parts.**

The different items are kept separate from each other by a **comma;** the last item is followed by a comma unless it is at the same time the last word of the sentence:

> The date was *Tuesday, December 3, 1976.*
>
> Please send my mail to *483 Tulane Street, Jackson, Oklahoma,* starting the first of the month.
>
> The quotation is from *Chapter V, page 43, line 7,* of the second volume.

Commas are also used to keep separate the different parts of *measurements* employing more than one unit of measurement. Here the last item is usually *not* separated from the rest of the sentence:

> The boy is now *five feet, seven inches* tall.
>
> *Nine pounds, three ounces* is an unusual weight for this kind of fish.

P 4d   Repetition and Contrast   ,/

Use commas between repeated or contrasted elements.

Use commas between expressions that are *identical or give two different versions of the same meaning.* Use the **comma** after a word or phrase to be repeated or to be followed by a definition or paraphrase:

> *Produce, produce!* This is a law among artists, or rather it is their inner compulsion.—Malcolm Cowley, "Artists, Conscience, and Censors," *Saturday Review*
>
> We were there in the nine days before Christmas, *the Navidad.*

Commas also separate words or groups of words that establish a *contrast:*

> *His wife, not his brother,* needs the money more.
> *The days were warm, the nights cool.*

Exercise

Check the following sentences for conventional punctuation of coordinate or closely related elements. After the number of each sentence, put *S* for satisfactory, *U* for unsatisfactory. Be prepared to explain why the satisfactory sentences were punctuated the way they were.

1. One of Ray Bradbury's astronauts had a wife on Mars, a wife on Venus, and a wife on Jupiter.

2. Mexicans have in them the placidity the gentleness and the patience of the Indian as well as the violence of the Spaniard.

3. He remembered the arenas with their intricate grillwork gates; the beautiful girls in festive gowns of red, purple, and every hue imaginable; and the excited crowds shouting "Bravo" to the fierce-eyed matador.

4. Her husband was always flying off to places like Chattanooga Tennessee or Missoula Montana.

5. The editorial offices of the magazine were located at 235 East 45 Street, New York, New York.

6. Aaron thought of himself as a noble, dedicated person persecuted by callous, materialistic teachers and employers.

7. Lee was known as a strategist not as a tactician.

8. The marooned astronauts came to know hunger, thirst, cold, and the continual throbbing headache of oxygen deprivation.

9. Ralph ran stumbling along the rocks, saved himself on the edge of the pink cliff, and screamed at the ship. (William Golding)

10. After a while the bagelman arrives with a large box full of breakfast: coffee, steaming hot; a triple order of bacon; two fried eggs; and bagels, split and buttered.

11. She had last been seen leaving church on Sunday, April 7, 1974, in Cleveland, Ohio.

12. The floor of the office was gritty with cigarette butts torn handbills and crushed cartons.

13. We had not expected to find such honest, public servants among such poor pessimistic people.

14. For them yoga was a way of life, not just a hobby.

15. One corner of the room is fitted with three worn turntables, a huge electric clock, and a cantilevered microphone that hangs over a console of switches, buttons, and dials.

P 5 Parenthetic Elements

Use dashes, parentheses, or commas to set off parenthetic elements.

To some extent, conventions of punctuation follow the rhythms of speech. This is true of conventional ways of setting off parenthetic elements, which *interrupt* a sentence without becoming grammatically a part of it.

P 5a Dashes

Use the dash—sparingly—to signal a sharp break in a sentence.

A speaker may stop in the middle of a sentence to supply some preliminary detail or additional clarification. In writing, such material is set off from the rest of a sentence by **dashes.** Use dashes for the following situations:

(1) A *complete sentence is inserted into another sentence,* without a connective or relative pronoun to join them:

Lady Macbeth—*has this been noted?*—takes very little stock in the witches.—Mary McCarthy, "General Macbeth," *Harper's*

(2) A *list* interrupts rather than follows a clause:

Women tolerate qualities in a lover—*moodiness, selfishness, unreliability, brutality*—that they would never countenance in a husband.—Susan Sontag, *Against Interpretation*

(3) After a list, a sentence starts anew with a summarizing *all, these,* or *those:*

The visual essay, the rhythmic album, the invitation to drop in on a casual conversation—these are the idiosyncratic traits by which television, as television, has come to be recognized.—Walter Kerr, "What Good Is Television?" *Horizon*

(4) A word or phrase is made to stand out for emphasis or for a *climactic effect:*

After twenty-three years, he was leaving Newston jail—*a free man.*

Every time you look at one of the marvels of modern technology, you find a by-product—*unintended, unpredictable, and often lethal.*

P 5b   Parentheses $( ) /$

Use parentheses to enclose unimportant data (or mere asides).

Parentheses are most appropriate for things mentioned in passing:

The University of Mexico was founded in 1553 *(almost a century before Harvard)* .

Kazan directed the rest of his considerable steam into studying English *(he graduated with honors)*, waiting on tables, and joining as many extracurricular campus clubs as he could.—Thomas B. Morgan, "Elia Kazan's Great Expectations," *Harper's*

Parentheses enclose dates, addresses, page references, chemical formulas, and similar information if it might be of interest to some readers but is not an essential part of the text. Here are some typical examples: *(p. 34)* *(first published in 1910)* *(now called Market Street)*.

Note: When a sentence in parentheses begins *after* end punctuation, end punctuation is required inside the final parenthesis:

Select your purchases with care. *(No refunds are permitted.)*

P 5c   Commas for Parenthetic Elements   ,/

> *Use commas for parenthetic elements that blend into a sentence with only a slight break.*

Take note especially of the following possibilities:

(1)   Use commas when you interrupt a statement to *address the reader* or to *comment on* what you are saying:

Marriage, *dear boy,* is a serious business.
Politicians, *you will agree,* were never popular in this part of the country.
Our candidate, *it seems,* is not very well known.

(2)   Commas set off the *introductory greetings and exclamations,* as well as the introductory *yes* and *no,* which frequently precede a statement in conversation and in informal writing:

Why, I don't even know that man.
Yes, you can now buy Pinko napkins in different colors.
Well, you can't have everything.

(3)   Commas set off the *"echo questions"* often added to a statement to elicit agreement or confirmation:

Punctuation

You are my friend, *aren't you?*
So he says he is sick, *does he?*

(4) Slight breaks similar to those caused by parenthetic elements are sometimes caused by *sentence elements that have changed their usual position in the sentence:*

Laws, *to be cheerfully obeyed,* must be both just and practicable.
The Spaniards, *at the height of their power,* were great builders of towns.

(5) Commas may take the place of dashes to set off a word for emphasis. They suggest a *thoughtful pause* rather than a dramatic break:

We should act, *and suffer,* in accordance with our principles.
People cannot, *or will not,* put down the facts.

Exercise

Check the following passages for conventional punctuation of parenthetic elements. After the number of each passage, write *S* for satisfactory, *U* for unsatisfactory. Explain why satisfactory passages were punctuated the way they were.

1. Well, you have made your point, Danny. The rest of us, you will agree, have the right to our own opinion.
2. Many discoveries though first made in wartime, were later put to peacetime uses.

3. Most of the energy we use—whether from coal, oil, or water —ultimately derives from the sun.

4. Why if I were you I would return the whole shipment to the company.

5. Geothermal power in your backyard, unless you have a geyser on your property, just can't be done.

6. Most energy (as leaders of the ecology movement have told us for years) comes from fossil fuels.

7. Nuclear fuel would create an enormous waste problem (as indeed there is already with our existing uranium plants.

8. Many people would agree, offhand, that every creature lives its life and then dies. This might, indeed, be called a truism. But, like some other truisms, it is not true. The lowest forms of life, such as the amoebae, normally (that is, barring accidents) do not die. (Susanne K. Langer)

9. Fashions (especially adolescent fashions) do not, as a rule outlast their generation.

10. Nowhere in the world has the old cliché of European romanticism—the assassin mind versus the spontaneous heart—had such a long career as in America. (Susan Sontag)

P 6   Quotation

Know how to punctuate different kinds of quoted material.

Often, you will need to indicate that you are reproducing information or ideas derived from a specific source, that you are quoting something first said or observed by someone else.

P 6a   Direct Quotation   "/

In repeating someone's exact words, distinguish them clearly from your own text.

Direct quotations are enclosed in **quotation marks.** They are usually separated by a **comma** from the credit tag (the statement identifying the source) :

She said, "Leave me alone."
"I don't care," he said.

Often the *credit tag interrupts the quotation.* Use **commas** both before and after the credit tag if it splits one complete sentence:

"Both marijuana and alcohol," *Dr. Jones reports,* "slow reaction times on a whole spectrum of tasks of varying complexities."

You need a comma before and a **period** after the credit tag if it comes between two complete sentences:

"All men are curious," Aristotle wrote. "They naturally desire knowledge."

The following variations are important:

(1) No comma is required with extremely *short quotations* or with *quotations worked into the pattern of a sentence* that is not a mere credit tag:

Your saying "I am sorry" was not enough to soothe his wounded pride.
The clatter of dishes and tableware, mingled with lusty shouts of "Seconds here!" and "Please pass the butter!", will

resound across the country.—John Crawford, "A Plea for Physical Fatness," *Atlantic*

No comma is required when the credit tag follows a question or an exclamation:

"Is everybody all right?" he shouted at the top of his voice.

(2) *Long or formal quotations* are often introduced by a **colon** instead of a comma. Whether you use a comma or a colon, capitalize the first word of the quotation if it was capitalized in the original source (or if it would have been capitalized if written down):

Saarinen's definition of architecture's purposes describes his work: "To shelter and enhance man's life on earth and to fulfill his belief in the nobility of his existence."

(3) *Long quotations* (more than ten typed lines) should be set off from the rest of a paper *not* by quotation marks but by indention and single-spacing. The same applies to quotations consisting of more than a full line of poetry. (See the sample research paper in Chapter 8 for examples of such **block quotations.)**

(4) Indicate when the person you are quoting is quoting someone else. In a quotation marked by the conventional set of double quotation marks, **single quotation marks** signal a *quotation within a quotation:*

He said, "Our Congressman's constant cry of 'Cut that budget!' deceives no one."

"Many subjects," one researcher says, "only get through the rather scary effects of the drug by reassuring themselves with the knowledge that they will 'come down' in a few hours."

P 6b   Terminal Marks in Quotations   𝒫

Observe conventional sequences when quotation marks coincide with other marks of punctuation.

Note the following guidelines:

(1) Commas conventionally precede the final quotation mark, whereas semicolons and colons conventionally follow it:

> As he said, "Don't worry about me," the ship pulled away from the quay. You said, "I don't need your sympathy"; therefore, I didn't offer any.

(2) End punctuation usually precedes the final quotation marks, as in all the examples given so far. Sometimes, however, you will have to use a question mark or an exclamation mark after the quotation has formally ended. This means that the quotation itself is not a question or an exclamation. Rather, you are asking a question or exclaiming about the quotation.

> Who said, "We are strangers here; the world is from of old"?
> Don't ever tell a girl, "There'll never be another woman like my mother"!

Note: A terminal mark is not duplicated at the end of a quotation, even when logic might seem to require its repetition. For instance, use only one question mark even when you are asking a question about a question:

> Were you the student who asked, "Could we hold the class on the lawn?"

P 6c   Insertions and Omissions $\mathcal{P}$

*In direct quotation, indicate clearly any changes
you make in the original text.*

Use special marks as follows:

(1) If for any reason you insert *explanations or comments of your own,* set them off from the quoted material
by **square brackets:**

> As Dr. Habenichts observes, "Again and again, they [the
> Indians] saw themselves deprived of lands of whose posses-
> sion they had been assured with solemn oaths."

> The note read: "Left Camp B Wednesday, April 3 [actually
> April 4]. Are trying to reach Camp C before we run out of
> supplies."

(2) When you *omit unnecessary or irrelevant material*
from a quotation, indicate the omission by three spaced
periods (called an **ellipsis).** If the omission occurs after a
period in the original text, retain the sentence period and
then insert the ellipsis.

> The report concluded on an optimistic note: "All three of
> the patients . . . are making remarkable progress toward
> recovery."

> "To be a bird is to be alive more intensely than any other
> living creature, man included. . . . They live in a world that
> is always present, mostly full of joy." So wrote N. J. Berrill,
> Professor of Zoology at McGill University.—Joseph Wood
> Krutch, "If You Don't Mind My Saying So," *The American
> Scholar*

To indicate extensive omissions (a line or more of
poetry, a paragraph or more of prose), you may use a single
typed line of spaced periods.

P 6d   Indirect Quotation $\mathcal{P}$

In indirect quotations, reproduce someone else's ideas or thoughts but translate them into your own words.

Indirectly quoted statements often take the form of noun clauses introduced by *that;* indirectly quoted questions take the form of noun clauses introduced by words like *whether, why, how,* and *which.* Such clauses are *not* separated from the statement indicating the source by a comma or colon. They are *not* enclosed in quotation marks:

> Aristotle stated *that all men naturally desire knowledge.*
>
> General Grant replied *that he doubted the wisdom of such a move.*
>
> The artist asked me *which of the drawings I liked best.*

Note two exceptions:

(1)   The following passage shows ways of *working the source statement into the indirect quotation as parenthetic material,* requiring commas:

> *As Gandhi remarked,* the first consequence of nonviolent action is to harden the heart of those who are being assaulted by charity. But, *he continued,* all the while they are being driven to a frenzy of rage, they are haunted by the terrible knowledge of how wrong they are.—Michael Harrington, "Whence Comes Their Passion," *The Reporter*

(2)   Even in an indirect quotation, you may reproduce some words or phrases exactly as they were used. To indicate that you are *preserving part of the original wording,* enclose such words and phrases in **quotation marks:**

A 24-year-old British student with an honor degree in law tried to "conquer time" by drilling a hole in his skull with a dental drill while under the influence of LSD.

P 6e   Words Set Off from Context

𝒫

Use quotation marks to indicate words and phrases that are not part of your normal vocabulary.

Mark expressions that are not your own, even though you may not be quoting them from any specific source:

(1) **Quotation marks** may identify words that you employ for *local color or comical effect*. They enable you to show irony by holding an expression, as it were, at arm's length:

> It would seem that every modern child's pleasure must have its "constructive aspects."—Lois Phillips Hudson, "The Buggy on the Roof," *Atlantic*

(2) Either quotation marks or italicized print (underlining in a typed manuscript) identifies *technical terms* probably new to the reader or *words discussed as words,* as in a discussion of grammar or meaning:

> She wore a "Mother Hubbard," a loose, full gown long since out of fashion.
>
> The word *mob* was attacked as slang by some eighteenth-century writers.

(3) **Italics** rather than quotation marks identify *words that have been borrowed from foreign languages* and have not become part of the general vocabulary of English.

> Young Latin American men are very touchy these days about *machismo,* best translated as "an emphasis on masculinity."—Linda Wolfe, "The Machismo Mystique," *New York*

Many legal and scientific terms borrowed from Latin belong in this category:

> A writ of *certiorari* is used by a superior court to obtain judicial records from an inferior court or quasi-judicial agency.
>
> The word "comet" comes from the Greek *aster kometes,* meaning long-haired star.

Exercise

Check the following passages for conventional punctuation of quoted material. After the number of each passage, write *S* for satisfactory, *U* for unsatisfactory. Explain why the satisfactory passages were punctuated the way they were.

1. Harry, a restauranteur, likes to support his local police with "something for their trouble."

2. The student's voice was loud and angry when she asked the dean, "What do you think we are, little kids."

3. "We've completely crossed the void," he told Ichor. "We are approaching the outer limits of a planetary system."

4. As Stan Steiner has said, "the Chicano can rightly claim that he has been humiliated by the textbooks, tongue-tied by teachers, de-educated by the schools."

5. The lady from Buffalo kept asking the guide "what he meant by primitive?"

6. "That was sweet of you, Gary," Beverly said, the candles flickering over the table.

7. When she came back from Mexico, she kept using words like *paseo* and *abrazo*.

8. "This," he explained to the group, "is what total recall is like."

9. "Something is wrong here," she said, "people are not following their instructions."

10. He remembered the chief psychologist telling him the accidents will be simulated.

11. She thought for a while and said, "All I remember is the announcement: 'Follow Code 305.'"

12. Would you have had the heart to tell him: "Time is up?"

13. The speaker charged "that the television audience resembled the ancient Romans, who liked to see the gladiators do battle to the death."

14. The speaker quoted Jefferson as saying that "our new circumstances" require "new words, new phrases, and the transfer of old words to new objects."

15. The constant war cry of my high school English teachers was give an example!

8

The Research Paper

For Quick Reference

When you write a research paper, you write for a reader who wants to *know*. Your job is to find reliable and up-to-date sources of information or evidence on a given subject. You then assemble, interpret, and correlate material from your several different sources.

The research paper differs from the ordinary theme in

outward form. It includes **documentation:** It fully identifies sources, usually in footnotes, and often again in a bibliography, a final alphabetical listing of sources consulted during the project. As the author of a research paper, you make your sources and procedures available for inspection and review. Your readers can consult the sources for themselves—to see if the sources were quoted correctly, or if the evidence was selected fairly.

Documentation helps you avoid **plagiarism**—taking over the results of someone else's research or investigation without acknowledgment. Plagiarism is to the scholar what shoplifting is to businesspeople. It is true that many facts and ideas are common property and need not be credited to any specific source. Major historical dates and events, key ideas of major scientific or philosophical movements— these are generally accessible in reference books. However, whenever you make use of information recently discovered or compiled, and whenever you adopt someone's characteristic, personal point of view, it is necessary for you to identify your source. *Never copy whole sentences or paragraphs without making it clear that you are quoting another writer.*

R 1 Choosing a Subject

Select a subject limited in scope and suitable for objective investigation.

As a student writing a research paper, you need to produce definite results in a limited time. Your first task, therefore, is to select a subject that you can profitably treat within the time and with the materials at your disposal. Remember the following guidelines:

(1) Stay away from *highly technical subjects*. Recent discoveries about the nature of the universe or about the biochemistry of our bodies make fascinating topics, but you may soon need more knowledge of physics or mathematics than you and your reader can command.

(2) Center your paper on *one limited aspect* of a more general subject. Restrict your general subject area until you arrive at something that you can explore in detail. "The early history of American universities" is a general subject area. "The training of Puritan divines at Harvard" is a specific subject.

(3) Make detailed use of *several different sources*. Avoid subjects that would tempt you to summarize pre-assembled information from one main source. Avoid subjects that you find conclusively treated in a textbook or encyclopedia.

(4) Stay *close to the evidence* you present. When you write a research paper, the stance you adopt toward your audience is: "Here is the evidence. This is where I found it. You are welcome to verify these sources and to check these facts."

Here are some general areas for research:

1. The history of dictionary making: the principles and practices of lexicographers like Samuel Johnson or Noah Webster; the history of the *Oxford English Dictionary;* the reception of Webster's *Third New International.*

2. Bilingualism: problems encountered by French Canadians, Mexican-Americans, or Flemish-speaking Belgians; assimilation vs. the preservation of a separate linguistic

and cultural tradition; the schooling provided for children who speak a different language at home.

3. The history of the American Indian: early contacts with whites; wars, treaties, and reservations; the role of church and missionary; assimilation vs. self-identity.

4. The education or the reading of a prominent early American: books that influenced Washington, Jefferson, Franklin, or Madison; the influence of the classics or of contemporary trends of thought.

5. The public reception of a controversial author: Henrik Ibsen, D. H. Lawrence, Gertrude Stein, Henry Miller, Jean Genêt, Sylvia Plath; changing standards of public taste and morals.

6. Censorship: public pressures encountered by artists and writers; the role of religious or patriotic groups; defining pornography or obscenity; the role of lawgivers and courts.

7. The self-image of the young black in white society as reflected in the writings of one or more black authors: Richard Wright, James Baldwin, Ralph Ellison, Lorraine Hansberry, Maya Angelou.

8. The history of prison reform: conditions in early American jails; punishment vs. rehabilitation; problems and proposed solutions.

Exercise

Write a tentative prospectus for a research paper in one of the general areas listed above. Describe whatever in your background or previous reading might help you with your chosen subject. Outline your tentative plans for *limiting* your subject:

What aspects of the general topic, or what issues within the general area, interest you most? Outline any preliminary thoughts about how you might tackle your subject: What might be your overall plan of organization, or your general strategy?

(Your instructor may ask you to delay your prospectus until you have had a chance to do a minimum of *exploratory reading.*)

R 2 Going to the Sources

Learn how to find and evaluate sources.

The experienced investigator knows where to look. Writing a research paper gives you a chance to find your way around a library and to get acquainted with its resources.

R 2a General Reference Works

Learn to use the reference tools available to every investigator.

Encyclopedias An encyclopedia is a good place to start—but not to finish—your investigation. The encyclopedia provides a convenient summary of what is generally known on your subject. The purpose of your investigation is to go *beyond* the encyclopedia—to take a closer firsthand look.

- The *Encyclopaedia Britannica,* now an American publication, is considered by many the most authoritative of the general encyclopedias. It provides extended articles on general subjects, with exceptionally full bibliographies at the end of articles. It is brought up to date each year by the *Britannica Book of the Year*. Although you would normally consult the most up-to-date version, you will occasionally find references to scholarly articles in earlier editions.

- The *Encyclopedia Americana* is sometimes recommended for science and biography. General subjects are broken up into short articles, arranged alphabetically. The annual supplement is the *Americana Annual*.

- *Collier's Encyclopedia* is another multivolume general encyclopedia, written in a more popular style.

- The one-volume *Columbia Encyclopedia* provides a bird's-eye view. It serves well for a quick check of people and places.

Bibliographies   At the end of many encyclopedia entries you will find a short bibliography, a list of important books and other sources of information. The encyclopedia may suggest only very general books, but these in turn will often contain more detailed bibliographical listings or direct you to book-length bibliographies. Any general survey of a subject is likely to provide information about more detailed studies. College textbooks often provide a short bibliography at the end of each chapter.

Take up first those books that a bibliography labels "standard," "indispensable," or "the best introduction" to your subject. If the bibliographies you have consulted merely *list* books, take up those that are most frequently mentioned. Study their tables of contents, prefaces, introductory or concluding chapters. Find out what each book is trying to do and whether all or parts of it would be useful for your project.

- The *Book Review Digest* contains short selections from book reviews written shortly after publication of the book reviewed. These can give you an idea of the intention and importance of books on subjects of general interest.

Periodical Indexes   When writing on a current problem, you may have to rely primarily on articles in both general and technical magazines. The card catalog of your library lists magazines but not individual magazine articles. You will have to locate the latter in the **periodical indexes.** These are published in monthly or semimonthly installments and then combined in huge volumes, each listing articles for a period of one or more years.

- The *Readers' Guide to Periodical Literature* indexes magazines written for the general reader. If you are writing on American policy in the Far East, the *Readers' Guide* will direct you to speeches by government officials reprinted in full in *Vital Speeches of the Day* or *U.S. News & World Report.* It will direct you to discussions of American foreign policy in such magazines as *Newsweek* and *New Republic.* The *Social Sciences and Humanities Index* (formerly *International Index*) lists articles in more scholarly magazines. If you are looking for recent studies of the black community, this index will direct you to articles in sociological and psychological journals.

Note: Whatever index or bibliography you use, read its introductory pages and study its list of abbreviations. *Study the list of the periodicals indexed*—it may not include a magazine that you have seen mentioned elsewhere and that you know to be important. Look at sample entries to study the listing of individual articles (usually by subject) and the system of cross-references.

R 2b Specialized Reference Works

Use the reference tools of a special area of study.

Every major area, such as education, history, or art, has its own specialized reference guides: yearbooks, specialized encyclopedias, dictionaries of names and technical terms, general bibliographies. To find specialized reference works relevant to your research project, turn to Constance M. Winchell's *Guide to Reference Books,* or another general guide to reference works.

Biography In addition to the biographical entries in the major encyclopedias, most libraries have ample material for this kind of project.

- *Who's Who in America,* a biographical dictionary of notable living men and women, provides a brief summary of dates and details on important contemporaries. The *Dictionary of American Biography (DAB)* contains a more detailed account of the lives of important persons. The British counterparts of these two volumes are *Who's Who* and the *Dictionary of National Biography (DNB)*.

- The *Biography Index* is a guide to biographical material in books *and* magazines. By consulting both recent and earlier volumes, you can compile a comprehensive bibliography of material on the married life of George Washington or on the evangelistic campaigns of Billy Graham.

Literature   A library project on a subject from literary history may deal with an author's schooling or early reading, recurrent themes in the books of a well-known novelist, the contemporary reputation of a nineteenth-century American poet.

- The fifteen-volume *Cambridge History of English Literature* and the *Cambridge Bibliography of English Literature* provide comprehensive information about English authors and literary movements.

- The Spiller-Thorp-Johnson-Canby *Literary History of the United States,* with its supplementary bibliographies, lists as its contributors an impressive roster of contemporary American literary scholars.

- *Harper's Dictionary of Classical Literature and Antiquities* is a comprehensive scholarly guide to Greek and Roman history and civilization. (Robert Graves' *The Greek Myths* and Edith Hamilton's *Mythology,* both available as paperbacks, provide an introduction to famous names and stories.)

Current Events   A number of special reference guides are useful for papers on a political subject or on current events.

- *Facts on File* is a weekly digest of world news, with an annual index. It gives a summary of news reports and comments with excerpts from important documents and speeches. It can serve as a convenient review of day-to-day happenings in politics, foreign affairs, entertainment, sports, science, and education.

- The *New York Times Index* (published since 1913) is a guide to news stories published in the *New York Times.* By looking up an event or a controversy in either of the above indexes, you can ascertain the approximate dates for relevant articles in newspapers and magazines.

- The annual index to the *Monthly Catalog of the United States Government Publications* lists reports and documents published by all branches of the federal government.

R 2c   Library Catalogs

Learn to make efficient use of the card catalog.

Your research projects will ordinarily be geared to the resources of your college library. Its central card catalog is a complete alphabetical index of the materials available to you. In most card catalogs, the same book is listed several times: by *author* (under the author's last name), by *title* (under the first word of the title, not counting *The, A,* or *An*), and by *subject.*

An **author card** will look like this:

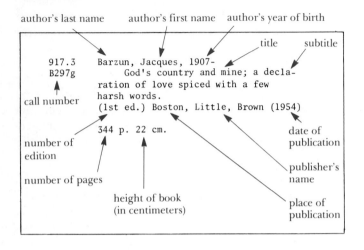

author's last name   author's first name   author's year of birth

title   subtitle

917.3 Barzun, Jacques, 1907-
B297g   God's country and mine; a decla-
ration of love spiced with a few
harsh words.
(1st ed.) Boston, Little, Brown (1954)

344 p. 22 cm.

call number

number of edition

number of pages

height of book
(in centimeters)

date of publication

publisher's name

place of publication

Sample catalog card

Look for the following clues to the nature of the book:

- *the number or description of the edition.* If the catalog lists both the original edition and another one marked "2nd ed." or "Rev. ed.," you will generally choose the one that is most nearly up to date.

- *the name and location of the publisher.* For instance, a book published by a university press is likely to be a scholarly or specialized study. The *date of publication is* especially important for books on scientific, technological, or medical subjects, since here new discoveries rapidly invalidate old theories.

- *the number of pages* (with the number of introductory pages given as a lower-case Roman numeral). It shows whether the book is a short pamphlet or a full-scale treatment of the subject. If the book contains *illustrations* or a *bibliography*, the card will carry a notation to that effect.

Often, a card lists the several major *subject headings* under which the book can be found. For instance, a catalog card for a sociological study of a town in the Middle West may carry the following notation concerning various headings under which the study is listed:

1. U.S.—Social conditions. 2. Cities and Towns—U.S. 3. Cost and standard of living—U.S. 4. U.S.—Religion. 5. Social surveys. 6. Community life.

Subject cards can direct you to many books that are relevant to your topic. Look for subject headings under which books on your topic might be listed. Books on progressive education might appear under *Education—Aims and Objectives,* under *Education—Experimental Methods,* or under *Educational Psychology.* Books on the Civil War might appear under *U.S.—History—Civil War,* under *U.S. —History—Military,* under *Slavery in the United States,* or under *Abolitionists.*

Once you decide that you should consult a book, copy its call number. The **call number** directs you, or the librarian, to the shelf where the book is located. Your library may use either of two numbering systems: the Library of Congress system or the Dewey decimal system. The **Library of Congress system** divides books into categories identified by letters of the alphabet. It then uses additional letters and numerals to subdivide each main category. For instance, the call number of a book on religion would start with a capital *B;* the call number of a book on education starts with a capital *L*. The **Dewey decimal system** uses numerals to identify the main categories. For instance, 400–499 covers books on language; 800–899 covers books on literature. The 800 range is then further subdivided into American literature (810–819), English literature (820–829), and so on. Additional numerals and letters distinguish among individual authors and among individual works by the same author.

Note: Most libraries have a separate, compact catalog for all periodicals to which the library subscribes. For each periodical it indicates the location of recent issues (often on the shelves of a separate periodical room) as well as of back issues (usually in bound volumes in the book stacks of the library).

R 2d   Bibliography Cards

> *Make your own card catalog of promising materials.*

Include a separate note card for each book, pamphlet, or magazine article you intend to use. Your instructor may suggest a minimum number of sources he wants you to consult. On each bibliography card, include the library call number or the place in the library where the publication is to be found. (This information is for your own personal use; do *not* reproduce it in your finished paper.)

A bibliography card for a book will look like this:

```
509      Conant, James Bryant
C743o
         On Understanding Science:   An
           Historical Approach

         New Haven:   Yale University Press, 1947
```

Sample bibliography card: book

Put the author's *last name first* to facilitate alphabetizing. If a work has been collected or arranged by a person other than the author you may start with that person's name, followed by "ed." for "editor." Ordinarily, however, the name of an editor or of a translator (followed by "trans.") appears on a separate line below the title. If an article in an encyclopedia is identified only by the author's initials, you may be able to find his full name by checking the initials against a list of contributors.

Start a new line for the *full title of the publication,* including a subtitle, if any. Underline the title of a book, pamphlet, or other work published as a separate entity. (Underlining in a typed manuscript corresponds to italics in print.) Put the title of an article or short poem in quotation marks and underline the title of the magazine or collection in which it appears.

Use a separate line for the *facts of publication.* For a book or pamphlet these may include:

(1) *number or description of the edition* (unless a book has not been re-edited since publication).

(2) *number of volumes* (if a work consists of several, and all are relevant to your investigation).

(3) *place of publication* (usually the location of the main office of the publishing house, or of the first branch office listed if several are given).

(4) *name of the publisher.*

(5) *date of publication* (which can usually be inferred from the copyright date, found on the reverse side of the title page).

(6) *number of the specific volume used* (if only one of several volumes is relevant to your investigation).

A bibliography card for an article may look like this:

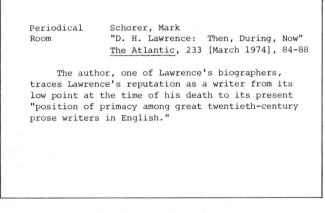

```
Periodical      Schorer, Mark
Room            "D. H. Lawrence:  Then, During, Now"
                The Atlantic, 233 [March 1974], 84-88

     The author, one of Lawrence's biographers,
traces Lawrence's reputation as a writer from its
low point at the time of his death to its present
"position of primacy among great twentieth-century
prose writers in English."
```

Sample bibliography card: article

For a magazine or newspaper article, the facts of publication ordinarily do *not* include the name of the publisher and the place of publication (though the latter is sometimes needed to identify a small-town journal). The pages of most professional or technical magazines are numbered consecutively through the several issues making up one volume, usually the issues published during one year. For an article in such a magazine, record the *number of the volume* (in Arabic numerals), the *date of the issue,* and the *page numbers of the article.* For articles in other magazines and in newspapers, record the date of the issue and the page numbers. If the pages in separate sections of a newspaper are not numbered consecutively, identify the section where the article is to be found.

Note that the above bibliography card for an article is an example of an *annotated card.* When you annotate your cards, you include brief reminders concerning your sources. You may want to note whether an article is written in a very technical or very popular style. You may want to note that a book has a glossary of technical terms, or a convenient summary of historical facts.

R 2e   Evaluating Your Sources

Learn to choose authoritative sources and to evaluate conflicting evidence.

Every investigator tries to find sources that are reliable and truly informative. When confronted with conflicting testimony, we learn to ask: Who is talking? How does the author know? What is he or she trying to prove? What side is this author on? When you evaluate your sources, consider points like the following:

(1) Is the author an *authority on his or her subject?* If you can, find out whether a book was written by an economist whose specialty is Russian agriculture or by a columnist who spent four weeks surveying Russian agriculture from the windows of a train.

(2) *Is the work a thorough study* or a sketchy survey of the topic? Is it short on opinion and long on evidence, or vice versa? Does it weigh the findings of other authorities, or ignore them?

(3) Does the author settle important questions by going to **primary sources**—legal documents, letters, diaries, eyewitness reports, transcripts of speeches and interviews, reports on experiments, statistical surveys? Or does he rely exclusively on **secondary sources**—other authors' accounts and interpretations of primary materials?

(4) Is the author's treatment *balanced or one-sided?* An early phase in the history of the American labor movement is likely to be treated one way in the success story of a famous industrialist, another way in the biography of a labor leader. An objective historian will weigh both pro-business and pro-labor views.

(5) Is the work *recent enough to have profited from current scholarship?* If it was originally published ten or twenty years ago, is the current version a revised edition? Consider the possibility that an author's views may have been invalidated by new findings and changing theories in a rapidly expanding field of study.

Exercises

A. Select one of the following subjects and compare its treatment in a general encyclopedia and in one of the more specialized reference works listed below. Choose one: atonality, surrealism, cybernetics, Zen, ESP, Savonarola, Hercules, Jacobins, Gestalt psychology, the Maccabees, Pan.

> *Grove's Dictionary of Music and Musicians*
>
> *Standard Dictionary of Folklore, Mythology and Legend*
>
> *Comprehensive Dictionary of Psychological and Psychoanalytic Terms*
>
> *Standard Jewish Encyclopedia*
>
> *New Catholic Encyclopedia*
>
> *Van Nostrand's Scientific Encyclopedia*
>
> *Cambridge Medieval History*
>
> *Cambridge Modern History*
>
> *McGraw-Hill Dictionary of Art*
>
> *Concise Encyclopedia of Living Faiths*

B. In the *Readers' Guide* or the *Social Science and Humanities Index*, find an article on one of the subjects listed below. Report on the intention of the author, level of difficulty of the article, and the author's use of sources. Choose one of the following general subjects:

> history of the American labor movement
> Freud and his disciples
> recent studies of black English
> dissent in the Soviet Union
> estimates of the world's fuel supply
> educational technology and our public schools

C. Transcribe and explain the information that the card catalog of your college library provides concerning *one* of the following books: Leonard Bloomfield, *Language;* H. W. Fowler, *A Dictionary of Modern English Usage;* Otto Jespersen, *Modern English Grammar;* H. L. Mencken, *The American Language;* Stuart Robertson, *The Development of Modern English.*

D. Study the arrangement of cards in the central card catalog of your college library in order to answer the following questions:

1. What are the major subdivisions for subject cards under the heading "Education"?

2. Where would you find a book by an author named John Mc-Millan (under *Mc, Mac, Mi?*), George St. John (under *St., Sa, Jo?*), Antoine de Saint-Exupéry (under *De, Sa, St.?*)?

3. Do subject cards for books on the Civil War precede or follow cards for books on the War of Independence? Is the arrangement alphabetical or chronological?

4. Are books about George Washington listed before or after books about the State of Washington, or about Washington, D.C.?

5. Check under *John Keats:* What is the relative order of the author's individual works, his collected works, and books about the author?

E. Through the card catalog of your college library, find one of the following books. Study its preface, table of contents, bibliography (if any), and any other introductory or concluding sections. Study its treatment of selected entries or of one or two limited topics. Then prepare a brief report on the intention, scope, and possible usefulness of the book. Choose one:

Leo Rosten, *The Joys of Yiddish*

G. M. Trevelyan, *History of England*

Edgar Z. Friedenberg, *Coming of Age in America*

Kenneth Rexroth, *Classics Revisited*

Clarence Major, *Dictionary of Afro-American Slang*

Margaret Mead, *Male and Female*

Alden T. Vaughan, *New England Frontier: Puritans and Indians*

Robert Coles, *Children of Crisis*

Thomas Pyles, *The Origin and Development of the English Language*

S. I. Hayakawa, *Language in Thought and Action*

Margaret M. Bryant, *Current American Usage*

Linda Goodman, *Sun Signs*

Joseph Campbell, *The Hero with a Thousand Faces*

R 3 From Notes to the First Draft

Learn how to take and use notes.

In putting a research paper together, you face two major tasks. You collect, from a variety of sources, material that all, in one way or another, bears on the question you are trying to answer, on the issue you are trying to explore. You sort out and arrange these materials in a coherent presentation, supporting the conclusions that your investigation has made you reach.

R 3a Taking Notes

Take accurate notes to serve as raw material for your first draft.

For a short research report, you may be able to take notes on ordinary sheets of writing paper. But for a longer research paper, 3 × 5 or 4 × 6 note cards will enable you to *shuffle* and arrange your information as the overall pattern of your paper takes shape. Make sure author and title of your source (in shortened form) appear on each card, along with exact page numbers. Use the tentative subdivisions of your paper as the common heading for each group of related cards. Remember:

- Use each card for a *single piece of information,* for a single quotation, or for closely related material. This way you won't have to split up the material on the card later, to use in different parts of your paper.

- Include the kind of *specific detail* that you will need to support generalizations: selected examples, statistical figures, definitions of difficult terms.

- Make sure the material you select is *representative* of the source—not taken out of context. The person you quote should be able to say: "Yes, I'll stand behind that. That's more or less what I meant."

In taking notes, do not simply copy big chunks of undigested material. *Adapt* the material to suit your purposes as you go along. Normally, you will be using three major techniques:

(1) *Summarize background information; condense lengthy arguments.* Here is a note card that condenses several pages of introductory information in John G. Neihardt's book *Black Elk Speaks:*

Last Battles

    In the fall of 1930, a Field Agent helped Neihardt meet Black Elk, a holy man of the Oglala Sioux who was a second cousin to chief Crazy Horse. Black Elk was nearly blind and knew no English. Neihardt, speaking to him through an interpreter, gained his confidence partly by respecting the holy man's long silences. In the spring of 1931, Black Elk took many days to tell his life story, including the story of his share in the defeat of General Custer, which Black Elk witnessed as a young warrior.

Neihardt, <u>Black Elk</u>, pp. vii-xi

Sample note card: summary

(2) **Paraphrase** *much of the material* that you are
going to use. Put it in your own words, emphasizing what is
most directly useful, cutting down on what is less important.
The following note card shows paraphrased material that
condenses the original text somewhat, with direct quotation used only for some striking phrases that help give the
material the "authentic touch":

Indian Education

    Indian children were put in crowded boarding
schools and fed at the cost of 11 cents a day (with
their diet supplemented by food that could be grown
on school farms). From the fifth grade up, children
put in half a day's labor on the school farm. They
were taught "vanishing trades of little or no economic
importance."

"Breaking Faith," p. 240

Sample note card: paraphrase

(3) *Use extended* **direct quotation** *for key passages.*
Quote an author directly when he sums up his position, or
when he takes a strong stand on a controversial issue:

```
Federal Policy

    "From the very beginnings of this nation, the
chief issue around which Federal Indian policy has
revolved has been, not how to assimilate the Indian
nations whose lands we usurped, but how best to
transfer Indian lands and resources to non-Indians."

Van de Mark, "Raid on the Reservations," p. 49
```

Sample note card: direct quotation

Use direct quotation sparingly or not at all in reproducing information, in outlining an author's argument, and
in covering minor or noncontroversial points. Frequent use
of undigested direct quotations tempts the reader to skip
the quoted material and to look in the accompanying text
for your main point.

Note: Make sure that your notes differentiate clearly
between paraphrase or indirect quotation on the one hand
and direct quotation on the other. In other words, *use
quotation marks to identify all material quoted verbatim.*

R 3b   Using Your Notes

Work the material from your note cards smoothly into your own text.

A paragraph in your finished paper will often combine material from several different note cards. Don't simply stitch the patches together. Spell out the conclusions that the evidence on your cards points to. Then *select* the material from your cards that will best back up your more general points. Study the way material from the following note cards has been selected to serve as evidence in a coherent paragraph:

Individual Note Cards:

```
Hamlet as thinker

      "Hamlet's character is the prevalence of
the abstracting and generalizing habit over the
practical.  He does not want courage, skill, will,
or opportunity; but every incident sets him
thinking; . . . I have a smack of Hamlet myself,
if I may say so."

                              4
```

The Research Paper

Hamlet as thinker

According to Coleridge (1818?), Shakespeare
meant to show the need for a healthy balance
between observation and thought, between reality
and the world of imagination. "In Hamlet this
balance is disturbed: his thoughts, and the
images of his fancy, are far more vivid than
his actual perceptions . . . Hence we see
a great, an almost enormous, intellectual
activity, and a proportionate aversion to real
action . . . he vacillates from sensibility,
and procrastinates from thought."

in Smith,

Hamlet as thinker

"It is we who are Hamlet . . . Whoever has
become thoughtful and melancholy through his own
mishaps or those of others; whoever has borne
about with him the clouded brow of reflection,
and thought himself 'too much i' th' sun;' . . .
whose powers of action have been eaten up by
thought, he to whom the universe seems infinite
and himself nothing; . . . this is the true
Hamlet." (pp. 287-88)

"His ruling passion is to think, not to act."
William Hazlitt, Characters of Sh.'s Plays (1817)
in Smith, pp. 287-91

Finished Paragraph:

The Romantic critics saw in Hamlet a man paralyzed by

thought. They saw in him a reflection of their own tempera-

ment: a love for solitude, an extreme sensitivity, a tendency

to be kept from effective action by melancholy reflections.

From Notes to the First Draft

①② "It is we who are Hamlet," said William Hazlitt. The true
Hamlet is someone "whose powers of action have been eaten up
③ by thought"--"whoever has become thoughtful and melancholy
through his own mishaps or those of others; whoever has borne
about with him the clouded brow of reflection, and thought him-
④ self 'too much i' th' sun.'"[7] Coleridge, who said "I have a
smack of Hamlet myself," saw in Hamlet a lack of balance be-
⑤ tween thought and reality--"a great, almost enormous, intellectual activity, and a proportionate aversion to real action."[8]

To keep your text moving smoothly, remember the following:

- Link quoted and paraphrased material *clearly to its source*. Where necessary, put in tags like "According to the governor . . ." or "As Erich Fromm has observed, . . ." When you quote several authors, make sure references like "he" or "the writer" point clearly to the one you have in mind.

- Steer your readers by telling them what *the point of a quotation* is or why you quote it. Prepare the reader to look for a key point:

Weak: In 1817, William Hazlitt expressed his views on Hamlet's character *in the following manner:* "He seems incapable of deliberate action and is only hurried into extremities on the spur of the occasion. . . ."

Better: Hazlitt, like Coleridge, *saw Hamlet as a man kept from action by excessive thought:* "He seems incapable . . ."

The Research Paper

- *Quote key words and phrases* as part of your own sentence. In addition to full-length quotations, use apt quoted words and phrases in wording your own conclusions, comments, interpretations:

The eloquent Renaissance prince became for Romantic critics like Charles Lamb "the shy, negligent, retiring Hamlet."

- When a quotation becomes part of a sentence of your own, *fit it into the grammatical pattern* of your own sentence—without changing the wording of the part quoted directly:

Unsatisfactory: Pope Pius described a just war in this way: "If it has been forced upon one by an evident and extremely grave injustice that in no way can be avoided."

Satisfactory: Pope Pius stated that a war is just "if it has been forced upon one by an evident and extremely grave injustice that in no way can be avoided."

R 3c   Organizing Your Notes

Group together note cards that contain related material.

Often a group of cards will record details pointing to a common generalization, evidence backing up the same major point. Often a group of cards will record related causes combining to produce a common result. Two related groups of cards may contain parallel sets of data for detailed comparison.

As your paper begins to assume definite shape, remember the following advice:

(1) *Work toward a unifying thesis.* Ask yourself: "What is this paper as a whole going to tell the reader?" Suppose you are writing a paper on the present state of gambling in the United States. Your problem will be to keep your paper from becoming a repository of miscellaneous facts about gambling laws, famous gamblers, different games of chance, and tourist life in Las Vegas. To unify your paper, you might concentrate on the legal aspects of gambling. You could then review in some detail the laws of Nevada as exceptions to antigambling laws in other states, the legal status of horse and dog races, the question of lotteries and games conducted for charitable purposes. Everything you say in the paper could support one single major point:

Thesis: Gambling laws in the United States are paradoxical and unpredictable.

To give thrust and direction to your paper, state the thesis early—at the end of a brief introduction.

(2) *Work out a definite overall strategy.* When writing about critical interpretations of Hamlet's character, do not simply give a dreary survey following straight chronological order. Instead, try to identify three or four major schools of thought. Group together critics interested in the *lone* Hamlet, who listen to his monologues and solitary musings. Group together critics interested in the *social* Hamlet, who are absorbed by his playacting and verbal fencing. Group together critics interested in the *child* Hamlet, who listen, in psychoanalyst's fashion, for hints of his early psychological history.

(3) *Write a preliminary outline.* Formulate a tentative thesis sentence summarizing the conclusion that your paper

seems to suggest. Your outline and your thesis sentence will enable you to decide which of your note cards contain irrelevant material and should be set aside. They will also help you to decide in which areas your notes need to be supplemented by further reading. A definitive outline preceding the final paper usually shows whether the paper has a unifying purpose, whether the major subdivisions of the paper contribute to that purpose, and whether unrelated odds and ends have been eliminated. (For forms of outlines, see O 7e.)

R 3d   Revising the First Draft

Allow time for a final rewriting of your first draft.

A first draft usually makes jerky reading. The writer is likely to have concentrated on getting the paper as a whole into shape, without always making it clear to readers how he or she got from one paragraph to the next. To help guide your final revision, do the following:

- Check for *clear overall intention.* Make sure that the main points you are trying to bring out are not merely implied but clearly and fully stated. State them preferably at the beginning of the paper following your introduction or, if more appropriate, toward the end of the paper in the form of a summary.

- Check for *adequate support.* Make sure you have the details and examples that your reader would accept as adequate evidence for your major points.

- Check for adequate *interpretation.* Many papers suffer from too much quotation, too much paraphrase, and not enough explanation and comparison. Examine key terms to see whether they need to be more explicitly defined. Explain terms like *Hellenistic, psychosomatic,* or *lingua franca.*

- Check for *coherence.* Make your reader see the relationship between different parts of your paper. Anticipate and answer the questions of a reader mired in a mass of details: "How did this get in here?" "Why do I have to study this particular set of statistics?" Make sure there is a clear **transition,** implied or stated, from paragraph to paragraph.

Exercises

A. Select an article or a chapter in a book on one of the general topics listed below. Assume that you are extracting important information or notable opinions for use in a larger research project. Prepare ten note cards, grouped around two or three major headings and illustrating the various techniques of note-taking. Choose one:

- the history of advertising
- secret wartime codes and how to break them
- the history of photography
- the Long March
- Hollywood's early stars
- the Cherokee nation
- the suffragette movement
- rape and the law

B. After finishing the first draft of a research paper, write a *one-page abstract* that spells out the thesis and summarizes the argument. (Your instructor may ask you to submit a *preliminary* summary of findings at an earlier stage of your investigation.)

R 4   Footnotes and Bibliographies

Follow the style of documentation required by your instructor.

Documentation enables your readers to identify, trace, and check your sources. Its purpose is to provide exact and comprehensive information in condensed form.

R 4a   Footnotes

Use footnotes to indicate the origin of facts, opinions, and illustrative material.

Use footnotes not only when you quote an author directly, but also when you merely paraphrase or summarize what was said.[1] A footnote is *not* necessary when the author has merely repeated something that is widely known or believed:

[1] Not all footnotes serve exclusively for documentation. Explanatory footnotes, of which this note is an illustration, may define technical terms unfamiliar only to some of the readers. They may provide information not necessary to the main trend of the argument.

Footnotes and Bibliographies

No Footnote: George Washington was elected to the Virginia assembly in 1758. (This is "common knowledge," the kind of fact likely to be recorded in public documents and found in many history books.)

Footnote: Samuel Eliot Morison describes Washington as "an eager and bold experimenter" in new agricultural methods.[17] (This is a judgment the historian made on the basis of first-hand investigation. The text already mentions his name; the footnote, not reprinted here, will give the exact source.)

Number your footnotes consecutively. Place the **footnote number** outside whatever punctuation goes with the sentence or paragraph to which it refers. Indent the footnote itself like a paragraph, and start it with the raised footnote number. Normally, capitalize the first word and use a period or other end punctuation at the end. In your typed manuscript, *single-space* your footnotes and put them in one of three positions:

- between two unbroken lines *immediately below the line of typed material* to which they belong.[2]

---

[2]Even when a different system of placing footnotes is required in the final paper, students may find the system of which this footnote is an illustration the most convenient one to follow in the first draft. It prevents errors when footnotes have to be renumbered because of changes in the manuscript.

- *at the bottom of the page,* separated from the text by an unbroken line or triple spacing. To estimate the amount of space required at the bottom of the page, you may have to type your footnotes on a separate sheet of paper first.

- on a separate sheet *at the end of your paper*. This system is usually required when a manuscript is submitted for publication.

R 4b   First References

Fully identify a source the first time you refer to it.

The most common type of footnote gives full information about a source the first time it is mentioned or drawn on in the text. The following sample footnotes illustrate the standard form for such a first reference, as well as the most important variations.

(1) *Standard reference to a book.* Give the author's full name, putting the first name *first.* After a comma, add the title of the book—*underlined* in typescript (italicized in print). Give the facts of publication in parentheses. (Include place of publication, name of publisher, date of publication.) After a comma, add the page reference ("p." for single page; "pp." for several pages: pp. 163–65).

[7] Mary McCarthy, <u>Memoirs of a Catholic Girlhood</u> (New York: Harcourt, 1957), p. 23.

[4] Neil Postman and Charles Weingartner, <u>Teaching as a Subversive Activity</u> (New York: Delacorte, 1969), pp. 158–59.

(2) *Newspaper or magazine article.* Enclose the title of the article in quotation marks; underline the title of the newspaper or magazine: "How to Deep-Freeze Bait," *The Fisherman's Monthly.* Give the date of issue, separated from what precedes and follows by commas. If a magazine provides a volume number, give it as an Arabic numeral, en-

close the date in parentheses, and give the page reference *without* using "p." or "pp.": 15 (Sept. 1975), 47.

³"U.S. Asked to Air Youth Exchanges," New York Times, 15 June 1968, p. 8, col. 1.

²Peter Collier, "The Red Man's Burden," Ramparts, 8 (Feb. 1970), 27.

(3) *Partial footnote.* If the text of your paper has given the author's full name, start your footnote with the title. (Do the same even if your text has given both name and title.) If your text attributes a quotation about American dialects to its author, the footnote might look like this:

²American English (New York: Oxford Univ. Press, 1958), p. 17.

(4) *Work with subtitle.* Separate the subtitle from the title by a colon unless the original has other punctuation. Underline the subtitle of a book; enclose both the title and the subtitle of an article in the same set of quotation marks.

¹¹Marshall McLuhan, Understanding Media: The Extensions of Man (New York: McGraw-Hill, 1964), p. 20.

¹³Horace Sutton, "Drugs: Ten Years to Doomsday?" Saturday Review, 53 (14 Nov. 1970), 19.

(5) *Edited or translated work.* Insert the editor's or translator's name after the title, separating it from the title by a comma. Use the abbreviation "ed." or "trans." The editor's name may come *first* if the author is unknown, if the editor has collected the work of different authors, or if the editor has brought together an author's work from different sources.

²H. L. Mencken, The Vintage Mencken, ed. Alistair Cooke (New York: Vintage, 1956), p. 49.

⁶Konrad Lorenz, On Agression, trans. Marjorie Kerr Wilson (New York: Harcourt, 1966), p. 7.

⁵Arna Bontemps, ed., American Negro Poetry (New York: Hill and Wang, 1963), p. 183.

(6) *Revised editions.* If a work has been brought up to date since its original publication, indicate the number of the edition you are using. Place it before the facts of publication, separating it from what precedes it by a comma.

²Albert C. Baugh, A History of the English Language, 2nd ed. (New York: Appleton, 1957), pp. 7-8.

¹¹M. B. Forman, ed., The Letters of John Keats, 3rd ed. (London: Milford, 1948), pp. 67-68.

(7) *Work published in several volumes.* Specify the number of the volume you are citing. Use a capital Roman numeral, insert it after the facts of publication, and separate it from what precedes and follows it by commas. Remember that after a volume number "p." and "pp." are omitted.

³Vernon Louis Parrington, Main Currents in American Thought: An Interpretation of American Literature from the Beginnings to 1920 (New York: Harcourt, 1930), III, 355.

(8) *Article in a collection.* Identify fully both the article and the anthology of which it is a part.

⁴Carl R. Rogers, "Two Divergent Trends," in Existential Psychology, ed. Rollo May (New York: Random, 1969), p. 87.

(9) *Encyclopedia entry.* Page numbers and facts of publication are unnecessary for *short* entries appearing in alphabetical order in well-known encyclopedias or dictionaries. Date or number of the edition used, however, is sometimes included because of the frequent revisions of major encyclopedias.

[2]M. J. Politis, "Greek Music," <u>Encyclopedia</u> <u>Americana</u>, 1956.

[4]"Drama," <u>Encyclopaedia</u> <u>Britannica</u>, 1958, VII, 596.

(10) *Bible or literary classic.* References to the Bible usually identify only book, chapter, and verse. The name of a book of the Bible is *not* underlined or put in quotation marks. References to a Shakespeare play available in many different editions may specify act, scene, and line; references to an epic poem book, canto, and stanza.

[4]Judges 13:5. (or) [4]Judges xiii.5.

[3]<u>Hamlet</u> ll.ii.311-22.

Note, however, that you will have to specify the edition used if textual variations are important, as with a new translation of the Bible. No identification is necessary for well-known or proverbial lines: "To be or not to be"; "The quality of mercy is not strained"; "They also serve who only stand and wait."

(11) *Quotations at second hand.* Make it clear that you are not quoting from the original or complete text.

[5]William Archer, letter of October 18, 1883, to his brother Charles; quoted in Henrik Ibsen, <u>Ghosts</u>, ed. Kai Jurgensen and Robert Schenkkan (New York: Avon, 1965), p. 135.

(12) *Pamphlets and unpublished material.* Indicate the nature and source of materials other than books and magazines: mimeographed pamphlet, unpublished doctoral dissertation, and the like. Start with the title if no author or editor is identified. Use quotation marks to enclose unpublished titles.

[6]Walter G. Friedrich, ed., "A Modern Grammar Chrestomathy" (Valparaiso, Indiana, mimeo., 1961), p. 12.

[7]U. Fuller Schmaltz, "The Weltschmerz of Charles Addams," Diss. Columbia 1959, p. 7.

[8]Grape Harvesting (Sacramento: California Department of Viticulture, 1969), pp. 8–9.

R 4c   Later References

Keep subsequent references short but clear.

There is no need to repeat the full name and title, or the facts of publication. Here are the most common possibilities:

(1) *Shortened reference.* Once you have fully identified a book, use the author's last name to identify it in later footnotes. Separate the name from the page reference by a comma.

[11]Baugh, p. 9.

When you are using *several works by the same author,* use the author's last name and a shortened form of the title:

[11]Baugh, History, p. 9.

(2) *One footnote for several quotations.* Avoid long strings of footnotes giving different page references to the

same work. If several quotations from the same work follow one another in the same paragraph of your paper, incorporate the page references in a single footnote. Use this method only when *no* quotations from another source intervene.

¹³Harrison, pp. 8-9, 12, 17.

(3) *Page references in the text.* If all or most of your references are to a single work, you may put page references in parentheses in the body of your text: (p. 37). Identify the source in your first footnote and explain your procedure.

¹Jerome S. Bruner, <u>On Knowing: Essays for the Left Hand</u> (New York: Atheneum, 1965), p. 3. All page references in the text of this paper are to this source.

(4) *Latin abbreviations.* An alternative system for shortened reference is frequently found in earlier scholarship but no longer in frequent use. Instead of repeating, in a shortened form, the author's name or the title, the writer may use *ibid.,* an abbreviation of Latin *ibidem,* "in the same place." When used by itself, without a page reference, it means "in the last publication cited, on the same page." When used with a page reference, it means "in the last publication cited, on the page indicated." Like other Latin abbreviations used in footnotes, *ibid.* is no longer commonly italicized. It can refer only to *the last source cited.*

¹G. B. Harrison, <u>Introducing Shakespeare</u> (Harmondsworth, Middlesex: Penguin Books, 1939), p. 28.

²Ibid., p. 37.

If a reference to a *different* work has intervened, the author's name is followed by *op. cit.,* short for *opere citato,* "in the work already cited." (This abbreviation cannot be used when *several works* by the same author have already been cited.)

[1]G. B. Harrison, <u>Introducing Shakespeare</u> (Harmondsworth, Middlesex: Penguin, 1947), p. 28.

[2]B. Ifor Evans, <u>A Short History of English Drama</u> (Harmondsworth, Middlesex: Penguin, 1948), pp. 51–69.

[3]Harrison, op. cit., p. 37.

R 4d   Abbreviations

Know scholarly abbreviations and technical terms that you may encounter in your sources.

The meaning of many of these will be clear from their context or position: *anon.* for "anonymous," *ch.* and *chs.* for "chapter" and "chapters," *col.* and *cols.* for "column" and "columns," *I.* and *II.* for "line" and "lines," *n.* and *nn.* for "note" and "notes." Others are not self-explanatory:

©	copyright (© 1961 by John W. Gardner)
c. or ca.	Latin *circa,* "approximately"; used for approximate dates and figures (c. 1952)
cf.	Latin *confer,* "compare"; often used loosely instead of *see* in the sense of "consult for further relevant material" (Cf. Ecclesiastes xii.12)
et al.	Latin *et alii,* "and others"; used in refer-

	ences to books by several authors (G. B. Harrison et al.)
f., ff.	"and the following page," "and the following pages" (See pp. 16 ff.)
loc. cit.	Latin *loco citato,* "in the place cited"; used without page reference (Baugh, loc. cit.)
MS, MSS	manuscript, manuscripts
n.d.	"no date," date of publication unknown
passim	Latin for "throughout"; "in various places in the work under discussion" (See pp. 54–56 et passim)
q.v.	Latin *quod vide,* "which you should consult"

R 4e   Final Bibliography

In your final bibliography, include all the information required to identify a source when first cited.

Your final bibliography will be based on your bibliography cards. Its main purpose is to describe in one single alphabetical list all sources you have used. You may include sources that you have found helpful or enlightening but have not actually quoted in your paper.

Entries in the bibliography *differ* from footnotes as follows:

(1) The *last name of the author* (or of the first author listed when a book has several authors) is placed first—since the bibliography is an *alphabetical* listing. The full name of the author is separated from what follows by a period.

(2) The *facts of publication* for a book are *not* enclosed in parentheses and are separated from what precedes and what follows by periods.

(3) Entries for books do not include page references; entries for parts of books or items in magazines give the *inclusive page numbers* for the whole selection.

The following might be sample entries from a final bibliography for a paper on photography as social document. Study the different kinds of entries. (See also the bibliography at the end of the sample research paper.)

Capa, Cornell, ed. The Concerned Photographer, Vol.
    II. New York: Grossman, 1972.

Capa, Robert. Images of War. New York: Grossman, n.d.

Dillard, Annie. "Sight into Insight." Harper's, 248
    (Feb. 1974), 39–46.

Eisenstaedt, Alfred. The Eye of Eisenstaedt. New
    York: Viking, 1969.

Gernsheim, Helmut, and Alison Gernsheim. Creative
    Photography: 1826 to the Present. Detroit:
    Wayne State Univ. Press, 1963.

Nairn, Ian. The American Landscape: A Critical View.
    New York: Random, 1965.

"A Photographer's Odyssey." The Oakland Herald,
    26 Aug. 1974, p. 9, col. 3.

Note: In a typed manuscript, single-space each individual item but leave a double space between items. Indent five spaces for the second and for subsequent lines of each item. If you list *several publications by the same author,* substitute a line composed of six consecutive hyphens for his name in second and subsequent entries. If *no name of author or editor is known to you,* list the publication alphabetically by the first letter of the title, not counting "The," "A," or "An."

Exercise

Interpret the information provided in the following footnotes:

⁶ C. E. Silberman. *Crisis in the Classroom: The Remaking of American Education.* (New York: Random, 1970), p. 26.

³ Robert E. Spiller et al., *Literary History of the United States,* rev. ed. (New York: Macmillan, 1953), p. 1343.

¹ William McGuire, ed., "The Freud/Jung Letters," *Psychology Today,* 7 (Feb. 1974), 41.

⁹ Euripides, *The Trojan Women,* trans. Richmond Lattimore, in *Greek Plays in Modern Translation,* ed. Dudley Fitts (New York: Dial, 1947), p. 161.

⁴ "Prison System Breaking Down?" *U.S. News and World Report,* 11 Aug. 1967, p. 61.

⁸ Kenneth Muir, ed., *Collected Poems of Sir Thomas Wyatt* (Cambridge, Mass.: Harvard Univ. Press, 1950), p. xx.

⁷ 1 Corinthians iii. 18–20.

¹³ Simone Weil, "The *Iliad,* or The Poem of Force," trans. Mary McCarthy, in *The Mint,* ed. Geoffrey Grigson, No. 2 (1948), p. 85.

¹² Cf. *The Complete Works of William Hazlitt,* ed. P. P. Howe (London: Dent, 1932), XI, 88 ff.

⁸ Paul Goodman, "The New Reformation," *New York Times Magazine,* 14 Sept. 1969, p. 14.

Review Exercise: Sample Research Paper

Study the following sample research paper, adapted from a student-written paper. Pay special attention to the way the author has adapted and worked into the text a variety of quoted material. Compare the different kinds of footnotes used. Contrast the way sources are identified in the footnotes and in the final bibliography. How successful has the author been in meeting the standards outlined in the preceding chapter?

THE FUROR OVER IBSEN

by

John Balfour

English 2, Section 5

March 22, 1969

OUTLINE

Thesis: Ibsen's plays were denounced as immoral and at
          the same time celebrated as advancing a new
          morality.

Introduction: The divisive effect of Ibsen's plays

      I.   Ibsen's plays and his time

           A. The morality of his plays

           B. The moral views of his contemporaries

     II.   The attack on Ibsen

           A. Scott's denunciation

           B. Archer's collection of criticism

    III.   Shaw's defense of Ibsen's plays

     IV.   Ibsen's portrait of his critics

           A. The moralist in his plays

           B. Ibsen's letters

Conclusion: Ibsen as father of the modern drama

THE FUROR OVER IBSEN

What did Henrik Ibsen do? According to Granville-
Barker, he "split the English theater in two."[1] Indeed,
"as everyone knows, the introduction of Ibsen into England
was not a peaceful one. In its wake came one of those great
outbursts of critical frenzy and inflamed controversy which
at regular intervals enliven literary history."[2] In England,
as in the rest of Europe, the public was split into two
factions: those who placed Ibsen on the blacklist as
"immoral"; and those who saw in him the champion of a new
morality.

Ibsen's plays aroused both indignation and enthusiasm
because he fought against maintaining appearances at the
expense of happiness, or what he termed hypocrisy. Una
Ellis-Fermor, a translator and lifelong student of Ibsen,
said that he "took upon himself the task of exposing the
makeshift morality of his contemporaries in private and
public life":

---

[1]Harley Granville-Barker, "When Ibsen Split the English
Stage in Two," Literary Digest, 28 April 1928, p. 24.

[2]"A Retrospective Eye on Ibsen," Theatre Arts Monthly,
12 (March 1928), 199.

379

-2-

> In The Pillars of the Community he examines
> the lie in public life, the tragic struggle
> of Karsten Bernick to hide his sin and pre-
> serve his reputation at the expense of another
> man's good name. . . . In A Doll's House and
> Ghosts the subject is the lie in domestic life;
> the first shows the destruction of a marriage
> by an unreal and insincere relationship between
> husband and wife, and the second the destruction
> of the lives and souls of the characters by the
> oppressive tyranny of convention.[3]

In Ghosts, a dutiful and unloving wife keeps up an elaborate

façade of respectability for a profligate husband. She

finds herself defeated when her cherished son returns home

suffering incurably from the syphilis he has inherited from

his father. According to Bernard Shaw, the play was "an

uncompromising and outspoken attack on marriage as a useless

sacrifice," the story of a woman who had wasted her life in

manufacturing a "monstrous fabric of lies and false appear-

ances."[4]

Against the tyranny of middle-class standards, Ibsen

pitted his own concept of individual integrity. He felt,

according to Georg Brandes, that "the individuality of the

human being is to be preserved for its own sake, not for

---

[3] Henrik Ibsen, Three Plays, trans. Una Ellis-Fermor
(Hammondsworth, Middlesex: Penguin Books, 1950), pp. 9-11.

[4] The Quintessence of Ibsenism, 3rd ed. (New York: Hill,
1957), pp. 86, 88.

the sake of higher powers; and since beyond all else the
individual should remain free and whole, all concessions
made to the world represent to Ibsen the foul fiend, the
evil principle."[5] One of the main ideas fused into Ibsen's
plays, according to an article in the Encyclopaedia
Britannica, is "the supreme importance of individual character, of personality: in the development and enrichment
of the individual he saw the only hope for a really cul-
tured and enlightened society."[6]

A Doll's House was particularly loaded with the "first
duty to oneself" theme. Nora, in the last act, wakes to the
fact that she is not worthy to be a good mother and wife
because she has been merely a submissive servant and foil
first for her father and then for her husband; she has been
so protected and guided by them that she has no individual
conception of life and its complexities. Nora realized that
she did not know enough about the world and her place in it
to be really "a reasonable human being," and she felt a
duty to become one.[7] Her life all at once seemed so

---

[5]Creative Spirits of the Nineteenth Century, trans.
Rasmus B. Anderson (New York: T. Crowell, 1923), p. 373.

[6]"Ibsen, Henrik Johan," Encyclopaedia Britannica, 1958,
XII, 38.

[7]Henrik Ibsen, Four Great Plays by Ibsen (New York: Dutton,
1959), p. 65.

-4-

artificial and meaningless to her that she felt like a doll living in a doll's house, Nora left her husband and children to try to gain an understanding of real life, and when she "banged the door of A Doll's House, the echo of that violence was heard across the continent."[8]

Ibsen wrote these plays at a time when people felt a general ferment, a "spirit of the age" or "movement of the century" that had introduced everywhere a tendency toward change. Spokesmen for the modern age referred to the "new phase into which humanity is passing" and expressed the conviction that "society must undergo a transformation or perish."[9] But the voices resisting the clamor for "innovations" were equally strong. Their watchword was devotion to duty--toward God, country, one's family and husband. Self-denial for the sake of greater forces was the commendable action. The churches taught it was sinful to assert one's own wishes and desires. The people, especially the dominated wife with whom Isben frequently deals, were exhorted to live for the good of everyone but themselves.

---

[8]"Drama," Encyclopaedia Britannica, 1958, VII, 600.

[9]William Barry in The Nineteenth-Century (1889); quoted in Michael Goodwin, ed., Nineteenth-Century Opinion: An Anthology (1877-1901) (Hammondsworth, Middlesex: Penguin, 1951), pp. 124,122.

Spokesmen for the emancipation of women were told in the public press that "men are men and women, women"; that "sex is a fact--no Act of Parliament can eliminate it"; that "where two ride on a horse, one must needs ride behind."[10] They were told that in women's hands "rests the keeping of a pure tone in society, of a high standard in morality, of a lofty devotion to duty in political life." If she were to enter openly into political conflict, she would "debase her sex" and "lower the ideal of womanhood amongst men."[11]

The old-fashioned moralists were shocked by the "Ibsenist" view that self-fulfillment is more important than the sanctity of marriage, one's duty to others, and even business success. According to Arthur Bingham Walkley, drama critic for the London _Times_, "Ibsen became a bogey to many worthy people who had never read or seen a single one of his plays." To these people, "Ibsenism was supposed vaguely to connote 'Woman's Rights,' Free Love, a new and fearful kind of wildfowl called 'Norwegian Socialism,' and

---

[10]Quoted in _Nineteenth-Century Opinion_, pp. 103, 109.
[11]_Nineteenth-Century_ _Opinion_, pp. 103-104.

generally, every manifestation of discontent with the existing order of things."[12] Clement Scott, a prominent drama critic, led such formidable opposition against Ibsen's dramas, especially A Doll's House and Ghosts, that they were actually banned for a time from English stages. "Ibsen fails," Scott says, "because he is, I suppose, an atheist, and has not realized what the great backbone of religion means to the English race." Scott continues, "He fails because his plays are nasty, dirty, impure, clever if you like, but foul to the last degree; and healthy-minded English people don't like to stand and sniff over an ash-pit."[13]

Many of the people causing the uproar against Ibsen used similar exaggerated and irrational language. William Archer, the first English translator of Ibsen, collected some of the attacks appearing in the English press when Ghosts was first produced. The play was called "disgusting," "loathsome," "gross," and "revoltingly suggestive and blasphemous." It was compared to "a dirty act done publicly"

---

[12]"Ibsen in England," Living Age, 12 (Sept. 21, 1901), 790.
[13]Quoted in "Inside Views of Ibsen in the Nineties," Literary Digest, 12 May 1928, 24.

and was called "a piece to bring the stage into disrepute and dishonour with every right-thinking man and woman."[14]

Those who defended Ibsen--Shaw, Archer, Walkley-- blamed his unpleasant reception in England on both his revolutionary themes and his new dramatic technique. We shall steer away from Ibsen's new dramatic technique and instead discuss the defense of Ibsenism as a new moral philosophy. Shaw himself has been called one of the men "who summon their generation to act by a new and higher standard." He made Ibsen his hero because Ibsen championed the view that Shaw made the basis for many of his own plays:

> By "morals" (or "ideals") Shaw means conven-
> tional, current standards. Because these stand-
> ards are universal and inherited from the past,
> they often do not fit particular situations and
> present-day societies. Therefore good men--like
> some of Ibsen's characters--often choose to act
> "immorally," contrary to accepted morality.[15]

To Shaw, Ibsen became the first of the two types of pioneers classified by Shaw in The Quintessence of Ibsenism. This type of pioneer asserts "that it is right to do some- thing hitherto regarded as infamous." Ibsen felt that it was right to think first of building himself and secondly

---

[14] Quoted in Shaw, Quintessence, pp. 91-93.

[15] Reuben A. Brower, "George Bernard Shaw," in Major British Writers, ed. G. B. Harrison (New York: Harcourt, 1959), II, 687.

of building the institutions of society. To Shaw, this
change explained the unkindly reception of Ibsen's new
thoughts in England: "So much easier is it to declare the
right wrong than the wrong right. . . . a guilty society
can more readily be persuaded that any apparently innocent
act is guilty than that any apparently guilty act is innocent."[16] Shaw seems to feel that Ibsen would have had more
success telling people it was wrong to work on Monday than
he would have had saying it was right to work on Sunday.
Men could not accept the idea that the obligation of self-
sacrifice could be removed from them--that it would be all
right for them to consider a duty toward themselves first.

Shaw complained of the difficulty of finding "accurate
terms" for Ibsen's new "realist morality." To Shaw, it was
Ibsen's thesis that "the real slavery of today is slavery to
ideals of goodness." Ibsen had devoted himself to showing
that "the spirit of man is constantly outgrowing the ideals,"
and that "thoughtless conformity" to them is constantly
producing tragic results. Among those "ridden by current
ideals," Ibsens plays were bound to be denounced as immoral.
But, Shaw concluded,

---

[16]Shaw, pp. 23-25.

> There can be no question as to the effect
> likely to be produced on an individual by
> his conversion from the ordinary acceptance
> of current ideals as safe standards of conduct,
> to the vigilant openmindedness of Ibsen. It
> must at once greatly deepen the sense of moral
> responsibility.[17]

Ibsen himself knew well and satirized in his plays the moralists who inveighed against "the undermining of family life" and the "defiance of the most solemn truths." In Ghosts, Pastor Manders, who represents a timid regard for convention, warns people against books that he vaguely associates with "intellectual progress"--and that he has not read. Rörlund, the schoolmaster in The Pillars of the Community, sums up the position of the guardians of conventional morality when he says:

> Our business is to keep society pure . . . to keep
> out all these experimental notions that an impatient
> age wants to force on us.[18]

Ironically, Rörlund provides a moral façade for "practical men of affairs" like the ship owner Bernick. Bernick, who talks about his "deep-rooted sense of decency," has abandoned the woman he loved in order to marry a wealthy girl

---

[17]Shaw, pp. 147-49, 152, 154.

[18]Ibsen, Three Plays, pp. 27-28.

and save the family business. He has abandoned to need and
shame a married woman with whom he has had a secret affair.
He has saved his own reputation in the community at the
expense of having a younger friend blackened as a libertine
and a thief. Bernick's defense of his conduct is that he
lives in a community in which "a youthful indiscretion is
never wiped out." The "community itself forces us into
crooked ways."[19] But Ibsen's heroes are people who rebel
against the "tyranny of custom and convention"; who hold
that "the spirit of truth and the spirit of freedom" are
the "true pillars of the community."[20]

Ibsen was not intimidated by the controversy caused by
his plays. In a letter to a friend he wrote in 1881, he
said: "Ghosts will probably cause alarm in some circles.
. . . If it didn't do that, there would have been no need
to write it." In a letter written a year later, he said:
"That my new play would produce a howl from the camp of those
'men of stagnation' was something I was quite prepared for."
Shortly afterward, he summed up his faith in the future
in a letter that said in part:

---

[19] Three Plays, pp. 48, 97-98.
[20] Three Plays, pp. 116, 137.

-11-

> In time, and not before very long at that,
> the good people up home will get into their
> heads some understanding of <u>Ghosts</u>. But all
> those desiccated, decrepit individuals who
> pounced on this work, they will come in for
> devastating criticism in the literary histories
> of the future. People will be able to sniff
> out the nameless snipers and thugs who directed
> their dirty missiles at me from their ambush in
> Professor Goos's mouldy rag and other similar
> places. My book holds the future. Yon crowd
> that roared about it haven't even any proper
> contact with their own genuinely vital age.[21]

It was Ibsen's assertion of man's duty to himself,

against the tradition of conformity to custom and con-

vention, that was the main grounds of significant controversy

over Ibsen's works. In presenting this view in his plays,

as a modern critic says, "Ibsen established realism as the

ruling principle of modern drama." Problems of the day had

been aired on the stage before, "but nobody before Ibsen

had treated them without equivocation or without stressing

secondary matters while ignoring primary ones." Because

he was the first, "Henrik Ibsen . . . has long held the

unofficial title of 'father of the modern drama.'"[22]

---

[21]Quoted in Henrik Ibsen, <u>Ghosts</u>, trans. Kai Jurgensen
and Robert Schenkkan (New York: Avon, 1965), pp. 126, 129-30.

[22]John Gassner, Introduction to <u>Four Great Plays</u>,
pp. vii-viii.

BIBLIOGRAPHY

Brandes, Georg. _Creative Spirits of the Nineteenth Century_.
Trans. Rasmus B. Anderson. New York: T Crowell, 1923.

Brower, Reuben A. "George Bernard Shaw." _Major British
Writers_. Ed. G.B. Harrison. 2 vols. New York: Harcourt
1959.

"Drama." _Encyclopaedia Britannica_. 1958, VII, 576-616.

Goodwin, Michael, ed. _Nineteenth-Century Opinion: An
Anthology (1877-1901)_. Hammondsworth, Middlesex:
Penguin, 1951.

Granville-Barker, Harley. "When Ibsen Split the English
Stage in Two." _Literary Digest_, 28 April 1928, 24-25.

Ibsen, Henrik. _Four Great Plays by Ibsen_. New York: Dutton,
1959.

-----. _Ghosts_. Trans. Kai Jurgensen and Robert Schenkkan.
New York: Avon, 1965.

-----. _Three Plays_. Trans. Una Ellis-Fermor. Hammondsworth,
Middlesex: Penguin, 1950.

"Ibsen, Henrik Johan." _Encyclopaedia Britannica_, 1958, XII,
37-41.

"Inside Views of Ibsen in the Nineties." _Literary Digest_,
12 May 1928, 24.

"A Retrospective Eye on Ibsen." _Theatre Arts Monthly_, 12
(March 1928), 199-211.

Shaw, Bernard. _The Quintessence of Ibsenism_, 3rd ed.
New York: Hill, 1957.

Walkley, A. B. "Ibsen in England." _Living Age_, 12
(21 Sept. 1901), 790.

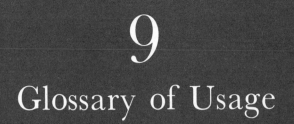

9
Glossary of Usage

Note: The following glossary reviews the status of words, word forms, and constructions that are frequently criticized as careless, illogical, excessively informal, or otherwise limited in appropriateness and effectiveness.[1]

a, an The *a* should appear only before words that begin with a consonant when pronounced: *a desk, a chair, a house, a year, a C, a university.* The *an* should appear before words that begin with a vowel when pronounced (though, in writing, the first letter may be a consonant): *an eye, an essay question, an honest man, an A, an M, an uninformed reader.* In the latter position, *a* is nonstandard.

above, above-mentioned, aforementioned, aforesaid Avoid the use of *above, above-mentioned, aforementioned,* and the like, to refer to something previously mentioned. These phrases suggest the wooden, bureaucratic style of some business letters, many government publications, and most legal documents. Use a less mechanical expression like *this point, this fact, these considerations.*

allusion, illusion An "allusion" is a hint or indirect reference (to call an athlete a "Goliath" is to use a Biblical allusion). An "illusion" is a deceptive sense impression or a mistaken belief. When an illusion is serious and persistent enough, it may become a "delusion."

amount, number *Amount* is sometimes used loosely instead of *number* in reference to things counted individually and as separate units.

---

[1] For confusing words often included in a Glossary of Usage, see SP 1c; for a list of idiomatic prepositions, see D 1e.

Satisfactory: A large number [not *amount*] of people were waiting.

Satisfactory: The *number* [not *amount*] of unsold cars on dealers' lots was growing steadily.

and and but at the beginning of a sentence When *and* and *but* are used at the beginning of a sentence, or at the beginning of a paragraph, they have the effect of partly canceling out the pause signaled by the period or by the paragraph break. They can therefore suggest a sudden or an important afterthought. But many modern writers start sentences with *and* or *but* merely to avoid heavier, more formal connectives like *moreover, furthermore, however,* and *nevertheless.*

and/or *And/or* is an awkward combination sometimes necessary in commercial or official documents.

angle, approach, slant *Angle, approach,* and *slant* are overused as synonyms for "attitude," "point of view," "position," or "procedure."

apt, liable, prone In informal speech and writing, *apt, liable,* and *prone* all appear in the sense of "likely." In formal usage, *apt* suggests that something is likely because of someone's aptitude ("He is apt to become a successful artist"); *liable* suggests that what is likely is burdensome or undesirable ("He is liable to break his leg"); *prone* suggests that something is almost inevitable because of strong habit or predisposition ("He is prone to suspect others").

as *As* as a substitute for *that* or *whether* ("I don't know *as* I can come") or as a substitute for *who* ("Those *as* knew her avoided her") is nonstandard. As a substitute for *be-*

cause or *while, as* is often criticized as ambiguous, unemphatic, or overused:

> *As* [better: "because"] we had no money, we gave him a check.

attribute, contribute *Contribute* means "to give one's share" or "to have a share" in something; *attribute* means "to trace or ascribe something to a cause or source" ("He *attributed* the crossing of the letters in the mail to the intervention of a supernatural power") .

being as, being that As substitutes for *because* or *since, being as* and *being that* ("*being that* I was ill") are nonstandard.

between, among *Between* is historically related to *twain,* which in turn is a variant of *two.* As a result, grammarians have often restricted *between* to references to two of a kind (distinguish *between* right and wrong) and required *among* in references to more than two (distinguish *among* different shades of color). *Between* is also appropriate when more than two things can be considered in pairs of two:

> He had sand *between* his toes.
> Bilateral trade agreements exist *between* many European countries.

blame for, blame on There are two idiomatic uses of the word *blame:* "He blamed the passenger *for* the accident" and "He blamed the accident *on* the passenger." The first of these is preferred in formal English.

calculate, reckon, expect, guess In formal written English, *calculate* and *reckon* imply computing or systematic reasoning; *expect* implies expectation or anticipation; *guess* implies conjecture. In the sense of "think," "suppose," or "consider," these verbs are colloquial or dialectal.

can and may   Formal English uses *can* in the sense of "be able to" or "be capable of," *may* to indicate permission. The use of *can* to indicate permission, increasingly common in speech and writing, is often considered informal:

Formal: You *may* (have my permission to) take as much as you *can* (are able to) eat.

Informal: *Can* I speak to you for a minute?

cannot help but   Although occasionally found in writing, *cannot help but* is widely criticized as illogical or confused:

Satisfactory: I *cannot help* wishing that I had never met you.

Satisfactory: I *cannot but* wish that I had never met you.

compare with, compare to   We compare two cities *with* each other to see what they have in common, but we compare a city *to* an anthill to show what a city is like.

continual, continuous   To be "continuous," something must extend without interruption in space or in time. People may keep up a "continual" conversation, interrupted because they have to pause for breath.

couple of   In formal writing, *couple* refers to two of a kind, a pair. Used in the sense of "several" or "a few," it is colloquial. Used before a plural noun without a connecting *of,* it is nonstandard.

Colloquial: We had to wait *a couple of* minutes.

Nonstandard: We had only *a couple* dollars left.

credible, credulous, creditable   Stories may be credible or incredible; the people who read them may be credulous or incredulous. An act that does someone credit is a creditable act.

cute, great, lovely, wonderful   Words like *cute, great, lovely,* and *wonderful* so often express thoughtless or insincere praise that their use in formal writing can suggest immaturity. *Cute* is colloquial.

different than   *Different from* is characteristic of formal written English. Nevertheless, *different than,* widely used in speech, is becoming acceptable in writing ("Life in cadet school for Major Major was no *different than* life had been for him all along."—Joseph Heller, *Catch-22*). *Different than* is the more economical way of introducing a clause:

Economical:	We tried a different method *than* we had used last year.
Less Economical:	We tried a different method *from the one* we had used last year.

disinterested, uninterested   In formal writing, *disinterested* usually means "unswayed by personal, selfish interest" or "impartial" ("We were sure he would be a *disinterested* judge"). *Disinterested* used in the sense of "uninterested" or "indifferent" is objectionable to many readers.

do form for emphasis   Verb forms with *do, does,* or *did* can serve as emphatic variants of the simple present and the simple past: "She may not wear the latest fashions, but she *does* know how to cook." In student writing, the emphatic *do* is sometimes overused:

Overdone: I really *did appreciate* the teacher's help an awful lot.

Better: I *appreciated* the teacher's help.

double comparative, double superlative Short adjectives usually form the comparative by adding the suffix *er* (*cheaper*), the superlative by adding the suffix *est* (*cheapest*). Long adjectives, and adverbs ending in *ly*, usually employ the intensifiers *more* and *most* instead (*more expensive, most expensive; more carefully, most carefully*). Forms using both the suffix and the intensifier are non-standard (*more cheaper, most cheapest*).

double negative Double and triple negatives—the use of additional negative words to reinforce a negation already expressed—are nonstandard: "I *didn't* do *nothing*," "*Nobody* comes to see me *no more*."

due to as a preposition *Due to* is generally accepted as an adjective: "His absence was *due to* ill health." "His absence, *due to* ill health, upset our schedule." As a preposition meaning "because of," *due to* is often criticized:

Objectionable: He canceled his lecture *due to* ill health.

Safe: He canceled his lecture *because of* ill health.

each other, one another Conservative writers distinguish between *each other* (referring to two persons or things) and *one another* (referring to more than two).

enthuse *Enthuse* is a "back formation" from the noun *enthusiasm* and is used in colloquial English as a convenient shortcut for "become enthusiastic" and "move to enthusiasm." Similar back formations, like *reminisce* from *reminiscence,* have become generally acceptable. *Enthuse* still has a long way to go.

etc.   *Etc.,* the Latin abbreviation for "and so on" or "and the like," often serves as a vague substitute for additional details, examples, or illustrations. Furthermore, *ect.* is a common misspelling; "and etc." and "such as . . . etc." are redundant.

farther, further; all the farther   A traditional rule required *farther* in references to space and distance ("We traveled *farther* than we had expected"), *further* in references to degree and quantity ("We discussed it *further* at our next meeting") and in the sense of "additional" ("without *further* delay"). *Further* is now widely accepted as appropriate in all three senses.

All the farther in the sense of "as far as" ("This is *all the farther* we go") is variously classified as colloquial, non-standard, or dialectal.

get, got, gotten   The verb *get* is used in many idiomatic expressions. Some of these are colloquial:

> *have got* (for "own," "possess," "have available")
> I *have got* ten dollars; she *has got* blue eyes; you *have got* ten minutes.
>
> *have got to* (for "have to," "must," "be obliged")
> I *have got to* leave now; we *have got to* think of our customers.
>
> *get to* (for "succeed")
> I finally *got to* see him.
>
> *get* (for "understand")
> *Get* it?

get (for "arrest," "hit," "kill")
> The police finally *got* him.

get (for "puzzle," "irritate," "annoy")
> What really *gets* me is that he never announces his tests.

Some grammarians commend the use of *get* in sentences like "He *got hit* by a truck" as an emphatic and unambiguous alternative to the ordinary passive, formed with *be, am, was, were* ("He *was hit* by a truck"). This use of *got* is still widely considered informal.

In American English, *have gotten* is an acceptable alternative to *have got,* except when the latter means *have* or *have to.*

hadn't ought to   In formal English, *ought,* unlike some other auxiliaries, has no form for the past tense. *Hadn't ought* is informal; *had ought* nonstandard.

Informal: You *hadn't ought* to ask him.
Formal: You *ought not to have* asked him.

hopefully   When used instead of expressions like "I hope" or "let us hope," *hopefully* is considered illogical by conservative readers.

Informal: *Hopefully,* the forms will be ready by Monday.
Formal: *I hope* the forms will be ready by Monday.

if, whether   Conservative readers object to *if* when used to express doubt or uncertainty after such verbs as *ask, don't know, wonder, doubt.* The more formal connective is *whether:* "I doubt *whether* his support would do much good."

in, into Formal writing often requires *into* rather than *in* to indicate direction: "He came *into* [not *in*] the room."

in terms of A vague all-purpose connective frequent in jargon: "What have you seen lately *in terms of* new plays?"

Jargon: *Virtue* originally meant "manliness" *in terms of* [better: "in the sense of"] warlike prowess or fortitude.

infer, imply In formal usage, *imply* means to "indicate or suggest a certain conclusion"; *infer* means "to draw a conclusion on the basis of what has been indicated or suggested." A statement can have various implications, which may lead to inferences on the part of the reader.

irregardless Used instead of *regardless, irregardless* is often heard in educated speech but is widely considered nonstandard.

it's me, it is I Traditional grammarians required *it is I* on the grounds that the linking verb *is* equates the pronoun *I* with the subject *it* and thus makes necessary the use of the subject form. Modern grammarians accept *it is me* on the grounds that usual English word order (he hit *me*; she asked *me*) makes the object form natural. *It's me* is now freely used in informal speech; other pronouns (*us, him, her*) are still occasionally criticized as uneducated usage.

Informal: I thought it was *him*. It could have been *us*.
Formal: It was *he* who first raised the subject.

judicial, judicious A "judicial" decision is a decision reached by a judge or by a court. A "judicious" decision shows sound judgment. Not every judicial decision is judicious.

later, latter "Although both Alfred and Francis were supposed to arrive at eight, the former came earlier, the *latter later.*"

learn, teach In standard English, the teacher *teaches* (rather than *learns*) the learner; the learner is *taught* (rather than *learned*) by the teacher.

leave, let In formal usage, *leave* does not mean "allow" or "permit"; you do not "leave" somebody do something. Nor does *leave* take the place of *let* in suggestions like "Let us call a meeting."

less, fewer *Less* is often used interchangeably with *fewer* before plural nouns. This use of *less* was once widely condemned. The safe practice is to use *less* in references to extent, amount, degree (*less* friction, *less* money, *less* heat) but not in references to number (*fewer* people, *fewer* homes, *fewer* requirements) .

like as a connective In informal speech, *like* is widely used as a connective replacing *as* or *as if* at the beginning of a clause:

Informal: Do *like* I tell you.
Formal: Do *as* I tell you.
Informal: The patient felt *like* he had slept for days.
Formal: The patient felt *as if* [or *as though*] he had slept for days.

401

Note that *like* is acceptable in formal usage as a preposition: "The girl looked *like* her mother."

moral, morale　We talk about the "moral" of a story but about the "morale" of troops. People with good morale are not necessarily very moral, and vice versa.

most, almost　*Most* is informal when used in the sense of "almost" or "nearly": *"Most* everybody was there." "Mrs. Jones considers herself an authority on *most* any subject."

on account of　Nonstandard as a substitute for *because.*

Nonstandard:　Once she is married, a teacher is likely to stop teaching *on account of* [should be "because"] she will have to take care of her own children.

plan on　In formal usage, substitute *plan to.*

Informal:　My father had always *planned on* him taking over the farm.

Formal:　My father had always *planned to* have him take over the farm.

possessives with verbal nouns　A traditional rule requires that a verbal noun (gerund) be preceded by a possessive in sentences like the following:

Formal:　He mentioned *John's winning* a scholarship.

Formal:　I am looking forward to *your mother's staying* with us.

This rule is widely observed in formal writing. In informal speech and writing, the plain form is more common:

Informal:　Imagine *John winning* a scholarship!

A combination of a pronoun and a verbal with the *-ing* ending may express two different relationships. In the sentence "I saw *him returning* from the library," you actually saw *him*. In the sentence "I object to *his using* my toothbrush," you are not objecting to *him* but merely to one of *his* actions. *My, our, his, their* use the possessive pronoun when the object of a verb or of a preposition is not the person himself but one of his actions, traits, or experiences:

> We investigated the chances of *his* being elected.
>
> There is no excuse for *their* not writing sooner.
>
> I do not like *your* associating with the neighborhood children.

preposition at the end of a sentence   Teachers no longer tell students not to end a sentence with a preposition. The preposition that ends a sentence is idiomatic, natural English, though more frequent in informal than in formal use.

Informal:	I don't remember what we talked *about*.
Informal:	She found her mother-in-law hard to live *with*.
Formal:	Let us not betray the ideals *for* which these men died.
Formal:	Do not ask *for* whom the bell tolls.

prepositions often criticized   *Inside of* (for *inside*), *outside of* (for *outside*), and *at about* (for *about*) are redundant.

Back of for *behind* (*back of* the house), *inside of* for *within* (*inside of* three hours), *off of* for *off* (get *off of* the table), *outside of* for *besides* or *except* (no one *outside of* my friends), and *over with* for *over* (it's *over with*) are colloquial.

403

As to, as regards, and *in regard to* are generally acceptable, but they can seem heavy-handed and bureaucratic when used as indiscriminate substitutes for briefer or more precise prepositions.

Awkward:	I questioned him as to the nature of his injury.
Preferable:	I questioned him *about* his injury.

As to whether, in terms of, and *on the basis of* flourish in all varieties of jargon.

Per (a dollar *per* day), *as per* (*as per* your request), and *plus* (quality *plus* service) are common in business and newspaper English but inappropriate in a noncommercial context.

provided, provided that, providing *Provided, provided that,* and *providing* are interchangeable in a sentence like "He will withdraw his complaint, *provided* you apologize." However, only *provided* has escaped criticism and is therefore the safest form to use.

reason is because In informal speech, *the reason . . . is because* often takes the place of the more formal *the reason . . . is that.* The former construction is often criticized as redundant, since *because* repeats the idea of cause already expressed in the word *reason.* Either construction can make a sentence unnecessarily awkward.

Informal:	*The reason* that the majority rules *is because* it is strongest.
Formal:	*The reason* that the majority rules *is that* it is strongest.
Less Awkward:	The majority rules *because* it is strongest.

respectfully, respectively *Respectfully* means "full of re-spect"; *respectively* means "with respect or reference to each of several things in the order in which they were mentioned" ("*Un* and *deux* mean one and two respec-tively").

shall, will In current American usage, *will* usually indi-cates simply that something is going to happen:

> I *will* ask him tomorrow.
> You *will* find it on your desk.
> Mr. Smith *will* inform you of our plans.

The more emphatic *shall* often indicates that something is going to happen as the result of strong determination, definite obligation, or authoritative command:

> I *shall* return.
> We *shall* do our best.
> Wages of common laborers *shall* not exceed twenty dollars a day.

Shall is also common in questions that invite the listener's approval or consent:

> *Shall* I wait for you?
> *Shall* we dance?

Formal English used to require *shall* for simple future in the first person: "I *shall* see him tomorrow." Current hand-books of grammar no longer require the observance of this convention.

405

so and such In *formal English, so* and *such* show that something has reached a definite point, producing certain characteristic results:

> She was so frightened *that she was unable to speak.*
>
> There was such an uproar *that the chairman banged his gavel in vain.*

Informal English often omits the characteristic result. *So* and *such* then function as **intensifiers:** "I am *so* glad." "He is *such* a lovely boy." You can make such sentences generally acceptable in two different ways. Substitute an intensifier like *very* or *extremely:* "I am *very* glad." Or add a clause giving the characteristic result: "He is such a lovely boy *that all the girls adore him.*"

split infinitives Occasionally a modifier breaks up an infinitive; that is, a verbal formed with *to* (*to come, to promise, to have written*) . The resulting split infinitive has long been idiomatic English and occurs in the work of distinguished writers. The traditional rule against it is now all but obsolete. However, a split infinitive can be awkward if the modifier that splits the infinitive is more than one word:

Awkward: He ordered us *to* with all possible speed *return* to our stations.

Better: He ordered us *to return* to our stations with all possible speed.

subjunctive *In formal usage* subjunctive forms occur in clauses concerned with possibilities rather than with facts:
After *if, as if,* and *as though,* use *were* instead of *was*

if the possibility you have in mind is *contrary to fact or highly improbable:*

> The bird looked as if it *were* a plane.
> If I *were* you, I would try to improve my language habits.
> He acts as if his name *were* John D. Rockefeller.

Use *is* or *was* if you are considering a genuine possibility:

> If your brother *was* ill, he should have notified you.
> It looks as if the plane *is* going to be late.

Use subjunctive forms in noun clauses *after verbs indicating that something is desirable or necessary* but has not yet come about. "I wish I *were* [not "I *was*"] a wise old man." Forms like *answer* instead of *answers, go* instead of *goes* or *went,* and *be* instead of *is* or *was* occur after verbs signaling a suggestion, a request, a command, or a resolution:

> His wife insists that he *spend* more time at home.
>
> We demand that he *repay* all his debts.
>
> I move that this question *be* referred to one of our innumerable committees.

superlative in reference to two In informal speech and writing, the superlative rather than the comparative frequently occurs in comparisons between only two things. This use of the superlative used to be considered illogical:

Informal: Which of the two candidates is the *best* speaker?
Formal: Which of the two candidates is the *better* speaker?

take and, try and, up and *Take and* (in "I'd *take and* prune those roses") and *up and* (in "He *up and* died") are dialectal. *Try and* for *try to* ("I'd *try and* change his mind") is colloquial.

these kind Agreement requires *"this kind* of car" or *"these kinds* of fish." *"These kind* of cars" and *"those kind* of cars" are informal.

titles: Dr., Prof., Reverend In references to holders of academic degrees or titles, *Dr. Smith* and *Professor Brown* are courteous and correct. *Professor* is sometimes abbreviated when it precedes the full name: *Prof. Paul F. Brown.* In references to a clergyman, *Reverend* is usually preceded by *the* and followed by the first name, by initials, or by *Mr.* (*the Reverend William Carper; the Reverend W. F. Carper; the Reverend Mr. Carper*).

type, type of, -type The practice of omitting the *of* in expressions like "this *type* of plane" is colloquial. *Type* is increasingly used as a suffix to turn nouns into adjectives: "an escape-type novel," "a drama-type program." Such combinations strike many readers as barbarisms, foreign to idiomatic, natural English. Often they are used to turn simple ideas into fuzzy, wordy phrases: "A subsidy-type payment" says no more than "subsidy."

unique, perfect, equal It used to be argued that one thing cannot be *more unique, more perfect,* or *more equal* than another; either it is unique or it isn't. Formal English often substitutes *more nearly unique, more nearly perfect, more nearly equal.*

used to, didn't use to, used to could *Used to* in questions or negative statements with *did* is informal and only occasionally seen in print ("the strident . . . anti-police slogans which *didn't use to* be part of the hippie mode" —*National Review*).

Informal: She *didn't use to* smoke.
Formal: She *used not to* smoke.

Used to could is nonstandard for *used to be able.*

where, where at, where to   In formal English, *where* takes the place of *where to* ("*Where* was it sent?" and *where at* ("*Where* is he?"). *Where* used instead of *that* ("I read in the paper *where* a boy was killed") is colloquial.

who, which, and that   *Who* and *whom* refer to persons ("the man *whom* I asked"). *Which* refers to ideas and things ("the car *which* I bought"). A *who, whom,* or *which* introducing a **restrictive modifier** may be replaced by *that* (but *need* not be):

The man *that* I asked liked the car *that* I bought.

A *whom* or a *which* that is the object in a restrictive modifier is often left out:

The man *(whom)* I asked liked the car *(which)* I bought.

Of which and *in which* can easily make a sentence awkward. *Whose* is therefore widely used and accepted in reference to ideas and things: "the Shank-Painter Swamp, *whose* expressive name . . . gave it importance in our eyes" (Thoreau).

-wise   The practice of converting a noun into an adverb by tacking on *-wise* is characteristic of business or advertising jargon. Use *grammatically* for *grammar-wise*, *linguistically* for *language-wise*.

without   *Without* is nonstandard when used as a connective introducing a clause.

Nonstandard: The landlord won't let me stay *without* I pay the rent.

Standard: The landlord won't let me stay *unless* I pay the rent.

you with indefinite reference   Formal writing generally restricts *you* to the meaning of "you, the reader." Much informal writing uses *you* with indefinite reference to refer to people in general; formal writing would substitute *one:*

Informal: In ancient Rome, *you* had to be a patrician to be able to vote.

Formal: In ancient Rome, *one* had to be a patrician to be able to vote.

10
Grammatical Terms

Note: Use the index to locate a fuller discussion of many of the grammatical terms listed in this glossary.

absolute construction A word or phrase that is grammatically independent of the rest of the sentence. Typically, a verbal or verbal phrase: *"The guests having departed,* Arvin locked the door."

active See VOICE.

adjective A class of words that can point out a quality of a noun (or noun equivalent). They occur characteristically as modifiers of nouns ("the *happy* child") and as predicate adjectives ("The child was *happy*"). They normally have distinctive forms for use in comparisons (*happier, happiest; more reasonable, most reasonable*).

adjective clause A dependent clause serving an adjective function: "The man *who had startled us* apologized."

adverb A class of words used to modify verbs, adjectives, other adverbs, or a sentence as a whole:

> He ran *quickly.*
> He was *strangely* silent.
> He sang *moderately* well.
> *Surprisingly,* he did not answer.

Many adverbs show the distinctive *-ly* ending.

adverbial clause A dependent clause serving an adverbial function: "We left *after the rain had stopped."* *"When the bell had ceased to ring,* I opened the door."

agreement Correspondence, mainly in number, between grammatically related elements. Use of matching forms of a subject and its verb (the *dog barks*—the *dogs bark*); choice of a pronoun matching its antecedent (*"Each* member must be aware of *his* responsibility").

antecedent The noun (or equivalent) for which a pronoun substitutes: *"Aunt Hertha* fell sick soon after *she* arrived."

appositive A noun (or equivalent) placed as a modifier next to—usually after—another noun: "Mr. Brown, *the registrar,* proved most helpful."

articles *A* and *an* (the **indefinite** articles) and *the* (the **definite** article), used as noun markers: *a* book, *an* honest man, *the* door.

auxiliaries "Helping" verbs used in forming complete verbs: *be (am, are, was,* etc.), *have, shall (should), will (would), can (could), may (might), must, ought.*

case Inflected forms of nouns and pronouns, signaling certain grammatical relationships within a sentence: the **possessive** of nouns (*George's* friend), the **subject forms** and **object forms** of pronouns (*I—me, he—him,* etc.).

clause A subject-predicate unit that may combine with other such units in a sentence. **Independent** clauses are grammatically self-contained and can be punctuated as complete sentences:

> *I think; therefore, I am.*
> *I think. Therefore, I am.*

Dependent clauses are grammatically subordinate to an independent clause (main clause) :

> Arvin had a dog, *which barked all night.*
> *After the rain stopped,* we went home.

See also ADJECTIVE CLAUSE, ADVERBIAL CLAUSE, NOUN CLAUSE.

collective noun   A group noun that is singular in form but may require a plural verb:

Singular: The *jury votes* tomorrow. (thought of as a unit)
Plural: The *jury are* out to lunch. (thought of as individuals)

comparative   The form of adjectives and adverbs that is used to indicate higher degree: "Blood is *thicker* than water."

complement   A sentence element completing the predication of the verb. The complements of action verbs are called **objects:**

> Arvin called *the sheriff* (**direct** object) .
> She wrote *my father* (**indirect** object) *a letter* (**direct** object) .

The complement of a linking verb is a noun or adjective describing the subject (**subjective complement**):

> Her father was *a businessman* (**predicate noun**).
> The girl looked *pale* (**predicate adjective**).

After some verbs, an object is followed by a description of the object (**objective complement**):

The editorial called the project *a failure.*
Arvin labeled the charges *ridiculous.*

conjunction   See CONNECTIVES.

conjunctive adverb   See CONNECTIVES.

connectives   Words that connect sentence elements or clauses: **coordinating connectives** (*and, but, for, or, nor*) ; **subordinating connectives** (*if, when, because, though, whereas*) ; **adverbial connectives** (*however, therefore, consequently*) .

coordinate adjectives   Two or more adjectives describing different qualities of the same noun, with a comma taking the place of *and:* "a *noisy, unruly* crowd."

correlatives   Pairs of connectives coordinating sentence elements or clauses: *either . . . or, neither . . . nor, not only . . . but also, whether . . . or.*

determiners   Noun markers including **articles** (*a, an, the*) , **demonstrative pronouns** (*this, these; that, those*) , and **possessive pronouns** (*my, your, his, her, its, our, their*) .

elliptical constructions   Constructions in which missing elements can be supplied to facilitate grammatical analysis:

The paintings [*that*] he collected filled a large room.
When [*she was*] interviewed, the actress denied rumors of an impending engagement.

expletives   The *it* and *there* used as mere introductory words in *it-is, there-is, there-are* sentences.

finite verb A term used to distinguish a complete verb from a verbal, which cannot by itself function as a predicate.

function words Words whose major function is to establish grammatical relationships within a sentence: articles, connectives, prepositions.

gender The quality of nouns and pronouns that determines choice between *he, she,* or *it;* between *actor* and *actress, alumnus* and *alumna, fiancé* and *fiancée.*

gerund See VERBAL.

idiom An expression that does not conform to general grammatical patterns but is established by usage as the habitual way of conveying a given meaning: *bear in mind, have a mind to, keep in mind.*

infinitive See VERBAL.

inflection Changes in the form of words to reflect changes in grammatical relationships: the plural *-s* of nouns; the *-s, -ed,* or *-ing* of verbs; the *-er* or *-est* of adjectives.

intensifier Words that modify adjectives or adverbs and express degree; also called **intensive adverbs:** *very* hot, *quite* calm, *rather* young.

interjection A grammatically independent element used to express attitude or emotion: *ah, oh, ouch,* etc.

kernel sentences The minimum sentences from which more complicated structures are derived in transformational grammar. They are the **source sentences** from which actual sentences are generated by successive transformations.

linking verb See VERB.

modifier A word, phrase, or clause that develops or restricts the meaning of another sentence element or the sentence as a whole (see also ADJECTIVE, ADVERB). **Restrictive** modifiers contribute to identification and need no punctuation; **nonrestrictive** modifiers provide additional information not essential to identification and are set off, normally by commas:

Restrictive: The man *who returned my wallet* was a complete stranger.

Nonrestrictive: Mr. Norton, *who found my wallet,* is an old friend.

mood The classification of verb forms as **indicative** (plain or factual: "I am ready"); **imperative** (request or command: "Be quiet"); and **subjunctive** (hypothetical or contrary to fact: "I wish he were here!").

noun A class of words that name or classify people, animals, things, ideas. They occur typically as subjects of clauses or as objects of verbs and prepositions. Their appearance is often signaled by noun markers like the **articles** (*a, an, the*). Many nouns add *-s* to the plain form to form the plural: *dogs, cars, houses, colleges.*

noun clause A dependent clause taking the place of a noun: *"That he was late* does not surprise me."

noun equivalent   A sentence element (pronoun, infinitive, gerund, noun clause) that is grammatically equivalent to a noun.

number   Choice of appropriate forms to express **singular** (one of a kind) or **plural** (more than one).

object   See COMPLEMENT.

object form   See CASE.

participle   See VERBAL.

passive   See VOICE.

past   See TENSE.

perfect   See TENSE.

person   Choice of appropriate forms to express the person speaking (**first person:** *I know, we know*); the person spoken to (**second person:** *you know*); or the person spoken about (**third person:** *he knows, they know*).

phrase   A group of related words, typically a preposition or a verbal accompanied by its object or other related material.

Prepositional Phrase: Irene sat *at the window.*
Verbal Phrase: Father gave up *smoking cigars.*

predicate   The second basic element of the typical written sentence, making an assertion about the subject. The predicate consists of a complete (finite) verb and its possible complements and modifiers.

preposition A class of words that relate a noun (or equivalent) to the rest of the sentence: "Arvin left *after* dark."

present See TENSE.

principal parts The basic forms of a verb: simple present (*know*), simple past (*knew*), past participle (*known*).

progressive construction Verb form expressing action in progress: "Fred *was lighting* a cigarette."

pronoun A class of words taking the place of nouns; classified as **personal** (*I, you, he*), **possessive** (*my, your, his*), **reflexive** or **intensive** (*myself, yourself, himself*), **demonstrative** (*this, that*) **relative** (*who, which, that*), **interrogative** (*who, which, what*), and **indefinite** (*one, anyone, everyone*). See also CASE.

relative clause A dependent clause related to the main clause by a relative pronoun: "The article *that I mentioned* begins on page 5."

restrictive See MODIFIER.

sentence A grammatically complete and self-contained unit of thought or expression, set off from other such units by end punctuation. The typical written sentence contains at least a subject and a predicate ("Birds sing"). The most common exception is the subjectless request or command, in which the subject is said to be understood ("Show him in").

Sentences combining two or more independent clauses are called **compound**. Sentences combining an independent and one or more dependent clauses are called **complex**. A combination of the two types is called **compound-complex.**

Compound:	He hummed, and she sang.
Complex:	He hummed when she sang.
Compound-Complex:	When they heard the news, he hummed and she sang.

source sentence   See KERNEL SENTENCE.

subject   The first basic element of the typical written sentence, about which the predicate makes an assertion.

subject form   See CASE.

subjunctive   See MOOD.

superlative   The form of adjectives and adverbs used to express highest degree: "Fred is the *fastest* runner on the team."

tense   The system of verb forms expressing primarily different relationships in time:

Present:	I know	Perfect:	I have known
Past:	I knew	Past Perfect:	I had known
Future:	I will (shall) know	Future Perfect:	I will (shall) have known

transformation   One of the successive steps by which more complicated structures are produced from simple ones in a transformational grammar. The reshuffling, addition, or deletion of grammatical elements needed, for instance, to turn present into past tense, active into passive voice, or an affirmative into a negative statement. See also KERNEL SENTENCE.

transitive   See VERB.

verb   A class of words that signal the performance of an action, the occurrence of an event, or the presence of a condition. Verbs appear in typical verb positions: "Let's *leave.*" "The boys *left* the scene." They typically take an *-s* in the third person singular of the present tense *(asks, leaves, condones)*. They use characteristic **auxiliaries** in forms consisting of more than one word *(have left, was asked, will be leaving)*. **Action verbs** are modified by adverbs; **linking verbs** are followed by adjectives:

Action Verb: He *responded* quickly.
Linking Verb: His response *seemed* quick.

Regular verbs use the same form for the simple past and the past participle:

Regular: I *laughed*   I have *laughed*
Irregular: I *knew*   I have *known*

Transitive verbs normally require an object:

Transitive: He *raises* chickens.
Intransitive: He *rises* early.

Grammatical Terms

See also TENSE, MOOD, VOICE.

verbal A form that is derived from a verb but does not by itself function as a predicate: **infinitive** (*to* form), **present participle** (*-ing* form used as an adjective), **gerund** (*-ing* form used as a verbal noun), **past participle** (*-ed* form in regular verbs, irregular in others). Verbals appear as noun equivalents, modifiers, and *parts* of verbs.

Infinitive:	He liked *to dream*.
Present Participle:	Her *dreaming* look entranced him.
Gerund:	*Dreaming* got him nowhere.
Past Participle:	He had *dreamed* of childhood days.

voice The verb form that shows whether the subject is acting (**active**) or acted upon (**passive**):

Active:	Eileen *feeds* the children.
Passive:	The children *are fed* by Eileen.

Appendix
Practical Prose Forms

For Quick Reference

X 1   Summaries

Train yourself to grasp the structure of written material and to concentrate on essentials.

Practice in writing summaries will benefit you in important ways as a student and as a writer:

- It will give you practice in *close, attentive reading.* Too many writers are ineffectual because they have not learned to listen first, to think second, and to formulate their own reactions third.

- It will strengthen your sense of *structure* in writing. It will make you pay close attention to how a writer organizes his material, how he develops a point, how he moves from one point to another.

424

- It will develop your sense of what is *important* in a piece of writing. It will make you distinguish between a key point, the material backing it up, and mere asides.

In writing a summary, concentrate on three closely related tasks:

(1) *Make sure you grasp the main trend of thought.* Above all, you need to see clearly the *organization* of what you are asked to summarize. Identify key sentences: the thesis that sums up the major point of an essay (or section of an essay) ; the topic sentence that is developed in the rest of a paragraph. Formulate in your own words major points that seem to be *implied* but not spelled out in a single sentence. Distinguish between the major steps in an argument and merely incidental comment.

(2) *Reduce explanation and illustration to the essential minimum.* Omit passages that are mere paraphrase, restating a point for clarity or emphasis. Drastically condense lengthy explanations. Preserve only the most important details, examples, statistics. Reduce or omit anecdotes, facetious asides, and the like.

(3) *Use the most economical wording possible.* Where the original uses a whole clause, try to sum up the same idea in a phrase. Where it uses a phrase, try to use a single word. Where several near-synonyms restate the same idea, choose the one that best gives the central common meaning. Cut out all grammatical deadwood.

Unless the original version is already severely condensed, a summary of about one-third or one-fourth the original length can usually preserve the essential points. The shorter the summary, however, the greater the danger of oversimplification or outright misrepresentation. Be careful to preserve essential conditions and distinctions: *if-* and

Appendix: Practical Prose Forms

unless-clauses; differences between *is, will,* and *might;* words like *only, almost,* and *on the whole.* Preserve the relative emphasis of the original, giving more prominence to a point treated at great length than to one mentioned in passing.

Study the following passage. The running commentary suggests points you would have to note in writing an adequate summary.

We might characterize popular art first, as is most often done, with respect to its *form.* Popular art is said to be simple and unsophisticated, aesthetically deficient because of its artlessness. It lacks quality because it makes no qualifications to its flat statement. Everything is straightforward, with no place for complications. And it is standardized as well as simplified: one product is much like another. It is lifeless, Bergson would say, because it is only a succession of mechanical repetitions, while what is vital in art is endlessly variable. But it is just the deadly routine that is so popular. Confronted with that, we know just where we are, know what we are being offered, and what is expected of us in return. It is less unsettling to deal with machines than with people, who have lives of their own to lead. For we can then respond with mechanical routines ourselves, and what could be simpler and more reliably satisfying? —Abraham Kaplan, "The Aesthetics of the Popular Arts," *Journal of Aesthetics and Art Criticism*

(1) *Key idea:* Emphasis will be on *form* rather than content of popular arts.

(2) *Essential qualification:* "Most often done" and "is said to be" show this view to be widely held, but not necessarily fully shared by *author.*

(3) *Synonyms:* "Simple," uncomplicated," "artless," "flat," "straightforward" all reinforce same major point.

(4) *Added step:* Popular art is "standardized" as well as "simplified."

(5) *Another added step:* It is "mechanical" rather than "variable."

(6) *Major transition:* The "mechanical" element in the popular arts is what makes them popular.

(7) *Explanation:* Why is "deadly routine" easy to live with?

Here is the summary you might write after close study of the passage:

Summary: According to a widely held view, popular art is simple and uncomplicated in form, and therefore "artless." It is standardized, and it lacks life because of mechanical repetition. But it is just the mechanical quality that is popular, because it is simple to react to what we know, but unsettling to deal with something that has a life of its own.

Exercises

A. Study the differences between the full text and the summary in each of the following pairs. Would you have noted the same major points and essential qualifications?

Original:
The invention of the process of printing from movable type, which occurred in Germany about the middle of the fifteenth century, was destined to exercise a far-reaching influence on all the vernacular languages of Europe. Introduced into England about 1476 by William Caxton, who had learned the art on the continent, printing made such rapid progress that a scant century later it was observed that manuscript books were seldom to be met with and almost never used. Some idea of the rapidity with which the new process swept forward may be had from the fact that in Europe the number of books printed before the year 1500 reaches the surprising figure of 35,000. The majority of these, it is true, were in Latin, whereas it is in the modern languages that the effect of the printing press was chiefly to be felt. But in England over 20,000 titles in English had appeared by 1640, ranging all the way from mere pamphlets to massive folios. The result was to bring books, which had formerly been the

expensive luxury of the few, within the reach of all. More important, however, was the fact, so obvious today, that it was possible to reproduce a book in a thousand copies or a hundred thousand, every one exactly like the other. A powerful force thus existed for promoting a standard uniform language, and the means were now available for spreading that language throughout the territory in which it was understood.—Albert C. Baugh, *A History of the English Language*

Summary:

Printing from movable type, invented in Germany about 1450 and brought to England about 1476, had a far-reaching influence on all European languages. Within a hundred years, manuscript books had become rare. Though at first most printed books were in Latin, over 20,000 titles in English had appeared by 1640. Books were now within the reach of everyone and could exert a powerful standardizing influence upon language.

Original:

The tendency to erect "systems"—which are then marketed as a whole—affects particularly the less mature sciences of medicine and psychology. In these subjects we have had a succession of intellectual edifices originally made available only in their entirety. It is as if one cannot rent a room or even a suite in a new building, but must lease the whole or not enter. Starting with a substantial contribution to medicine the authors of such systems expand their theories to include ambitious explanations of matters far beyond the original validated observations. And after the first pioneer, later and usually lesser contributors to the system add further accretions of mingled fact and theory. Consequently systems of this kind—like homeopathy, phrenology, psychoanalysis, and conditioned reflexology (the last dominant for years in Russia) —eventually contain almost inextricable mixtures of sense and nonsense. They capture fervid adherents, and it may take a generation or several for those who preserve some objectivity to succeed in salvaging the best in them while discarding the dross.—Dr. Ian Stevenson, "Scientists with Half-Closed Minds," *Harper's*

Summary:
Medicine and psychology have produced a number of intellectual systems that one is asked to accept as a whole or not at all. The ambitious authors and adherents of such systems go beyond original valid findings to produce a mixture of truth and error that attracts enthusiastic supporters. Objective observers may not succeed in separating the valuable from the worthless till much later.

B. Select a passage of about 250 words from a history or science textbook. Prepare a summary running to about a third of the original length. Provide a copy of the original.

X 2 Letters

Make the appearance and style of your business letters suggest the qualities prized by business people: competence and efficiency.

Correspondence creates special problems of manuscript form. In writing or answering a formal invitation, you will do well to follow forms suggested in a book of etiquette. In writing a personal letter, you may allow yourself considerable freedom, as long as you keep your handwriting legible and use presentable stationery. Between these extremes of formality and informality is the kind of letter that you may have to write to a teacher, to a college official, or to a future employer. In applying for a scholarship or for a job, follow a conventional letter form.

X 2a   Format and Style

Make sure your business letters are neat and consistent in format, clear and courteous in style.

The specimen letter on page 431 illustrates a format widely used in business correspondence. Use it as a model for spacing, indention, and punctuation.

Notice the following possible variations:

(1) When you are not using the letterhead of a firm or institution, type in *your address* above the date, as follows:

```
                         138 South Third Street
                         San Jose, California  95126
                         January 12, 1968


Mr. Ralph J. Clark, Jr.
Personnel Manager
San Rafael Independent-Journal
185 Washington Street
San Rafael, California

Dear Mr. Clark:
```

(2) A *married woman* may wish to put (*Mrs.*) in front of her typed name.

Try to write clearly and naturally; do not adopt a special business jargon when you write a business letter. Avoid especially the following: a *stodgy,* old-fashioned businessese ("wish to advise that," "beg to acknowledge," "am in receipt of," "pursuant to," "the aforementioned"); a *breezy* "shirtsleeve" English ("give it the old college try," "fight tooth and nail," "give them a run for their money").

CALIFORNIA STATE COLLEGE, ⌐ letterhead

809 East Victoria Street • *Dominguez Hills, California 90247* ⌐

heading ┠──→ June 14, 19___

Institute for Better Business Writing, Inc.
1000 University Way
Los Angeles, California   90025   ←──⎰ inside address

Gentlemen: ◄──⎰ salutation

I was happy to receive your request for information
regarding business letter formats.

The format of this letter is the one most frequently
used in business. It's called the <u>block format.</u>
With the exception of the heading and the signature
block, all its elements begin at the left hand margin,
even the first word of each paragraph. The body of
the letter is single-spaced, with double spacing
between paragraphs.
    ─⎰ body
Secretaries generally like the block format better
than the older indented formats. It has a clean and
precise appearance, and is quicker to type -- no
fiddling around with indentations.

There are other formats in use, but the block format
seems to have the widest appeal. You won't go wrong
adopting it for all your official correspondence.

signature block ⌐   Sincerely yours,

  complimentary close
  signature   *Walter Wells*
  signature identification   Walter Wells
                       Department of English

WW:mea   ←──── ⌐ IEC block
cc: Dean Howard Brody

                  initials (of author and typist)
                  enclosures (if any)
                  carbon copies

X 2b   The Request

State inquiries and requests clearly and positively, and aim them at the intended reader.

Many of the business letters you write will ask someone else to *do* something for you: to provide information, to perform a service, to correct a mistake. Make such letters clear, businesslike, and persuasive.

(1) Make sure you state your request clearly and directly *early* in the letter. The basic question in your reader's mind is "What do you want?"

(2) If you are making *several* requests in the same letter, or if several points need attention, make sure *each* stands out clearly. Consider numbering them for emphasis. Too often, only the first major point gets attention; other matters, buried later in a letter, are forgotten.

(3) Whenever possible, relate your request directly to the *interests and responsibilities* of the person you are writing to. Avoid a "To-Whom-It-May-Concern" effect; avoid using form letters if at all possible.

(4) Even when you have a legitimate complaint, remain *courteous*. Emphasize the mutual satisfaction to be derived from a mistake corrected, rather than the mutual frustration occasioned when an error is first made.

The following sample letters attempt to put these principles into practice:[1]

---

[1] Most of the sample letters in this section are adapted from Walter Wells, *Communications in Business* (Belmont, California: Wadsworth, 1968) .

Letter 1

Dear Mr. Bliss:

Largely because of the success of The Muse, your new
campus literary magazine, we at Colfax College feel
the time is right for a similar publication on this
campus. Your help on a few important questions would
get us moving in the right direction.

We would like to know

    1. How you went about soliciting manuscripts
    for your first edition.
    2. How you decided upon the proportions of
    space to devote to fiction, poetry, criticism,
    reviews, and advertising.
    3. Whether you use university or commercial
    printing facilities.
    4. What mailing list you used to solicit
    charter subscriptions.
    5. Why you decided to price The Muse at $1.25.

Our enthusiasm runs high over the possibility of a
literary review at Colfax. Target date for the first
issue is October 1 of this year. We've got the administration's green light and the faculty is solidly
behind us. With your aid, we can be that much closer
to realizing our goal--a first-rate campus publication
capable of standing beside the best from the larger
schools, The Muse most certainly among them.

               Sincerely,

               Jeffrey Cantwell
               Student Body Vice-President

Appendix: Practical Prose Forms

Letter 2

Gentlemen:

I was surprised to receive your recent request for more transcripts to complete my application to the Graduate School. I will, of course, have them sent if absolutely necessary, but I do feel that your request penalizes me.

Upon coming to State as a transfer undergraduate in 1965, I paid two dollars, for transcripts in dupli- cate, to each of the three institutions I had pre- viously attended. At that time, you informed me that all my papers were in order, and you admitted me. Now you request the very same transcripts in support of my graduate application.

Would it not be possible for you to refer to the transcripts already in your possession? Or if copies must be sent to the graduate advisor, could you not duplicate my transcripts and send me the bill? In either case, you would save me the time of recon- tacting each institution, and perhaps preclude a delay in their responding.

I hope this request is in no way unjustified. It should be more expedient for both of us as you process my application.

Sincerely yours,

Kenneth Darwin

Kenneth Darwin

X 2c   The Letter of Application

Make your letter of application suggest competence, confidence, and a genuine interest in the position for which you apply.

Employers look for employees who will prove an asset to their organization and who are at the same time good to work with and good to know. They shy away from applicants who seem to promise problems, trouble, complexes, or an overinflated ego. Remember the following advice:

(1) If possible, be *specific* about the position for which you apply. Introduce the letter by mentioning the advertisement or the person that informed you of the vacancy (but do not mention leads that smack of the "grapevine").

(2) Stress *previous training* and practical experience that you can show to be relevant to the job. Give a factual tone to the account of your qualifications, while at the same time presenting them to advantage.

(3) Give your letter *character*. Establish your identity. Many job applications look very much the same, and the anonymous, average applicant has little chance to be remembered—and to be preferred. If you have positive convictions about the work of the organization to which you apply, state them in a paragraph or two. If you have some serious thoughts about the role of business, hazard them.

(4) If you list *references,* obtain prior permission from those whose names you use. Common sense suggests that you quietly drop from your list the name of any teacher or former employer who shows little enthusiasm when you tell him about your plans.

(5) If the account of your qualifications is extensive, put it on a separate "data sheet," or *résumé*.

Study the following sample letters:

Appendix: Practical Prose Forms

Letter 3

Dear Mr. Clark:

In answer to your advertisement, I wish to apply for a post as a general reporter. My credentials are that I am a journalism major, and I have had some practical experience of working for a newspaper.

On February 1, I shall graduate from San Jose State College. While getting a degree, I have taken a broad range of courses, representing all areas of editing and reporting. Also, I have been a general reporter for the <u>Spartan Daily</u> for two years and a feature editor for one year. Last summer I worked for thirteen weeks on the <u>Santa Clara Journal</u>, as an "intern" sponsored by the Journalism Department of my college. I did general reporting and some photography.

The following gentlemen have agreed to supply references:

> Dr. John Williams
> Department of Journalism
> San Jose State College
> San Jose, California
>
> Mr. Thomas Bigelow
> General Manager
> <u>Santa Clara Journal</u>
> Santa Clara, California
>
> Mr. Richard H. James
> Editor
> <u>Los Angeles Examiner</u>
> Los Angeles, California

I am prepared to be interviewed when you find it convenient.

Yours truly,

Gerald P. Johnson

Gerald P. Johnson

Letter 4

Mr. Daniel Levin, Attorney at Law
Peale, Corman, Bishop, Levin & Dilworthy
80 Lomita Canyon Boulevard, Suite 7630
Beverly Hills, California   92025

Dear Mr. Levin:

Edith Winters informs me of an opening in your secretarial staff, a position for which I should very much
like to become a candidate.

I understand that you need a legal secretary with a
rapid stenographic skill and the ability to handle a
large volume of correspondence. Along with my degree
in legal stenography from Foothill Junior College, I
have four years of secretarial experience in retail
dry goods and in insurance. My shorthand speed is
145 words per minute. On my present job, I handle
between forty and sixty letters every day. Both at
Foothill and on the job, I have had training sufficient to prepare me to handle routine letters without
supervision.

Appendix: Practical Prose Forms

My present job at Southwestern Life & Indemnity has
been quite satisfactory, but, having taken my degree
recently, I seek the further challenges and rewards
of a top-flight legal firm. Miss Winters' enthusiasm
for her work assures me that I would like the job. I
hope the enclosed résumé will help interest the firm in
me.

I can be in Los Angeles for an interview any afternoon
convenient for you. May I look forward to speaking
with you about the position you have available?

Yours sincerely,

Laura Edmondson

Laura Edmondson

Sample Résumé

ADAM PIERCE

Demmler Hall	Age: 23
Valhalla University	Ht: 6-1 Wt: 170
Kent, Ohio 26780	Single
613 KE 8 7600	Willing to relocate

Education

B.S. in Industrial Engineering, Valhalla University,
June 1969; top 10% of class, with special course
work in statistics, motivational psychology,
business law, and communications.

Won U.S. Paint Company Scholarship 1968
Member of Industrial Relations Club

Elected Secretary of the Student Council
On Dean's Honor Roll since 1966

Also attended Colfax College, Colfax, Indiana, 1964-65

Experience

    Staff Supervisor, Cleveland Boys' Club Camp, Kiowa, Ohio,
summer 1968; responsible for housing, activities
scheduling and occasional discipline of fourteen
counselors and 110 campers.

    Camp Counselor, Cleveland Boys' Club Camp, Kiowa, Ohio,
summers of 1966 and 1967.

Personal Interests

    Politics, world affairs, camping, chess, junior chamber
of commerce member, and volunteer hospital worker.

Military Service

    Served six months' active duty, U.S. Army, Fort Dix,
New Jersey, Oct. 1965 to April 1966. Presently
on reserve duty, attending one weekend meeting
per month.

References

    Will gladly be provided upon request.

X 2d   The Follow-Up Letter

*Keep interest alive, or reinforce a good first
impression, by a timely follow-up letter.*

Though many business people pride themselves on being hard-headed calculators, in practice business is often 51

439

percent relations. The follow-up letter serves important human needs: it shows positive interest and thus *reassures* the recipient; it serves as a *reminder,* keeping alive an impression that is beginning to pale as other business calls for attention.

Study the following sample letter, written by an applicant *after* a job interview:

Letter 5

Dear Mr. Goodfellow:

Just a note of thanks for the many courtesies shown me during my interview on Monday. Seeing National Motors from the inside has, as I said then, made the Executive Training Program all the more attractive to me.

Incidentally, I located a copy of Michaelson's The Corporate Tempo and found his chapter on training programs as fascinating and as eye-opening as you did. Needless to say, I am looking forward to hearing from you. After Monday's meeting, I am confident I can bring to the program the energy and ability for success at National Motors.

Sincerely,

Adam Pierce

Adam Pierce

X 2e   The Letter of Refusal

Write letters of refusal that create goodwill rather than antagonism.

There are many ways of saying no. The basic difference is between "No, thank you" and "No—and good riddance."

A refusal that at the same time shows an appreciation of the interest expressed generates goodwill and at the same time leaves the door open for future contacts.

Study the following sample letter:

Letter 6

Dear Mr. Tibbins:

I want to thank you for your letter of July 20 and for your generous offer of the post as market-research analyst at Continental.

With more qualms than I thought myself capable of, I have decided to forsake that offer and accept one made me by the Grollier Food Company of San Francisco. While the salary they offer is slightly less than Continental's, their market-research department is small, making possible, I feel, more rapid advancement. The decision was made quite difficult by the obvious attractiveness of your offer, not to mention the congeniality of your staff. Only time will prove if it's a wise one.

Once again, let me express my genuine thanks for all the consideration you and the Continental staff have given my candidacy.

Very sincerely yours,

Michael Henriques

Michael Henriques

Exercises

A. In an effective business letter, as in all effective persuasion, the writer shows his ability to imagine himself in the place

Appendix: Practical Prose Forms

of the reader. Compare and contrast the letters in each of the following pairs. Which letter in each pair is the more successful in this respect?

1(a) Enclosed is our draft in the amount of $31.90, which is the amount over your deductible for which Smith Motors, the garage of your choice, agreed to repair your automobile. You will also find enclosed a copy of the estimate on the basis of which they agreed to repair.

1(b) I'm happy to send you our draft for $31.90. It represents the repair cost for your car in excess of the deductible amount in your policy. The enclosed repair estimate was, as you requested, made by Smith Motors in Dalhart.

2(a) Just what kind of outfit are you people running? We place a simple order, delivery takes forever, and when it finally gets here, half the pieces are broken. To top it all off, in the same day's mail we get your bill. Some joke!

We feel we can do without this kind of rotten service. There's no time left for us to place an order with a decent company (although we'd like to), so get on the ball and send us a replacement order right away.

2(b) On January 10, we placed an order with you for 500 pieces of glassware in various patterns. Yesterday the order arrived with only 234 pieces in salable condition. All the rest were chipped or broken.

You can understand our disappointment, I am
sure. Customers have been requesting your
glasses, and we have been promising them a
prompt supply. Now some of them will probably
go elsewhere--their faith in us destroyed, and
our potential profit lost--unless you take
immediate action.

We ask that you send us an immediate duplicate
order, and allow us to adjust our payment to
cover only the salable glassware. We are confident that you will be able to get this shipment to us as soon as possible.

B. Find a project or recent development that merits publicity or support. Write a letter about it to the editors of a
newspaper or magazine, to a legislator, or to a responsible
official. Observe conventional letter form.

C. Write a letter of inquiry or request in connection with
some project in which you are currently interested. Observe
conventional letter form.

D. Write a letter of application for a position in which you
have at one time or another taken an interest. State the qualifications that you might have by the time you are ready to apply for
the position in earnest.

E. Write a follow-up letter or a letter of refusal in connection with some business contact that you can imagine yourself
being engaged in after your graduation from college. Observe
conventional letter form.

X 3   The Essay Examination

*Learn to write a structured essay examination
that makes the best possible use of what you know.*

For many students, the most direct test of their writing ability is the essay examination. To improve your own performance on such examinations, remember the following points:

(1) Study not for total recall but for a *writing* test. In studying the material, identify the key terms that might provide the focal point for a paragraph or short essay: *alienation, irony, agrarianism.* Fix firmly in your mind the three or four points you would cover if asked to trace the major step in an argument, or the key stages in a process. Then, for each key term or major point, try to retain *supporting detail* that would help you define or illustrate it. Do not merely memorize material; ask yourself practice questions that make you *select and arrange* materials in different ways to prove a point, to trace a comparison.

(2) Memorize *verbatim* at least some key phrases, definitions, or short passages. These will give an authoritative, authentic air to your writing. Nothing more reliably identifies the student who aims at better than *C* than the sentence that follows a pattern like this:

The term _____, which Frederick Marcus defines as "_____," has developed two important new applications: . . .

Michael Henchard, whom Thomas Hardy describes as "_____," was aware of his own capacity for impulsive action. . . .

(3) Determine exactly what the *instructions* ask you to do. Do not simply get a general notion of what the question is "about." Assume the question in a history course is "What do you consider the most important difference between the fall of Greece and the fall of Rome?" Do not simply put down everything you can remember about the fall of Greece and the fall of Rome. Focus on the key word in the instructions: *difference*. What *is* the difference? How can you line up material that will bring out this difference as clearly and convincingly as possible? Look also for specific writing instructions: Are you being asked to *summarize,* to *define,* to *compare,* to *evaluate*—or merely, more vaguely, to *discuss?*

(4) No matter what the pressure of time, take time to *structure* your answer. Come straight to the point. Especially in a one-paragraph answer, make your very first sentence sum up your key point, or your answer to the question being asked. Then use the rest of a paragraph to explain, support, or argue your point. Select what is clearly relevant; try to avoid a mere rambling effect. Whenever you can, work from a brief *outline* jotted down on scratch paper before you begin to write.

In addition to these basic points, here are a few practical hints:

- Bring an extra pen.

- Budget your time, especially if there are several questions. If you gain five points by treating one question at great length, and then lose twenty-five points by slighting the next two questions, you are twenty points behind.

- Get a general picture of the examination before you start writing. If there are several questions or topics, work first on those that you feel best qualified to take up.

• Relax. You will need a cool head to read the instructions without missing an important point.

Study the following essay exam, rated as above average by the teacher. The comments that follow it point out some features likely to have made a favorable impression on the reader.

Exam question: A common type of character in much contemporary literature is the individual who is trapped by a trick of fate, by environment, or by his own nature. Choose such a character from a short story you have recently read. Define the trap in which the character is caught. Describe the way in which he struggles, if he does, to free himself.

Answer: Miss Brill finds herself trapped by her spinsterhood and the advancement of age. She is old, as the story tells us; she's as old as her out-of-date fox fur. She is alone, with no friends, relatives, or close neighbors. This is her trap. Like a bird that will create its own prison in its own territory, Miss Brill makes hers. She does not socialize, nor does she try to make something useful out of her life but rather preys like a parasite on other people's more interesting, colorful lives. In her own way Miss Brill struggles to escape her prison. She daydreams. The world that she lives in is a fantasy world where all people are friendly and related. She "belongs" in this world whereas in the other world, the real world, she actually belongs to no one.

Quite successfully Miss Brill loses the real world for a time, but she cannot escape the real world entirely. The real world sticks its head in, in the form of a boy who says "Ah, go on with

446

you now." So she goes home, more aware than ever of her prison's boundaries and helpless (by her own nature) to do anything else. She can only fly on home to the security and solitude of her cold dark nest.

Note the following points about this answer:

(1) It responds directly to the *key term or key idea* in the assignment. The assignment asks about a character who is *trapped*. Note how this word and its synonyms keep echoing *throughout* the student's answer: "trapped," "prison," "boundaries."

(2) The first sentence serves as a *topic sentence* for the answer as a whole. It gives the brief, clear definition of the "trap" that the question asks for.

(3) The point about the character's trying to escape through daydreaming responds to the *second* part of the question. But note that this point is worked *organically* into the first paragraph. The student has *planned* this answer; there are no afterthoughts, no "Oh-I-forgot" effect.

Exercises

A. Study the following assignment for an essay examination and the two answers that follow it. One of the answers was rated good, the other poor. Which is which? Defend your choice in detail.

Assignment The following lines by Walt Whitman bear a close relationship to several ideas contained in essays you have read in this course. Explore, in an essay of 300 words, the connections you discern.

> When I heard the learn'd astronomer,
>
> When the proofs, the figures, were ranged in columns before me,
>
> When I was shown the charts and diagrams, to add, divide, and measure them,
>
> When I sitting heard the astronomer where he lectured with much applause in the lecture-room,
>
> How soon unaccountable I became tired and sick,
>
> Till rising and gliding out I wander'd off by myself,
>
> In the mystical moist night-air, and from time to time,
>
> Look'd up in perfect silence at the stars.

Answer 1 Several points in Walt Whitman's lines are important in exploring the connections between his ideas and the ideas pertaining to humanism in the essays we have read. First, we get the image of a man of letters attending a lecture of a man of science. Secondly, the lecture material consists of certainties—proofs and figures, charts, diagrams. Finally, we get a feeling of complete isolation and peacefulness as Whitman stands outside in the night air.

In C. P. Snow's essay on "The Two Cultures," the author states that our intellectual society is divided into two sections—scientific and literary. Each section believes the other is unaware of man's condition in life and shows no regard for its fellow men. Each section believes it has the "right" answer for society. Each section is so intense in its feelings that no communication is possible between the two sections. C. P. Snow says that we must "rethink education" to achieve a broad outlook on life in contrast to the narrow outlook that is the result of specialization and technicalities in science and in literary studies. This is the thought that I get when Whitman attends the astronomer's lecture.

The lecture material contains figures, charts, diagrams to prove the astronomer's theories. I believe Whitman is putting across the same point as Saisselin in his essay on "Humanism, or the Eulogy of Error." Saisselin claims that there are no proofs or certainties for the humanist. Man is a single entity; he lives alone and dies alone. This is man's fate. Man must recognize his isolation and his potential for error. Man must be flexible, but the astronomer suggests rigidity. Furthermore, man must not confine himself to one area in life but must be aware of the whole world about him. When Whitman steps outside into the night air and gazes at the stars, he feels the vastness of the universe. The astronomer looks at the universe to collect proofs and figures for his small world of lecture and research. He does not comprehend man's fate.

Answer 2 In the lines by Walt Whitman I am given the general impression that this person cannot comprehend the meaning of the lecture, the figures, or the charts and diagrams. It seems as though he is not scientifically inclined in his thinking and cannot grasp even a thread of the knowledge the lecturer is trying to communicate to him.

In his discussion of "The Two Cultures," C. P. Snow points out some of the reasons for the division between the literary and scientific scholars. One of these reasons is a lack of communication. The literary scholars feel that they are an elite intellectual group and that they should not talk to such illiterates as scientists. The scientists, on the other hand, have a much more exacting knowledge and think they are doing more for the world than reading or writing books.

Remy Saisselin said that humanism can't be defined. It is lived. I think this is true, and it shows in Walt Whitman's poem. The lines don't say anything about wanting to learn a little about philosophy or art or literature. Walt Whitman just wanted to look around. He had no real reason. He didn't want to become educated for a reward. He merely wanted to explore and become educated in something besides strict science for his own satisfaction and enjoyment.

Students today are made to specialize, and this cuts down on a general well-rounded education. If one lives in a small world of one type of life day after day, he cannot fully enjoy life. Diversity makes for more enjoyment. By learning a little in both science and the arts, a person becomes more happy with himself and those around him.

    B. Do you have a copy of an essay examination you have written recently? Select one or more passages totaling 250–300 words. Rewrite the material in accordance with the suggestions in this section. If you can, submit the original assignment, the original answer, and the improved version.

Index

Index

Index

Index

Handbook Key